Putin vs Putin

ALEXANDER DUGIN

PUTIN VS PUTIN

Vladimir Putin Viewed from the Right

ARKTOS
2014

ARKTOS

⊕ Arktos.com fb.com/Arktos arktosmedia arktosjournal

First edition published in 2014 by Arktos Media Ltd.

Copyright © 2015 by Arktos Media Ltd.

All rights reserved. No part of this book may be reproduced or utilised in any form or by any means (whether electronic or mechanical), including photocopying, recording or by any information storage and retrieval system, without permission in writing from the publisher.

ISBN
978-1-917646-37-6 (Softcover)
978-1-910524-12-1 (Hardback)
978-1-912975-78-5 (Ebook)

Translation
Gustaf Nielsen

Editing
John B. Morgan
The Russian edition was compiled and edited by N V Melentyeva

Layout
Tor Westman

Contents

Editor's Note 7

1. The Making of Putin 8
   Putin: The Unknown Revealed 9
   Patriot Plays 13
   The Twelve Labours of Putin 17
   Putin becomes an Ideal Ruler of the Period 22

2. Putin's Ideology 34
   Putin Owes Us All 34
   Ideological Expertise of the Political Environment 38
   Putin's Formula: Evolution of a Political Image 42
   On Putin's Responsibility before Christ and on Elite Rotation 61
   The Anti-American Consensus 73
   Putin's Munich Speech — a Turning Point in Russian History 76
   Putin's Mandate for a Revolution in Consciousness 82

3. Putin's Test 86
   Putin against the 'Sisters' 86
   Temptation by the Void 90
   Putin and the Void II: Political Solitude 93
   Putin's Grey Zone 97
   Unexpected Visitors 104
   No Time to Relax: New Network Challenges 107
   The Objective and Subjective in Putin's Course 110
   If Spring Comes Tomorrow 112

4. Putin's Geopolitics 118
   Shift in Foreign Policy 118
   Territorial Thinking 119
   Patriotic Enlightenment 125
   Putin: I Renounce the Devil 130

    President Putin's Liberal Reform 132
    Vladimir Putin as a Man of Destiny 139

5. Putin's Eurasian Revolution 145
    Vladimir Putin and the Conservative Revolution 145
    Putin, Conservatism and the *Siloviki* 157
    Vladimir Putin and the Empire 159
    Eurasianism as the New President's Ideology 163
    Putin and Eurasian Integration 165
    Eurasianism 170
    The Russian Order: The Relevance of the New *Oprichnina* 183

6. Putin: What Next? 188
    Putin's First Eight Years: A Conservative's Balance 188
    The Crisis of Representation 195
    End of a Political Cycle: Beyond the Grey Pole 199
    A Chain Reaction of the Authorities' Legitimacy 213
    A People's Front without the People 215
    Putin's Dead End 218
    The Putin that we have Lost: Criticisms from Above 233

7. Criticism of Putin from Above 249
    Hegemony and Counter-Hegemony: A Battle of Minds 252
    The Historical Pact 262
    4PT 281
    Conclusion 288

Appendix I 294

Appendix II 305

Index 311

Editor's Note

This book was originally compiled and published in Russian in 2012. Some of its texts were written after Putin's re-election, some were written during Medvedev's term, and some were written during Putin's first presidency (between 2000 and 2002). Readers should keep this in mind as the tense in which Prof Dugin refers to particular events sometimes shifts. The appendices were all written in the first half of 2014.

Most of the footnotes to the text have been added by me for this edition. A small number were part of the original Russian text, and these are denoted with an 'AD' following them. Where sources in other languages have been cited, I have attempted to replace them with existing English-language editions. Citations to works for which I could locate no translation are retained in their original language. Website addresses for on-line sources were verified as accurate and available during the period of August and September 2014.

The appendices were translated by volunteers from the Eurasia Movement.

JOHN B MORGAN IV
Budapest, Hungary, September 2014

CHAPTER 1

The Making of Putin

'Putin is the ideal ruler for the current period. He is a tragic figure. He has a horrible entourage, made up of exhausted people, a sea of despicable worms who are fouling up the entire field of his movement. And he is methodically and steadily, bit by bit, clearing away all this dismal legacy. He is like an alchemist turning black into white. It is only getting grey so far but this is just the beginning. The dawn is breaking, the dawn in boots. I believe in Putin and I entirely support him.'

— An extract from an interview with Alexander Dugin for the Website Dni.ru, 19 January 2001

'Mr Putin is a product of the Tsarist-Soviet security system, a traditionalist who believes that the only way to sustain order and protect the state is through authoritarianism. Therefore his political, legal, and military reforms are going to impede progress'.

— Boris Berezovsky, 'The Problem with Putin', *The Financial Times*, 28 May 2002

Introduction
Putin: The Unknown Revealed

As soon as Putin appeared, several significant factors contributed from the outset to a positive assessment of his personality. First, a harsh resentment towards the new Russian leader was expressed by ultra-liberals, the 'democratic schizos', as they were called at the time, spearheaded by the notorious Sergei Adamovich Kovalev.[1] Their message was, 'Putin belongs to the murderous KGB, he is a throwback to the past. He is a Red-Brown.'[2] The attack from their side immediately meant for us that Putin was 'our man': he was a patriot and a decent man to boot.

The ultra-'democratic schizos' were joined, with less gleeful abandon, by the more moderate 'democratic schizos' — Gusinsky,[3] Yavlinsky,[4] and

---

1   Sergei Kovalev (b. 1930) was a former political prisoner from Soviet times. Following the collapse of the Soviet Union, he became active in politics, particularly in the promotion of human rights in the Russian Federation, and served as an advisor to Boris Yeltsin. He was critical of the Russian intervention in Chechnya in the 1990s, urging Russian soldiers to surrender rather than fight. In recent years he has been critical of the Putin administration.

2   Red-Brown refers to a political position that combines elements both of socialism and authoritarian nationalism.

3   Vladimir Gusinsky (b. 1952) was the owner of many Russian newspapers and radio and television stations during the 1990s that were frequently critical of the Kremlin. After taking loans from the gas company Gazprom, he was unable to repay them when Gazprom demanded it in 2000, shortly after Putin took office and swore to strip Russia's oligarchs of their power. After being forced to give up his media holdings, he left the country as an exile and constructed a new media empire in Israel. A liberal, he has maintained close ties with a number of American politicians.

4   Grigory Yavlinsky (b. 1952) is a Russian economist who devised a plan in 1990, entitled *500 Days*, that detailed how Russia could transition from a socialist to a free market economy in less than two years. Although it wasn't implemented, Yavlinsky has remained a critic of the Kremlin from a liberal perspective ever since.

the ultra-Atlanticists, as well as Primakov[5] and Luzhkov[6] who were affiliated with them at some point. They had the following message: Putin is a nationalist and pro-superpower, and a protégé of the Yeltsin family and the Berezovsky-Abramovich-Mamut[7] clan. But it was evident that his association with a certain clan was a consequence of their competition with another clan, and such criticisms also proved beneficial for Putin.

The 'patriots', such as Prokhanov[8] and Zyuganov,[9] very cautiously and almost officially proclaimed that Putin was a 'Yeltsinist'. But if they had said that Putin was a hero, nobody would understand them.

Those who were anti-Chechnya were pleased by Putin's tough stance. They did not understand the rest of his policies, because they were simple voters, who ultimately gave their collective votes to Putin.

The oligarch Berezovsky, who was responsible for the 'technical support' behind the handover of power, crafted a patriotic image for Putin. Then he inadvertently became a 'corruptor' of the Eurasian type' (not just a corruptor), because the channels of the official withdrawal of capital to the United States and NATO member states were closed to him. 'Now he will

---

5   Yevgeny Primakov (b. 1929) is a Russian politician who began his career in Soviet times. In 2000 he challenged Putin in the presidential election, but withdrew before the election took place. He then became an advisor to and supporter of Putin.

6   Yuri Luzhkov (b. 1936) was one of the founders of the United Russia party, and was the Mayor of Moscow from 1992 until 2010.

7   Boris Berezovsky, Roman Abramovich and Alexander Mamut are all businessmen who were close to the Yeltsin administration and who favoured liberal reforms in Russia. Although they were all supporters of Putin in the beginning, they began to clash with him shortly after he took office. Berezovsky in particular, who controlled a great deal of the Russian media, became a bitter opponent of Putin and used his channels against him, ultimately causing Putin to threaten to destroy his media empire. He fled Russia in late 2000, and lived the rest of his life as an exile in the United Kingdom.

8   Alexander Prokhanov (b. 1938) is a writer and editor who has supported efforts to combine Communism with extreme nationalism in Russia.

9   Gennady Zyuganov (b. 1944) has been the First Secretary of the Communist Party of the Russian Federation (CPRF) since its foundation. The CPRF was founded in 1993 as a successor to the banned Communist Party of the USSR. It has attempted to formulate a new form of Communism with a more nationalist bent.

play with Asia', some thought at that point. He did not give a damn about liberal democrats.

It is clear that corruption is a bad thing, but the immediate eradication of corruption is impossible. It is a good slogan but every time one has to keep track of who benefits from it. Rooting out certain corrupt groups at a certain point is only beneficial to their competitors. Simple folk will not gain a single ruble from such manoeuvres. In order to eradicate it, a 'mental revolution' is necessary. The Eurasians think that corruption must be dealt with in stages, first crushing corruptors who work against the state for the benefit of the Atlantic hegemon, and then crushing the rest of them, including corruptors of the domestic Eurasian type. In fact, during the first stage of the fight against the Atlanticist corruptors one can side with the Eurasian type, and later get even with the latter.

Chubais[10] made an attempt to draw Putin over to the liberals using Putin's outspoken patriotism as a cover for the upcoming wave of liberal reform on the instructions of the West. This was the attempted strategy of the most liberal party of the period, The Union of Right Forces (SPS),[11] then headed by Sergei Kirienko.[12]

The fact that Putin was born in Saint Petersburg and worked with Chubais and Anatoly Sobchak[13] was an obvious drawback. The Russian people have always treated Saint Petersburg with suspicion. Moscow gained special importance when Constantinople fell, when Russia became the last Orthodox Tsardom, and the last Orthodox empire. The city always played a significant eschatological role in Orthodox Russia. It was said that 'Moscow is the Third Rome'. The meaning of the Tsardom was that of a state which

---

10   Anatoly Chubais (b. 1955) is a Russian economist who spearheaded the privatisation of the Russian economy in the early 1990s.

11   The Union of Right Forces was a party founded in 1999 with the aim of continuing the move toward a Westernised liberal market economy in Russia. It still exists but today claims to be a political public organisation rather than a party.

12   Sergei Kirienko (b. 1962) briefly served as Prime Minister under Yeltsin in 1998. He currently heads Russia's state nuclear energy programme.

13   Anatoly Sobchak (1937–2000) was the first democratically-elected mayor of Saint Petersburg from 1991 until 1996. Putin was one of his deputies during this period. Sobchak died under suspicious circumstances while campaigning for Putin.

recognises the truth of the Orthodox church in its entirety, and which is traditionally considered a barrier in the way of the son of perdition, the Antichrist, the katechon, 'the one who withholds' (the Second Epistle of Paul to the Thessalonians). The fall of Byzantium meant, from the apocalyptic Orthodox perspective, the dawn of apostasy and the universal rejection of Christianity. Moscow is the capital of an essentially new state: not national, but imperial, soteriological, eschatological, and apocalyptical. It is the last outpost of salvation, the Ark, the ground prepared for the descent of the New Jerusalem. 'And there will be no fourth.'[14]

'Peter',[15] Saint Petersburg, since day one established the Third Russia in terms of quality, structure and meaning. In a sense, this capital does not exist and cannot exist. 'There will be no fourth Rome.' This is already far from a national state or a soteriological Ark. This is a strange, giant chimera, a *post mortem* land and people who are existing and developing in a parallel realm located beyond history. This is a city from 'Navi,' the dark side, a city of moonlight, water, strange buildings, which are alien to the rhythm of history and the national and religious aesthetics. This is the reason why the authorities located in Moscow were seen as miracle-workers. In this case it was about the transmutation of the 'Peter-based' into the 'Moscow-based'.

The fact that Putin was born into a worker's family is remarkable. It was also rumoured that he was an Old Believer.[16] I personally liked Putin's psychological portrait in the *Zavtra* newspaper: 'A young wolf cub', a judo expert who is cruel and ruthless towards enemies. Very disciplined. The ruler of a great empire during a crucial point in history cannot be an intelligent and righteous Mr Nice Guy. There must be a 'crowned thunderstorm', the Terror of God. Everyone must shake with fear.

---

14   A sixteenth-century Russian monk named Filofei famously prophesied that Moscow would become the Third Rome. The first was Classical Rome, the second was Constantinople, but these cities had failed because their peoples failed to fully adopt Christianity. Filofei held that the mantle of upholding Christianity had now fallen to Moscow, and that there would be no fourth Rome since Moscow would fulfil its task where its predecessors had failed.

15   Peter is a common nickname for Saint Petersburg in Russian.

16   An Old Believer is a member of the Russian Orthodox Church who continues to follow the Church's practices that predate reforms that were instituted in the seventeenth century.

One thing is certain now: already at that point, after his emergence, I thought that Putin was not an answer but a task to be taken on, and the total balance of all his various facets is, overall, more Eurasian than Atlanticist. Putin could not break free from the objective laws of geopolitics. Even Yeltsin during his last years in office was not free from them, let alone Primakov during his ministerial term.

Of course, many things depended on his entourage and the battle of ideas around him. A huge part of Yeltsin's legacy was concentrated around Putin, the extirpation of which had to take a long time.

As a result, the debates around Putin's personality, since he had appeared seemingly out of nowhere, led to significant discord in all the political sectors of our society. He was named 'the great unknown' for a reason. But Putin was 'an unknown revealed', and with very sympathetic features. This is how we thought of him at the turn of the century.

Patriot Plays

How Putin Came to Power: PR-Patriotism

Vladimir Putin became Yeltsin's chosen successor under the following political scheme. Russia's pro-Western 'democratic' elite — oligarchs, mediacrats, liberal intelligentsia, and Moscow citizens who were sponging off of the interests of foreign powers and so on — realising that Yeltsin was unable to rule and that an explicit adoption of a liberal Atlanticist course would alienate the majority of the population, made up their mind to promote a manageable patriot with populist features. The same scenario had been prepared for Alexander Lebed.[17] Due to a number of factors, Putin was elected. This is an important fact: Putin was promoted by the Atlanticists, liberals and pro-Western oligarchs. His 'patriotism' was initially intended to be controlled and merely a front; it was in essence 'PR-patriotism'.

This PR-patriotism employed several components: its scenario, its directors, and its cast. The scenario was elaborated with the eager participa-

---

[17] Alexander Lebed (1950–2002) was a Russian Lieutenant General who went into politics in the 1990s. A critic of Boris Yeltsin, he ran against him in 1996, claiming that Russia needed a dictator, citing Augusto Pinochet as an ideal. He died in a helicopter crash.

tion of Boris Berezovsky; the directors were Alexander Voloshin,[18] Vladislav Surkov[19] and Gleb Pavlovsky,[20] and the principal roles were played by Putin and his Saint Petersburg entourage. It was clear from the outset that a demonstration of patriotism would require spectacular, large-scale action. The scriptwriters proposed to use Chechnya, which had previously played an important part in the Atlanticist project of Russia's disintegration. This part of the plan worked as planned: after the September 1999 apartment bombings in Moscow[21] the Russian army entered Dagestan, the second Chechnya campaign took place and Grozny was captured (1999–2000). The disintegration of the country and the separation of Chechnya were prevented. This is how Putin was legitimised. In retrospect it is clear that Berezovsky's iron grip was involved. He later became an outcast in London in 2001, where he was killed in March 2013.

The First Term: The Patriotic Jazz

Then one day, the directors decided to get rid of the scriptwriters of the first draft, labelling them 'enemy number two' ('enemy number one' being the Chechen terrorists). It started with the political liquidation of the media mogul Vladimir Gusinsky, who was a member of the first scriptwriters' team. Then Berezovsky was exiled. This further strengthened the overall system, making the directors the ultimate authority in Russian politics.

This period can be dubbed 'presidential-administration-ocracy'. In effect, the country was controlled by the presidential administration: Vo-

---

18   Alexander Voloshin (b. 1956) was Chief of the Presidential Administration both at the end of Yeltsin's term and at the beginning of Putin's. He was regarded as instrumental during the early years of Putin's administration.

19   Vladislav Surkov (b. 1964) was First Deputy of the Presidential Administration from 1999 until 2011, and is regarded as the chief ideologue and architect of the Russian political system as it exists today.

20   Gleb Pavlovsky (b. 1951) is a political scientist who has worked as an advisor to Putin.

21   In September 1999, following the Russian invasion of Dagestan, bombs were exploded on four occasions in apartment complexes in Moscow, Buynaksk, and Volgodonsk. 293 people were killed and over 600 injured. Although Islamist leaders in Chechnya denied responsibility for the attacks, despite having threatened attacks in Russia, Moscow blamed them and launched the Second Chechen War.

loshin and Surkov. They were the ones who determined the balance between 'patriotism' and 'liberalism'. This balance was constantly adjusted but one aspect was consistent: liberalism was the end and patriotism was the means to get to it. The national aspects of the drama were subject to Atlanticist interests (in foreign policy) and liberalism (in the economy). The patriotic rhetoric and demagoguery were not supposed to be backed up by any fundamental and irreversible substantive activity. The formula was built around superficial patriotism.

But after the removal of the 'scriptwriters' the patriotic posturing started to get some vague autonomous backing. This group was nicknamed 'the Peter Guys'.[22] The Peter Guys were not exactly a closely-knit group or a clear-cut ideological group, but the discharge of the initial scriptwriters opened up more space, strengthening the position of the actors and giving them more freedom. The overall action of the play, *The First Term*, was controlled by the directors, but the exit of the scriptwriters left some gaps in the script, which were immediately filled in by the 'improvisors'. The Peter Guys tried to turn a classical orchestra with a set score into patriotic jazz improvisation. Their main character was turning into a cult figure.

This was how a 'caprice' came about. The star started to meddle with the plot. The directors shook their heads. One of the last proposals of the Petersburg jazzmen was to butcher the patrons and entrepreneurs. In fact, it was quite logical because, overall, the performance was successful and became a box office hit. At the political level it meant that 'patriotism' gradually became as important as liberalism. It had become clear that they both now stood at the same level. The actors proclaimed that they were their own directors.

All Power to the Actors

Then new factors rushed into Russian political life. The 'new stagnation' was essentially over and we had to deal with the juxtaposition of three elements: a residual political scenario (liberal-democratic reforms in a slapstick patri-

---

[22] This refers to an entourage of advisors that Putin brought with him from Saint Petersburg when he became President.

otism sauce à la Zhirinovsky);[23] a residual political and economic leadership (the influence of the oligarchs, the Yeltsin family, mediacrats, and the community of experts — here the new 'patriotism' was kept under strict control) and the new improvisations (here patriotism for the first time got a chance to become fully-fledged).

So, these actors in the wrong play took power in the theatre. What were they facing? At this point the project required new directors and a new script. A dangerous illusion emerged that by poisoning the patrons, cutting off the electricity in the boxes and kicking the director out would mean a triumph for the President, the authorities and society. But behind a successful coup there are deep factors related to mass psychology: a coup must be backed by history, geopolitics, and the collective unconscious. Luckily, these repercussions (which were devised by the scriptwriters, who were estranged from the masses and, therefore, understood them perfectly) worked, but it was not the actors' achievement. Let's face it: if the Peter Guys (as a socio-psychological type) devised something along these lines on their own, they would still belong to the fringe of provincial law enforcement. They were hastily dressed, made up and jostled onstage. On the other hand, the scriptwriters and directors themselves underestimated the success of the performance. The spectators started wrecking the concert hall, shouting 'Encore! Bravo! Rub 'em all out in the outhouse!'[24] and the actors loved it. Rubbing 'em out is fun, but it is not enough.

So, a new script was needed. Luckily, the Peter Guys themselves realistically assessed the contents of what they had to work with. The slogan 'away with the director' also created a problem. It was now unclear what exactly

---

23   Vladimir Zhirinovsky (b. 1946) is the leader of the Liberal-Democratic Party of Russia, which he founded in 1990 as one of the first opposition parties allowed in the Soviet Union. An extreme nationalist of the populist variety, Zhirinovsky has long been known for his provocative statements and outrageous actions, which resonate with the frustrations of some Russian voters.

24   Following the apartment bombings in Moscow in September 1999, Putin, when he was still serving as Prime Minister under Yeltsin, famously said, 'We are going to pursue terrorists everywhere. If they are in the airport, we will pursue them in the airport. And if we capture them in the toilet, then we will waste them in the outhouse.' This phrase became closely identified with Putin during his election campaign the following year.

needed to be directed. The first thing that springs to mind is to invite the assistant director and the backstage crew to do it, or perhaps the prompters, so that they could make up the text in their box as the play went along. It was a reasonable idea, but it is not hard to guess who would have been their puppeteer (or, who would have called the tune). Those who had been fired did not vanish into thin air. Let us not forget: they owned the theatre. The only thing the rebelling actors were left with was the ecstatic crowd: the keys to the backstage, the cafeteria, and even the dressing rooms were gone.

The performance's programme had undergone significant changes. The years ahead raised a lot of questions, and it was important to note the objective factors, resources, and possibilities they presented. But the will and the intellect are a lot more important. Sadly, they are in very short supply. Given this situation, the default position of patriotism was a highly probable outcome, and this time a defeat could have been fatal. In all the hustle and bustle they could throw anyone forward: 'You write the script' and 'You will direct it'. But, as is often the case, these tasks were given to the actors themselves, as well as the stagehands, the lighting technicians, and even the ticket-takers. Creating a political elite with a new ideology is a time-consuming and laborious task. For the first eight years the Putin men were engaged in anything but this. Today the circumstances have made the issue of 'grey patriotic matter' especially relevant.

The Twelve Labours of Putin

Even at the outset of his first term, Putin accomplished labours worthy of Hercules, very concrete feats.

Labour No. 1: He prevented the disintegration of Russia in the Caucasus, built a bulwark against the Wahhabi[25] invasion of Dagestan, and repossessed two-thirds of Chechnya (leaving a third under the control of the rebels).

Labour No. 2: He cracked down on the parochialism fostered by the previous regime. In one swift move he cut the Federation Council down to

---

25 Wahhabism is an extremely strict, literal interpretation of Sunni Islam. Many militant jihadis around the world claim to follow its teachings, or an ideology derived from it.

size, which went from being a body of dissent to a quietly obedient organisation. He boxed the ears of the governors and booed the brash national separatists in the republics.

Labour No. 3: He introduced federal districts, tying the administrative-territorial structure of the Russian Federation (RF) to a military scheme, which gave ample, albeit nominal, powers to civil servants, who are not elected but appointed by Moscow, and who are responsible, first and foremost, for national security and who report directly to the federal government. These are the strongholds of Russia.

Labour No. 4: He exiled the two most notorious oligarchs from Russia, who had only a moment before manipulated the country, public opinion, the government, and the President in any way they wanted and gotten away with it. The rest were cut down to size.

Labour No. 5: He gave a green light to the integration processes in the Commonwealth of Independent States (CIS), proclaimed the creation of the Eurasian Economic Community (EurAsEC),[26] supported the Eurasian idea in his Astana speech (at Gumilev University),[27] and announced the establishment of the Common Economic Space (CES), including the RF, Belarus, Ukraine, and Kazakhstan.

Labour No. 6: He included the concept of a multipolar world[28] in his national security policy for the RF, which practically means that Eurasian-

---

26 The Eurasian Economic Community was proclaimed in 1996 and includes Russia, Belarus, Kazakhstan, Kyrgzstan, Tajikistan, and Uzbekistan.

27 In June 2004, Putin addressed a conference dedicated to the ideas of the Eurasian theorist, Lev Gumilev, and praised him for depicting the world in terms of a united Eurasia in opposition to the West, calling it an idea that was beginning to 'move the masses'.

28 A central concept of Dugin's Eurasianism is that since the collapse of the Soviet Union and the bipolar global order that had existed prior to that, geopolitics has been that of a unipolar world dominated solely by the United States, which has allowed the US to dictate the global order ever since. The Eurasianists favor a transition to a multipolar world, in which powers from all the major areas of the globe will stand at roughly the same level and look after the interests of their own regional blocs.

ism[29] has been legally recognised as the primary international strategy of Russia.

None of the above had been realised by Boris Yeltsin, who, in fact, did just the opposite on all six points: it was Yeltsin who gave birth to all the policies that Putin set out to eliminate.

It is evident that Putin has achieved a number of profound things. The bread-and-butter nature of his actions has brought me personally and the Eurasia Movement, which is headed by me, to support President Putin and the radical centre.

Unaccomplished Labours

The labours that Putin has not yet accomplished are:

Labour No. 1: He has not fully completed the first six points.

Labour No. 2: He has not finally made up his mind concerning relations with the United States.

Labour No. 3: He has not understood the dead-end nature of using the radical-liberal paradigm in economics.

Labour No. 4: He has not implemented a rotation of the political elite. The old political apparatus is still working according to the previous model and its seeming technical efficiency conceals its fundamental inadequacy.

Labour No. 5: He has not gathered an efficient team of his own that he could call upon for assistance in the process of further reform.

Labour No. 6: He has not yet tackled in earnest the strengthening of the Eurasian ideology as the basis of Russia's place in the world of the future.

These six accomplished and unaccomplished labours characterise Putin's current position. This is his status quo. Putin is like a tight-rope walker standing halfway over the precipice. Now he is facing a painful dilemma: which direction should he take, forward or backwards? But whatever deci-

---

29 Eurasianism first emerged as an idea among Russian émigrés in Europe following the October Revolution, believing that Russia is a unique civilisation that is neither European nor Asian, but possesses its own unique nature and destiny. Eurasianism re-emerged after the collapse of the Soviet Union and is the idea underlying Dugin's own Eurasia Movement. Eurasianists today also believe that it is Russia's duty to reintegrate those territories that were once part of the Russian Empire and/or the Soviet Union into Russia.

sion he makes, he will face significant risks. Following the logic of his first six feats, one has to go all the way and complete the other six. This definitely incurs risks, since opposition from all sides, especially the Atlanticists, will only grow, and the rope is thin. If it breaks there is a precipice underneath. Turning back is equally risky. Everything that he has done up to now will turn against him with all its might. Specifically, in this case he will have to stand against a burgeoning Eurasianism. In effect, the Putin majority that liberal analysts like to discuss so much is in fact the 'Eurasian majority'.

We applaud his first six feats, sympathise with the extremely complicated historical and political situation in which Putin operates, and we fully support the logic of his deeds and wish him success in realising the rest of them. We are ready to join him in this realisation in any capacity and on any basis. We want Putin to bring everything to a conclusion, to continue achieving his Herculean labours. Of course, if Putin decides to turn back by reversing his earlier deeds — if he gives Chechnya to the Wahhabis, for example, or offers sovereignty to those who just can't get enough of it, or brings the oligarchs back to Russia and begs for their forgiveness, releases Khodorkovsky,[30] annuls the federal districts, repents on NTV,[31] revises his conception of national security by accepting unipolar globalism and prioritises American interests over Russian national interests, or dissolves the CIS and EurAsEC — then it will be very hard to support him. But it will not be *the* Putin, the man over the precipice, but rather some kind of dark double. However, if you think about how much has changed, you will realise that today such a scenario is no longer likely.

On the Brink of Collapse

One has to admit that Putin's liberal economic policy is not exactly in accord with Eurasian orthodoxy which, for its own part, strives to develop the social sector, implementing economic planning in strategic areas and placing

---

30 Mikhail Khodorkovsky (b. 1963), an outspoken critic of Putin, was a Russian oligarch who was arrested in 2003 on charges of fraud and ultimately imprisoned. Putin pardoned him and he was released in December 2013 (after this was written).

31 A Russian television network created by Gusinsky which was known for its criticisms of Putin's policies.

national interests above a purely market-based logic. After 9/11 the issue of Russian–American relations became ambiguous, not to say conflicting, to the extent that short-tempered patriots, prone to panic, started talking about 'Putin's betrayal of Eurasian interests'. I tried not to jump to any immediate conclusions, but the tightrope walker's hesitation at the halfway point was all too evident.

Incidentally, the post-9/11 Putin majority was declared as dissolved by the political analyst Gleb Pavlovsky. He based this proposal on the ephemeral notion of 'civil society'[32] — a concept, created by an erratic liberal Atlanticist group, which is quite alien to Russia.

For my part, I have always reckoned that Putin will balance (undoubtedly within Eurasianism) between the two extremes: Left (socialist) Eurasianism and Right (liberal) Eurasianism. Alas, it subsequently emerged that the Atlanticist tendencies among the country's leaders were still in play. But the USA, by definition, does not have a positive geopolitical scenario to offer Russia. A good Russia for the US is a weak Russia: a shrivelled, emaciated, disjointed Russia, near dead, 'a black hole', as defined by Zbigniew Brzezinski.[33] This is why the Atlanticist course would inevitably lead to a dead end, and its disastrous and unpopular nature is becoming more and more evident to Putin, which means that his conversion to Eurasianism became inevitable. I thought that it should have happened much earlier, naturally and consistently, but history in the subjunctive is quite pointless. Reality corrected our forecasts relating to his labours: Putin failed to use the time of his first presidential term for a consistent and irreversible realisation of Eurasian reforms, and did not manage to achieve all twelve labours. In summing up Putin's overall activity during his first term from the Eurasian perspective, one has to acknowledge that, after adopting some Eurasian measures, Putin

---

32 Advocates of civil society in Russia favour a greater interaction between the government and those organisations which claim to advocate for the wishes of the citizenry, in particular Non-governmental organisations (NGOs).

33 Zbigniew Brzezinski (b. 1928) is a Polish-American political thinker who served as National Security Advisor to President Carter, where he advocated for greater confrontation with the Soviet Union, and who has been influential in several other American administrations up to the present day. He is still a well-regarded political and geopolitical commentator, where he defends American interests and is highly critical of Russia.

met with Eurasianism's lack of consistency in the professional, ideological, organisational and presentational sense, and under growing pressure from the Atlanticists he failed to consistently toe the Eurasian line. Naturally, the US, realising that Eurasianism was challenging its global domination, was not wasting its time.

Despite stating this I would like to note that the Eurasianists never gave up their hopes for Vladimir Putin, neither did they abandon their fight for him. At the same time, new horizons for difficult work were opened. Without a solid and dependable foundation — theoretical, political, organisational, administrative, and economic — Putin's Eurasian reforms have no chance of being realised. Therefore, we will have to continue working with our sleeves rolled up for Putin, and in the name of Putin, in order to have a truly popular leader supported by the 'Eurasian majority'.

Putin becomes an Ideal Ruler of the Period

In the year 1999, in the seventh month,
from the sky will come the great King of Terror,
bringing back to life the great King of the Mongols.
Before and after, Mars to reign by good fortune.

— Michel de Nostredame (Nostradamus)[34]

Instead of the great King of Terror, on 11 August 1999 there came Putin.

— Alexander Dugin, New Year's Speech to Arctogaia,[35] 31 December 1999

My principal field of activity is the exploration of ontology: I am interested in the field of meanings, nodes of being, and paradigms which manifest themselves everywhere and in everything. One can say that I am an ontological philosopher. All the other elements — sociology, history of religion, geopolitics, political science, cultural studies, literary studies, and so forth, stem from ontology.

---

34   Century 10, Quatrain 72.

35   A group dedicated to the study of religious and mystical ideas that was run by Dugin in the late 1990s and early 2000s.

For many strenuous years my hard-won ideas, which came at enormous cost and effort, were pilfered at every turn by hordes of intellectual jackals and mainstream plagiarists. These years brought me nothing but a barrage of criticism, suppression, abuse, and filth. I did not even manage to achieve things which mediocre social second-raters are usually able to achieve through far less effort.

Power from the Eurasian Perspective: Predetermination

In this context I understand power by Byzantine standards, as a kind of immanent absolute. Any power comes from God, but God does not always bring good news. Sometimes the power to do evil is granted to people as a test of their loyalty to God, as a temptation. Then, following the lead of Saint Joseph Volotsky[36] and Protopope Avvakum,[37] one must say 'no' to evil power, right down to regicide, even if a Tsar abnegates his faith, the sacred legacy of 'our venerable and God-bearing fathers'. But, albeit evil and satanic, their power still remains holy and sacral, but in a negative sense. It was on this basis that I initially assessed the emergence of Vladimir Vladimirovich Putin. Everything he said and did was perfectly in line with the reality of contemporary Russia, everything represented our salvation in the right way, the salvation of our motherland. Putin is the ideal ruler for the current period. He is a tragic figure: he has a horrible entourage made up of exhausted people, a sea of despicable worms who are fouling up the entire field of his movement. And he is methodically and steadily, bit by bit, clearing away all of this dismal legacy. He is like an alchemist turning black into white. It is only getting grey so far but

---

36 Saint Joseph Volotsky (1440–1515) was a monk who supported the idea that the Tsars were God's representatives on Earth, but he also believed that this authority was valid provided that the Tsar followed the Church's teaching and authority.

37 Avvakum Petrov (1620–1682) was a Protopope who led the opposition against Patriarch Nikon's attempts to reform the Russian Orthodox Church, believing it to be a deviation from the Church's mission. Avvakum was imprisoned several times and finally burned at the stake for his resistance. His followers persisted and later became known as the Old Believers.

this is just the beginning. The dawn is breaking, the dawn in boots.[38] I devoted that article to the way the new Eurasian order — the solar, transcendental, continental KGB — would establish the positive values of Eurasia. I thought at the time that this order should include a new breed of young people, merciless towards their enemies, ironic, with a crimson glimmer in their eyes and leather dragon wings behind their backs, with binoculars and walking sticks, poison rings and time bombs. My imagination painted a vision of a golden dawn, a dawn in boots. I came to the conclusion that turning the country toward a patriotic mood, retaining its territorial integrity and developing it independently along its own national path required people of a new type, a new social layer. Such people, I thought, would come not from political parties, the bureaucracy, or from the business sector, but from the secret service. I thought that they should be state officials who constantly deal with the dark, secretive side of things and who would become a staple of the Eurasian renaissance. As professional patriots, they should have begun a new round of nation-building — the realisation of the Eurasian project.

I still believe in Putin and support him. The fact that it was he who replaced Yeltsin seems like providence. Although sometimes I think that the Eurasian position that we talk about in reference to Putin would have been taken by (almost) any other successor to Yeltsin. And even Yeltsin in his later years very slowly, intermittently, and by beating around the bush, began to move in this direction.

Eurasianism is inevitable. Sooner or later everyone will have to admit that. But Putin heartily says 'yes' to this major tendency, without trying to shirk it or act as if he is merely serving time. With his eyes open, unblinking, he is listening to the call of our history, painstakingly trying to catch it. And even if he accidentally gets carried away in the process, he should be forgiven. Putin is looking for a way out of the precipice, *de profundis clamavi*,[39] 'out of the depths I have cried [unto Thee, O Lord]'. His eyes are sad, as Mamleev[40]

---

38 Alexander Dugin, 'Dawn in Boots', available at the *Arctogaia* Web site: www.arctogaia.com/public/zarya.html - an article about the role of former KGB officers in Russia's Eurasian renaissance.—AD (This article in Russian only.—Ed.)

39 From Psalm 130.

40 Yuri Mamleev (b. 1931) is a writer and a metaphysical realist.—AD

notes. It means that he has not lost the chain of being; it means that, to a certain extent, he is an ontologist... Anyone would become a little 'putin' if he were in Putin's shoes. It seems like he is an Old Believer by birth. There is a mystical diary written by the Old Believer Anna Putina, consisting of famous ancient Russian hieroglyphs that contain a cryptic narration about the forthcoming secret destiny of Russia and the end of time. It all fits...

Eurasianist tendencies will continue to grow ever stronger with Putin in power. There will be active relations with the Asian countries, and Russia will cautiously start moving towards a European policy as well. The integrationist impulses of the CIS will be palpable, especially in economics. Putin will prepare the most favourable conditions for Russia's return to the global arena as an active player. Not immediately, but '*trois pas en avant, deux en arriere, tel va le maître aux pieds fondus*'[41] (as apparently said by Jean Richepin),[42] but he will reestablish the deserved power and dignity of Russia.

Circumstances will be favourable to us. The US will proclaim that it will always have the priority in international affairs, which will cool down relations somewhat. That said, an anti-American mood will spread all over the world. The inevitable collapse of the dollar is not far off. Russia must stand at the forefront of anti-Americanism and lead the others. When the US, the real evil empire,[43] collapses, we will help the victims and welcome refugees. Sooner or later Carthage will be destroyed,[44] and Putin will take another step towards the realisation of this dream.

I have participated in Russian politics for many years. I am one of the oldest Russian politicians. My views have changed somewhat but not so fast as those of the others. All other people's views are changing so drasti-

---

41 'Three steps forward, two steps back.'—AD

42 Jean Richepin (1849–1926) was a French writer. The phrase comes from his 1884 play, *Les Blasphemes*.

43 President Reagan infamously referred to the Soviet Union as the 'evil empire' in a speech in March 1983 in which he called for greater confrontation with the USSR to counter its expansionist aims.

44 In the second century BC, 'Carthage must be destroyed' was a popular saying among the Romans during the Punic Wars, who believed that the long-standing threat posed by their rival could only be ended through the destruction of the city. The Romans finally did destroy the city in 146 BC.

cally and unpredictably that, forgive me for saying so, it seems that they don't have any views at all. Either that or their views do not change at all, against all odds, which is the same thing. I am the most consistent Russian politician: I started with traditionalism,[45] the Conservative Revolution,[46] the Third Way,[47] and Eurasianism, and I am still holding the same line. I veered to the Left a little during the 1990s, recognising the traditionalist archaic aspect in socialism and Communism, which I had not seen until socialism fell. After the collapse of the Soviet regime I turned from an anti-Soviet patriot into a pro-Soviet one.

In order to realise my worldview I travelled through various political milieus, and I left a significant trail everywhere I went. From the national patriot movement in the mid-1980s, the newspaper *Den* ('Day'), the Right-Left opposition, and the Front of National Salvation,[48] up to my participation in the development of the ideology of the CPRF (Communist Party of the Russian Federation) see the books and articles by Gennady Zyuganov, as whole passages in them have been copied from my work); from my associa-

---

45 Traditionalism, a school of thought initiated by the philosophers René Guénon, Julius Evola and Frithjof Schuon holds that there is a set of transcendental metaphysical principles which lies at the heart of all authentic religions and mystical traditions, and which remains the same even when there are differences in the exoteric practices and doctrines. Traditionalism is also deeply critical of the modern world.

46 The Conservative Revolution designates a loose confederation of anti-liberal German thinkers who wrote during the Weimar Republic. There was a great diversity of views within the ranks of the Conservative Revolutionaries, but in general they opposed both democratic capitalism and Communism in favour of a synthesis of aristocratic, nationalism and spiritual values with socialism.

47 The Third Way is a term used for a wide variety of political and economic ideologies that have attempted to to transcend the dichotomy between liberal democracy and socialism. The various fascist movements of the mid-twentieth century were iterations of the Third Way.

48 The Front of National Salvation was established in 1992 as an alliance of Communists and nationalists in opposition to the post-Soviet reforms being enacted by Yeltsin's administration. Yeltsin banned the party (the first time this occurred in post-Soviet Russia), but this was overruled by the courts a few months later. The Front played a key role in the constitutional crisis of September-October 1993. The Front collapsed in 1994.

tion with the ideological project of National Bolshevism[49] as represented by the Limonovites[50] (this National Bolshevist ideology was resurrected, updated, and ceremoniously served by me to the boorish rogues led by this Parisian grandpa, who later reduced it to primitivism and the absurd) to my creation of the original version of the ideology of the Party of Russia's Rebirth.[51] In the process, my ideas were largely borrowed by the LDPR (Zhirinovsky's Liberal-Democratic Party of Russia) and Our Home — Russia[52] (in a more 'civilised' form), as well as Fatherland — All Russia[53] (I published two major conceptual articles in Luzhkov's magazine *Moya Moskva*, whose theses Luzhkov later reiterated, although he misquoted them).

Today the members of Putin's entourage - minus a diminishing remnant of liberals - are speaking my language. True, I am little-known, but only because thieves never reveal the sources of their wealth. I think this is self-evident. The Eurasia Movement which I am leading is a kind of intellectual

---

49 Several groups claim to be National Bolshevik, both in Russia and abroad. National Bolshevik ideology, which emerged after the First World War as an attempt to synthesise Communism and nationalism, was originally formulated by some participants in Germany's Conservative Revolution, such as Ernst Jünger and Ernst Niekisch. National Bolshevism was also present among some members of the anti-Soviet White movement and even among some Soviet Communists in the days of the Russian Civil War, although Lenin and Stalin both opposed it. Regardless, elements of the ideology re-emerged in Stalin's brand of nationalism, which began to appear in the 1930s.

50 Eduard Limonov (b. 1943) is a Russian writer who lived as an expatriate in both the US and in Paris during the Soviet era. Limonov returned to Russia in 1991 and founded the National Bolshevik Party (NBP) the following year, and Dugin was an influential early member. Dugin soon left the party to found his own, the National Bolshevik Front, and later abandoned National Bolshevism altogether to form the Eurasia Movement in 2001, although he still acknowledges a debt to NB thought. The party was banned in 2007.

51 The Party of Russia's Rebirth was a Leftist nationalist party established in 2003 by Gennady Seleznev, who had been the Speaker of the Duma between 1996 and 2004 and a member of the Communist Party. It was dissolved in 2008.

52 Our Home — Russia was a political party that existed between 1995 and 2000. A liberal party, it was instrumental in Yeltin's re-election in 1996. It merged into the United Russia party in 2000.

53 Fatherland — All Russia was a political party between 1998 and 2002 that was founded by Yuri Luzhkov and supported the election of Putin. In 2002 it merged with the United Russia party.

order, and a scientific laboratory. More and more wealthy individuals have been joining us, who are seriously concerned with the future of our fatherland, who are interested in the models of development being put into practice by the country and the people and in the National Idea, and who are aware of the practical advantages and importance of Eurasianism.

Slowly, gradually, but inevitably we are moving towards our goal. Previously, the Eurasian movement in contemporary Russia had been represented solely by young non-conformist intellectuals. Today a significant layer of this movement includes academics, businessmen, industrialists, law enforcement officers, religious men (Old Believers, Muslims, mystics, etc.), administrative officials, journalists, oil traders, and, traditionally, a broad segment of the counter-culture.

The Conservative Revolution is on Its Way

I have always held to the same view: Russia must be a strong state, prosperous, powerful, and independent. We have to face many enemies globally and our principal enemy is the United States of America, which makes no particular secret of its hostile attitude towards Russian civilisation. The US is the heir to the Anglo-Saxon empire, and we spent whole centuries in a geopolitical standoff with it. In earlier times, when the Russian government veered towards pro-American and pro-Western values, I was among the patriotic opposition. But when the government changed and started going back to a normal course, which had already begun prior to Putin, such as when Yevgeny Primakov had been appointed Prime Minister, I became more loyal to our rulers. The appointment of Primakov gave me new hope.

As a patriot, when Putin arrived I was in a festive mood. I had high hopes for Putin, considering that he is a figure who had been historically predetermined. The political processes that had previously been unable to manifest to an adequate degree became 'normalised' with Putin. They include Moscow's hard line with Chechnya and the signing of the document that created the Eurasian Economic Community — things that I had talked about for many years. The critical point came with Putin's statement that 'Russia has always seen itself as a Eurasian country'[54] — all this fully coincides with my stance.

With the emergence of Putin I finally developed my worldview and ideological position, coining the term 'radical centre'. Basically, it refers to centrism, but of the Eurasian type. It is not about simple submission to the powers-that-be but about constructive and active cooperation with the Eurasian power — the power that consciously and wilfully moves in the direction that I had urged it to move in for all those years filled with hard and dramatic struggle. The only thing that remains from my previous phase is radicalism. The role of my radicalism is to establish Eurasian tendencies, ideas, and projects with all possible passion, earnestness, and strenuousness. Another facet of my centrist radicalism is that I (contrary to today's conformists) consider Putin to be unconditionally good. If there are any negative aspects of his presidency, I believe that they are totally subordinate to his positive qualities, to the extent that they are not even worth noting. Blemishes disappear naturally. We are witnessing now what is gradually happening to the oligarchs, who had been an eyesore. They turned out to be not nearly as scary as they seemed. And where is the parochialism of the republics and the governors' separatist ambitions now? They simply vanished into thin air.

With the emergence of Putin, the powers-that-be finally took note of the Eurasian theory and the idea of the Third Way. Look around you. Look at the language that power speaks and at the topics that are being discussed in the media. They could not have been discussed without the conceptual layer represented by the Third Way — social, geopolitical, and, finally, economic. It began and was introduced by this humble narrator. The proof is redundant. Just compare the current situation with the one 20 years ago, when these developments were only in the making. Third Way concepts are getting both their feet firmly on the ground. It is another matter that it happened not through one specific party but by way of delegating certain ideas

---

54   'Russia has always felt like a Eurasian country', Beta-PRESS, available at beta-press.ru/article/295.—AD (The article is in Russian only. Putin made this comment in November 2000, shortly after assuming the Presidency.—Ed.)

to different political forces. In other words, the conservative revolution[55] that traditionalist scholars had written so much about is happening before our very eyes. But it turned out to be a revolution not from below but from above, without a clearly defined social subject. The ideas only gradually entered our consciousness.

Look what the CPRF and United Russia[56] are talking about now and at what political analysts are writing, and then take a close look at the *Elements*[57] anthology and at my textbooks *The Foundations of Geopolitics* and *The Foundations of Eurasianism*,[58] and you will understand where these symbols, subjects, and terms stem from. For instance, note the origins of the words 'mondialism' (an aspiration to unite all countries under one global government) and 'conspirology' (a science dealing with conspiracy theories), which I first introduced into the Russian language. Those were simple loan words, but today they have been fully fleshed out and have been included in dictionaries. To quote the remarkable French poet Stéphane Mallarmé,[59] '*il faut changer la langue*' ('one has to change the language') and you will change the world. If we introduce our own linguistic rules, it will result in the changing of reality. After all, man is a linguistic being, inconceivable without language. 'Language is the house of being,'[60] said Martin Heidegger.

Ideological Evolution: The Eurasian Perspective

Practically all of the concrete and highly efficient steps that were undertaken by Putin were made at the very beginning of his first presidential term, in a dashing, unexpected, and rather tough manner. This manner became his political foundation. Just to remind you of what we had at that point:

---

55   Alexander Dugin, *The Conservative Revolution* (Moscow: Arctogaia, 1994).—AD (No English translation exists.—Ed.)

56   United Russia is currently the largest political party in Russia, and is the party of Putin.

57   *Elements* was a journal edited by Dugin.

58   None of these books has been translated into English as of yet.

59   Stéphane Mallarmé (1842–1898) was one of the major poets of the French Symbolist school.

60   Heidegger elaborates on this phrase in his 'Letter on "Humanism"', in *Pathmarks* (Cambridge: Cambridge University Press, 1998).

a liberal pro-Western elite, which hated Russia with all its heart, and the people which it dubbed 'this country'; the media, divided between scheming oligarchs who were waging wars against each other over the people's and the government's heads; the separatist hotbed in Chechnya; the blossoming totalitarian Islamist sects (the Wahhabis); the sovereignty of the regional barons; and a deep schism in society. The country was on the verge of a catastrophe: disintegration, terror, civil war and chaos, and society was stricken by apathy and silent resentment, while a grim, odious and sick tyrant was looming above it all.

Putin, when he came to power, gave a sharp and effective answer to all these challenges. He stopped the expansion of the Chechen Wahhabi separatists, and the Russians entered Grozny. He took the major media out of the hands of the most notorious oligarchs and placed them within the limits of minimal loyalty to the state and its people. He prevented Russia's disintegration into 'appanage principalities'[61] where the leaders of the Fatherland — All Russia were leading it. Putin reformed the Federation Council, deliberately weakening it, and strengthened the nation's territorial integrity, introducing the rigid structure of the federal districts. He created a better social atmosphere, harmonised the sharpest tensions and introduced the notion of 'fashionable patriotism'. He cracked down on the totalitarian religious sects. He suspended the seemingly imminent disintegration of the nation and gave the people a chance to catch their breath. This is the basis of his high approval ratings. This is the only Putin that the people accept and support.

Another aspect is his foreign policy. Here Putin followed two strategies at once: patriotic rhetoric and his vacillations between Europe and the US. Since Russia does not have the potential for a fully-fledged strategic autarchy of its own, the important choice lies between cooperation with the US or with Europe. Putin was indecisive in this regard. Since Russia's strategic interests, from a geopolitical standpoint, belong in the Russian-European strategic partnership, the President found himself in a difficult situation.

---

61   The ownership of territories which is passed to the children of a leader by right of heredity. Kievan Rus' established an appanage system in the eleventh century, which led to a great deal of infighting over the next four centuries and caused the fragmentation and weakening of the state.

The mighty US, using a carrot-and-stick approach, tried to suppress Russia, whereas indecisive Europe in its turn lent a helping hand before jerking it back. Theoretically, Putin needed to take a consistently Eurasian line and stick to it no matter what, be it the post-9/11 syndrome, the American aggression in Iraq, or even situations that arose prior to these events. All the steps he took in the Eurasian direction — the strengthening of relations with the Asian states, the integration processes within EurAsEC, the partnership with Europe, and so on can be regarded as successful. The concessions he made to the US were failures.

That being said, I have to admit the following: Putin had been extremely lucky all this time. Luck is a very curious quality. A question arose: what exactly was it that prevented the President from acting to the full extent of his power? I have formed an impression that Putin fought the counterattacks of the victims of his reforms, fighting a rear-guard action on the domestic political front. These counterattacks were very serious, and, to a large extent, Putin had to stay where he was or even step back a little on a number of points.

After the quick victory over the Chechen separatists, the operation assumed a protracted character: it was not quite a war, but neither was it a victory. Three years passed, and the initially besieged rebellious governors resurfaced among the ranks of United Russia as if nothing had happened, and, blackmailing the President with their election issues, started to seek their own profit. The federal districts proved to be largely inefficient and simply multiplied the ranks of hollow bureaucrats. The radical Islamist sects resumed their activities and spread all over the North Caucasus. 'Patriotism' and conservatism lacked any real substance and remained empty slogans and claptrap. Genuine political conciliation did not happen, and the Kremlin administration was still 'chasing Communists' and engaging in PR. In other words, Putin not only failed to develop and finalise his endeavours, but, on some issues, lost the positions that he had previously occupied.

Why did it happen? At first it seemed that Putin became President too fast. He simply did not have enough time to back himself ideologically, conceptually, in terms of his entourage, or politically, as befits such a high position. This severe personnel shortage and the absence of new blood in the political elite played an enormous role. Putin's protégés in most cases proved to be unable to handle their tasks properly, and as a result, the process of rotating the members of the political elite came to a standstill: the officials who had held office before Putin had been more efficient and had more experience, but they belonged to a different political paradigm; Putin's people were loosely-knit and haphazard, and their personal loyalty would have been enough only if the President had had a clear ideological base or dictatorial tendencies. There were some external reasons as well: the pressure from the West reached unprecedented heights. Any action aimed at strengthening Russia's position made the US unhappy, and it became a natural rallying point for all the internal agents of Western influence as well to the external levers of power, both economic and political.

Putin had yet to create a new political system, to implement fundamental reforms, to get the creation of a new political elite going, and to find traces of an actual counter-elite in contemporary Russian society that he could draw upon, either by growing it artificially or by redeploying some of the more efficient managers into the state's political sector. Without new blood, the country may have faced a collapse.

While Putin symbolises a respite, his place in history is uncertain. I am convinced that Russia has only one future — the Eurasian way, and I believe that Putin can only realise himself as a Eurasian President. It will be extremely difficult but it will be the right way.

CHAPTER 2

Putin's Ideology

Putin Owes Us All

Some analysts call Putin a patriot, others call him a liberal. The question remains: 'Who is Mr Putin?' Who is he, after all? Who or what influences his opinions? There are two factors that Putin has to reckon with in his decision-making. On the one hand, it is necessary to sustain a high level of credibility domestically, which manifests itself in high ratings, positive public opinion, support from the voters, and so on. On the other hand, there are external factors: support from the West, closer relations with Europe and NATO, and adequate performance in the area of foreign policy. These two factors are intertwined in a complex way and are almost inversely proportional.

The people of Russia have traditionally been expecting a tough stance from Putin, wishing for a stronger state, a patriotic orientation and the pursuit of a national identity, as indicated by numerous polls. At the same time, the outside world, especially Europe and the US, wants exactly the opposite: the introduction of dynamic liberal reforms, the establishment of pro-Western values, and compliance with the norms of the European community. According to the Russian Public Opinion Research Centre, 71% of Russians think that Russia belongs to a distinct, 'Eurasian' or Orthodox civilisation, and that therefore development in a pro-Western direction does not suit the country. Only 13% of respondents named Russia as part of Western civilisation. As liberal reforms are progressing, the negative backlash from patriotic voters (the so-called 'Putin majority') is growing against Putin and his actions. Even the Western press takes note of this: 'What makes Putin pursue an aggressively pro-Western policy at a time when most of his people do not want anything of the kind?' asked the *Los Angeles Times*.[1]

The Liberalism of the Between-election Cycle

Having been elected with the help of patriotic slogans, Vladimir Putin took advantage of the so-called 'between-election period' and acted in a liberal vein, scoring many points with the West. Apparently, Putin reckoned on the balance of the two vectors, not simply on a dogmatic 'patriotism' or an equally dogmatic 'liberalism'. In the process, the positions of the so-called 'Orthodox Chekists'[2] (patriotism) strengthened as the next elections approached. His midterm was a kind of peak in liberalism, after which, as the elections draw nearer, his liberal pro-Western inclinations tended to give way to the patriotic side. Accordingly, the balance of power in the Kremlin changed, namely toward empire-building initiatives, advocacy for a strong state, and increased momentum, which is also reflected in the strengthening of certain groups at the expense of other groups.

In order to maintain his strong position as the leader of the State, Putin has always striven to keep the pre-election balance in his political practice at 71% patriotism and 13% liberalism (strictly in accordance with the Russian Public Opinion Research Centre's results). This guaranteed his easy re-election. During all four years of Putin's second presidential term (as well as during Medvedev's presidency) we observed a reverse situation, where 71% of the state policy was oriented toward the West and 13% leaned toward patriotism.

---

1 'Pro-West Putin Snubs His Public' (16 May 2002), available at articles.latimes.com/2002/may/16/world/fg-russia16.

2 The Cheka was the original secret service of the Communist Party in the USSR, during the time of the Russian Revolution. The term 'Orthodox Chekists' refers to a circle of people who, like Putin himself, have or had connections to the secret police, but who today, unlike in militantly atheist Soviet times, are staunchly pro-Orthodox Church.

The Peter Chekists — the Myth Unrealised

That having been said, the patriotic pro-state ideology is a very vague category. The Peter Guys, as an actual group of proponents of this ideology, does not exist as such. There are various personalities from Saint Petersburg who are close to Putin, but we do not observe an alliance on the grounds of common viewpoints. The myth about the 'Orthodox Chekists' appears to me to have been a newspaper hoax. Past association with the secret service does not in itself constitute an ideology. It is rather a style, a type, which in certain situations may accommodate different belief systems, both patriotic and liberal pro-Western. It should be noted that the authors of the 'patriotic doctrine' from Putin's entourage, who are considered to be the 'Orthodox Chekists', are not yet backed by any ideological think tank or serious intellectual group. Besides, in their ersatz blueprints they keep relying on the traditional community of liberal spin doctors who ultimately, with careful reservations, call for globalisation and defend liberal reforms adapted to Russian conditions, which is not exactly patriotic and not at all Orthodox. And, vice versa, the group in power, which is not from Peter at all, has lately bolstered the process of the development of patriotic and ideological projects. In my opinion, the authorities today are more pragmatic than ever. There is virtually no one in power who has any distinct, colourful and consistent convictions, apart from the ultra-Atlanticist Chubais. But the need for ideology is there, so somebody will eventually step in and deal with this: if not sympathisers, then pragmatists.

A liberal course always reveals its negative aspects, be it the people's dissatisfaction with housing and utility reform, the monetisation of benefits, rising fuel tariffs, the liberalisation of natural monopolies or anything of that kind. In addition, a Western-oriented course will ultimately prove futile. This strengthens the importance of the patriotic factor: if Putin does not use it, all dividends will go to the opposition. Given the powerful potential of patriotism, which served as a basis for Putin's first election, this potential has still not acquired a clear-cut political shape. Today the institutions capable of offering an adequate political and ideological backing to Vladimir Putin are virtually non-existent. There is a group which proclaimed itself 'the party in power' in the form of the United Russia party, but politically and ideologically it is full of problems. This party has been diluted by extremely diverse characters, both Left and Right, regional rebels and pro-state officials, charismatic politicians and humble civil servants. But United Russia is not so much a political supporter as a barometer of Putin's own election prospects, and this does not make his life any easier. I do not consider that a party such as United Russia is capable of taking on any sort of coherent ideology (which has yet to be developed), nor of giving Vladimir Vladimirovich Putin additional support. It is something more along the lines of a preventive measure against rebelliousness, as well as an administrative resource complying with the party line. This is a good start, but far from sufficient. I think that Eurasianism will deal with the problem of ideology much more successfully; it has gradually become a very popular doctrine: it combines conservatism with a certain openness, being a kind of 'scientific patriotism' based on geopolitics. I am sceptical towards attempts to inculcate the Eurasian idea into the patented 'party of power'. That's why the idea of an independent 'Eurasia' party was born some time ago — a pro-Putin patriotic party with a distinct ideology.

The Strengths of the Eurasian Ideology

One strength of Eurasianism is that it is applicable to foreign policy. The Eurasia Movement from its outset made it a principal aim to create a Eurasian union as a direct equivalent to the European Union.

While we pursue closer relations with Eastern countries we also support tighter links with Europe. This is what Eurasianism is all about. Other types of Putin supporters are doomed to be a pale shadow of the pragmatism of his external policy, which drastically limits room for manoeuvre. As for relations with the US, Eurasianism by the very nature of its ideology cannot look to them for partners. Of all the political forces in the US we only support the isolationist Republicans because they are calling for the US to stop sponsoring globalisation, concentrate on internal problems and leave the rest of the world in peace. At the same time, Eurasianism believes that the future of Russia depends on an efficient conclusion of a series of strategic alliances with the states of the 'coastal zone' — from Europe through the Arabic world to Asia and the Far East. Pragmatism cannot be the content of a specific policy. It always operates within certain limits and must leave room for its practical operation. For Putin it is extremely important to have both the loyal Atlanticist party flank and the equally loyal Eurasian one. This combination will give him a free hand in any manoeuvre. The Atlanticists are doing well today but the vagueness and disjointedness of Eurasianism is being fully exploited by the opposition, but it is precisely Eurasianism that can help not only to improve the domestic situation in the country but also to make foreign policy much more consequent and effective.

At the beginning of his first term Putin had to grapple with what he had inherited. He came to power at a critical point in our national history and neither he nor society as a whole fully understood what had happened. What are we? Where should we go? Where are our enemies? Where are our friends? Does Russia have any friends at all? But I think that Vladimir Vladimirovich Putin owes us all: the Russian people, the country, and its history. Putin's mission is to create in Russia a stable political regime, consistent with Russian national interests, the interests of its people and the priorities of our geopolitics. And only then may he think about retirement. The current balance is deceptive and very fragile. It only exists at all thanks to Putin. Preferably it should be able to stand on its own on the basis of the political system and its mentalities. Creating an adequate, subtle and elaborate policy in the area of nation-building, patriotism and the National Idea is, arguably, the most important mission, and it can only be accomplished by Putin. As for us, we will do our best to help him with this.

Ideological Expertise of the Political Environment

In order to assess the political environment in which Putin started to operate, let me begin with some general definitions. One should differentiate the ideological leanings of the population (which are sometimes very obscure), the party forces and the political leaders. In contemporary Russia relations between the above are very strange, and are of a 'dialectical' type. In terms of intuitive sympathy the following groupings can be singled out: patriotic and non-patriotic, that is, liberal. In recent years the balance shifted dramatically towards patriotism, although the power elite, mass media and community of experts are still comprised of people with a rather squeamish attitude towards our country and our people. This is an apparent imbalance: the mainstream attitudes are markedly nationalistic, something that is shared by Vladimir Putin and his close circle, but the political paradigms remain liberal to a significant degree. One can discern a certain paradox here: the slow rotation of speechwriters or of their gradual adaptation to the changing situation has long forced Putin to use a strange language: he has been trying to voice the national-statist ideas using liberal jargon.

Whatever the case, politically the overwhelming majority of the population today is favourably disposed towards Russia's return as a superpower. How can these sympathies be categorised? The intuitive — apolitical, middlebrow — superpower sympathisers recognise one of their own in Putin. In this case the superpower orientation coincides with political centrism. This gives Putin more support: it is as if he unites both nationalist sentiments and centrist conformism.

Then there are the more politicised superpower supporters. The Left-wing ones are in a certain opposition to Putin. They are the CPRF and A Just Russia.[3] But this opposition — 'superpowerism' against 'superpowerism' — weakens the position of the Communists, who had been previously consolidated against the overt Russophobia of the Yeltsin regime. It appears that a portion of the Left-wing patriotic electorate can under certain conditions be incorporated into the pro-Putin movement. Zyuganov represents the dogmatic core of this sector but it seems to me people are starting to get tired of him.

Then there are the 'semi-superpowerist' liberals. These are former radical pro-Western reformers, who came to the pragmatic conclusion that they could not go on as they had due to the prospect of their ultimate collapse. They reluctantly and disgustedly took to Russian superpower slogans,

---

3 A Just Russia is a socialist party that was formed in 2006 and staunchly defends Russia's welfare programmes.

stressing 'economic liberalisation' (The Right Cause)[4] or 'humanitarian democracy' (Yabloko,[5] Yavlinsky). This electorate is not owned by the Right either and is likely, under certain conditions, to support Putin. However, this electorate is very small in size.

The above are followed by the lumpen superpower supporters, people with bad taste, petty criminals, and political imbeciles — they are the congregation of the LDPR. Superpowerism is filtered here through aggressive, stupid, albeit sometimes biting, humour. This is the audience of the TV shows *Okna*[6] or *Prozhektorperiskhilton*,[7] but more politically inclined. They have ersatz patriotism and superpowerism as a disease. They can partially support Putin if a couple of his spin doctors decide to use a patriotic agenda in his election campaign.

And finally there are dogmatic superpowerists. These are marginal ultra-patriots, skinheads, and everyday racists. This sector is colourful and brutal, but totally disjointed politically, its leaders being petty maniacs with atrophied muscles. As an electorate they are of little importance, but they are useful as a good argument in the PR campaigns that superpower opponents wage against superpower supporters. Who skinheads and ultra-nationalists will ultimately vote for is not important. Most likely, on the night prior to the election they will drink one too many and not make it to the ballot-boxes.

The final group is the anti-superpower liberals. They are represented by *Novaya Gazeta*,[8] the human rights movements, the economic sector of the government, the oligarchs, the liberal hallucinations of Chubais, *Ekho*

---

[4] The Right Cause is a party established in 2009 that favours liberal economic policies and democratic reforms.

[5] Yabloko is a party that was established in 1993 with the aim of supporting liberal reforms in Russia. It also favours closer relations with the US and Russian membership in the EU.

[6] *Okna*, or 'The Windows', is a talk show.

[7] 'Projector Paris Hilton' was a satirical news programme, the title of which was a spoof of a Gorbachev-era programme that had been called 'Projector of the Perestroika'.

[8] 'New Gazette' is a popular liberal and pro-Western opposition newspaper.

Moskvy,[9] Kasparov,[10] Venediktov,[11] the homosexual faction in the State Duma, and numerous other well-known media personalities. Today they have a tiny electorate which can be ignored as a statistical fluctuation (it is known that a relatively large percentage of voters in Russia tick the wrong boxes in the ballots due to stress or poor eyesight). The liberal electorate is almost non-existent. They are of course against Putin but he can disregard them. On the other hand, liberals still occupy strong positions among the political elite — in inverse proportion to their support in society. Since they have the support of external forces, they may inflict serious harm on Putin and the country, something they are unfortunately engaging in with some degree of success.

So, what do we have here? Putin as a Russian superpower supporter — without going into details about whether he is Right-wing, Left-wing or of any other denomination — is theoretically able to select his electorate from a huge field, significantly surpassing United Russia in size. This scenario was attempted under the All-Russian People's Front[12] project, but behind-the-scenes struggles over the control of this image-making tool has so far prevented it from being successfully realised.

Any shift, albeit minimal, by Putin from liberalism to socialism will be accompanied by a positive leap in his ratings, unless it gets falsified by the staff of *Ekho Moskvy* or their relatives, who will be scared stiff. This can be explained by the fact that in the realm of economic sympathies there is no necessary connection between them and purely political sympathies. Liberalism is attractive to a very small group of people and if it is still in favour with them, it is simply because many of them still don't understand what it is about. When they do, they will indignantly stay away from it even if it gets dressed up in superpower language. And, vice versa, Left-wing ideas such as social justice and the welfare state have a huge number of sup-

---

9   'Echo of Moscow,' a news radio station which also supports a widely-cited Website.

10 Garry Kasparov (b. 1963) is a chess Grandmaster and former World Chess Champion. In recent years he has become a staunch opponent of the Putin administration.

11 Alexei Venediktov (b. 1955) is the editor-in-chief of *Echo of Moscow*.

12 The All-Russian People's Front is an organisation inaugurated in 2011 by Putin with the stated aim of providing United Russia with new ideas and personnel.

porters — among both CPRF die-hards and those who have not yet chosen which party to join. Putin's appeal to this niche will be very fruitful from the point of view of an election strategy. It will not weaken but add more meaning to his status as a superpower supporter.

As for the age demographics of the electorate, it has until recently been dominated by pensioners, the elderly, the infirm and socially disadvantaged people — the 'dispossessed majority'. The election is the only day when they feel needed and when they can express themselves. They will determine the outcome. Needless to say, 90% of them are superpower and welfare state supporters. If they realise (which is very unlikely) that Putin's main ideologues are Right-wing liberals, the sight will not be pretty, because liberalism is not very popular among them, to say the least. This much-needed electorate is joined by middle-aged civil servants and state employees. They also have superpower and centrist sympathies, but a certain Left-wing inclination is also noticeable among them. Owners of small businesses that are sick of the situation also join this coalition. The clean-cut centrists have high hopes for the Army, the hospitals and the 'economic principalities' of the oligarchs (like Norilsk),[13] who always vote for the party in power, for obvious reasons. Young people don't vote at all, or very marginally, because they are not part of Russia's political life. Which leads us to the following conclusion: the majority will support Putin, the Left-wing superpower supporter. But if they become seriously confused, the electorate will support even other Putins.

Putin's Formula: Evolution of a Political Image

The Putin phenomenon is a phenomenon of *political science*, functionality and, to a certain extent, image-making. The question 'Who is Mr Putin?'[14] has been formulated in English for a reason and it was circulated in English, becoming a cliché. In the Russian context there is no question of «Кто

---

13 Norilsk is a mining city in northern Russia.

14 In English in the Russian edition.

Вы, господин Путин?»,[15] because the Russians themselves understand that *in the Putin phenomenon his personality is either insignificant or has been purposely hidden, or has not yet revealed itself.* There is no use toying with a metaphysical question such as what is Putin's personality like. Is it there at all? That is not relevant for us now: from the point of view of political science *it is almost irrelevant. Putin does not have a personal political portrait either*: he came to the top following a call from above, skipping over whole flights of stairs. He had no significant importance in politics, the party or the apparatus; he became the top official without relying on any consolidated teams, authorities or social strata. 'He who was nobody, became everything.'[16]

All Putin's decisions are based on *political logic*. They are free from *the voluntarist aspect* which was dominant with Yeltsin. The proof: *absence of a team*. Russian politologists have *artificially removed* the factor of the *Peter Guys* in their confrontation with the Yeltsin *Family*.[17] Putin's absence of voluntarism was hastily attributed to the counterbalancing of the two teams. But *there are no teams*. The *Peter Guys* and the *Family Guys* are so intertwined, standalone and devoid of common corporate, economic, political and other goals, that trying to single these groups out is a mere *convention*, if not *disinformation*. Its purpose is to try to explain the weakness of Putin's voluntarism in familiar terms. And voluntarism has been so typical of Russian history that it is hard to imagine its weakness, let alone absence.

Putin's personnel policy proves the correctness of this thesis. After coming to power, the new President, in fact, *did not carry out any rotation of personnel*, which had been expected and predicted by everybody. The almost three-year-long wait for the resignation of Voloshin was reminiscent of *Waiting for Godot* by Samuel Beckett.

---

15 The Russian for 'Who is Mr Putin'?

16 Paraphrased from the lyrics to the socialist anthem, 'The Internationale'. Part of the first stanza reads, 'We have been nothing; let us be all.'

17 A term for the people around Yeltsin; not just those who were actual relatives of his, but also many of their advisors and financial supporters.

Nationalism Plus Liberalism

From the outset Putin embodied the politological formula: *nationalism (patriotism) plus liberalism (economic reform)*. This formula became the staple of the Putin phenomenon. *It* matters more than his personality. One can argue that in this case it was his personality that was chosen to suit the formula and not the other way around. In order to understand this formula, one has to go back to the political scheme which underlay the logic of the political processes of the 1990s. After the collapse of the Soviet system two forces became clearly dominant in Russian politics: pro-Western liberals (reformers) and non-liberal nationalists (conservatives, mostly represented by Communists and socialists). After the 1991 coup the pro-Western liberals seized control (exploiting the authoritarian nature of Yeltsin), the economy (the Chubais and Gaidar[18] government), the media (Poptsov,[19] Berezovsky, Yakovlev,[20] Gusinsky), and the intelligentsia, and set about elaborating the norms (constitutionally protected andimplicit) of liberal-democratic political correctness. The formula of this period was 'market plus the West' and it was accompanied by a negative attitude towards Russia, its people, its history and its national identity. The victorious power was in the minority.

At the other end there was the *majority opposition* with an opposite ideology: *'Communism plus nationalism'* (*the Red-Browns*). They represented the majority beyond the confines of political correctness. The majority was discriminated against and separated from the uppermost authorities, the economy and the media. This system was very unstable and existed to a large

---

18   Yegor Gaidar (1956–2009) was Acting Prime Minister of Russia during the second half of 1992, and was the leader of many of the economic reforms which rapidly transitioned Russia away from Communism ('shock therapy'). He was held responsible by many Russians for the economic hardships of the 1990s.

19   Oleg Poptsov was the founder of the state-owned All-Russia State Television and Radio Broadcasting Company in 1990, and ran the TV station TVC for many years.

20   Alexander Yakovlev (1923–2005) was part of the Politburo, Secretariat of the Communist Party and an advisor to Gorbachev. Called the 'godfather of glasnost', he was the architect of many of Gorbachev's reforms. Following the collapse of the Soviet Union, he continued to fight for liberal reforms and was later a critic of Putin's policies.

extent *thanks to the authoritarian style of Yeltsin and his supporters among the politicians and oligarchs*. Basically, it was a kind of *liberal dictatorship*.

Throughout the 1990s this system shifted towards a *less severe confrontation*. After 1993 the ruling elite, enjoying the privileges of the victor, *did not engage in any full scale repression* and the Red-Browns did not end up completely eliminated. On the contrary, certain disparate elements of the *losers' ideology* were included in *the winners' discourse*. After this crucial moment power started *moving away* from its initial formula — 'market + the West'. In the second half of the 1990s some democratic politicians started to play with the *prevalent mood of the masses* (nationalism plus sociality). This led to the Luzhkov-Primakov coalition (and, more broadly, Fatherland — All Russia). Here we can already discern the 'non-liberalism plus nationalism' formula in *a moderately enlightened form*. Evgeny Primakov became *an emblematic figure* of this trend who was seemingly destined to succeed, in contrast with the weakening Yeltsin. *A simple continuation of the authoritarian liberal-democratic Yeltsinism* was not enough to stop this trend, which was gearing up to unite with the Red-Brown masses at a certain point.

And that is when the Putin formula, *'liberalism + nationalism'*, was born. Its real author is unknown to me: among its alleged authors are Boris Berezovsky, Gleb Pavlovsky, Vladislav Surkov, and so on. This position was *situated strictly between* the liberal elite and the nationally- and socially-inclined masses. It effectively released the enormous tensions between the social and political worlds. The uniting element between the elite and the masses is *nationalism*, the separating element is still the *liberal economy*. From the very beginning Putin communicated only this formula and nothing else. Disregarding the nuances, he adhered strictly to this position. It was *a formula of public consensus* and it gradually became a *preferred criteria of political correctness*. Only the *'ultras'* were left behind: the ultra-liberals, ultra-Yeltsinists, ultra-Westerners, ultra-nationalists, ultra-Communists, and the uneducated Red-Browns. Putin promptly marginalised these forces: some were exiled (Gusinsky, Berezovsky); others resigned (Yumashev,[21] Voloshin); some were imprisoned (Khodorkovsky); others were dissolved

---

21   Valentin Yumashev (b. 1957) was a close associate of Yeltsin and served as Chairman of the Presidential Executive Office in 1997–98.

(Russian National Unity [RNU],[22] the National Bolshevik Party [NBP]); some turned into buffoons (Nemtsov,[23] Kasyanov),[24] and others were forgotten (Gaidar, Novodvorskaya).[25] In the political sphere Putin established new limits of political correctness which stemmed from his formula. From then on *market orientation and patriotism*, defined very broadly, became the staples of loyalty, the basis of the ersatz ideology of the Putin era.

Putin as the Conductor of Liberal Reform: Oligarchs — Separating Functions

Putin's economic policy was initially designed in a strict liberal fashion. Putin did not allow even a hint of socialist measures. Actually, this is what sets him distinctly apart from the *economic populism* of Primakov and Luzhkov. All the key personalities in the economy were distinctly liberal: Gref,[26]

---

22 Russian National Unity is a far-Right, paramilitary party which calls for the expulsion of all non-Russians from Russia. Following a crackdown by the government in the late 1990s, the party is largely inactive now.

23 Boris Nemtsov (b. 1959) was Governor of the Nizhny Novgorod region from 1991 until 1997, where he oversaw a radical transition to the free market that earned the praise of Western politicians. After that he served as First Deputy Prime Minister. In recent years he has been arrested on multiple occasions for participating in unauthorised protests against Putin's administration.

24 Mikhail Kasyanov (b. 1957) became Minister of Finance in 1999 and then Prime Minister in 2000. He began to implement many reforms, but became unpopular with the Russian populace who felt that his pace of reform was too slow, and he was dismissed, along with Putin's entire cabinet, in 2004, just prior to the elections. Since then he has become a vocal critic of Putin.

25 Valeriya Novodvorskaya (1950–2014) was a famous dissident from the Soviet era who had been imprisoned in a psychiatric hospital. She later became a harsh critic of Putin, and once infamously said in an interview that it was Russian policies in Chechnya that had resulted in terrorism.

26 German Gräf (b. 1964) was the Minister of Economics and Trade from 2000 until his dismissal in 2007. Regarded as one of the liberals in Putin's cabinet, one of his less popular reforms was the monetisation of benefits.

Chubais, Kudrin,[27] Illarionov.[28] In this respect Putin is very *consistent* and harsh (we are not yet discussing the advantages and disadvantages of liberalism as such). From a sociological point of view, the potential of the masses' optimistic attitude towards liberal reform was, for a time, exhausted and was consolidating only the marginal electorate of the SPS. In United Russia the liberal element is not obvious. Its electorate is consolidated under a different principle — '*power + obscure patriotism*', and it contains very little of reform and market orientation. Nevertheless, during his first two terms Putin pursued a tough *anti-populist line* in economics in accordance with his formula. This is a distinctive aspect of his formula, and he follows it strictly and consistently.

The Yeltsin period was characterised by the fact that the main *subjects* of political and economic life were Russian oligarchs who concentrated in their hands the strands of power over the *political sphere, the media and the economy*. They also largely mastered the prevailing 'ideology', controlling and financing teams of experts (those that were not financed by Western intelligence agencies, that is). Besides, the activity of law enforcement ministries and agencies was to some extent controlled by the mechanisms of corruption, which were ultimately managed by the oligarchs.

The oligarchs were *the principal actors* of the politics at the time, capable of proposing both *sociopolitical and economic projects*, as well as of building the mechanisms and generating *resources* for their implementation. They were legitimised by *Yeltsin's individual voluntarism*. But this voluntarism was only a *necessary* requirement for the realisation of this or that undertaking, and without the *sufficient* requirement — involvement of the oligarchs and the enforcement of this undertaking. As a result, Yeltsin's initiatives consistently failed. The oligarchs were the crucial instrument in pre-Putin Russia. Everything that happened *was sanctioned and controlled by them*.

---

27   Alexei Kudrin (b. 1960) was the Minister of Finance from 2000 until 2011.

28   Andrei Illarionov (b. 1961) became Putin's senior economic advisor in 2000, and also acted as Putin's representative to the G8 summit. In 2005 he resigned on the grounds that Russia was becoming an undemocratic state under Putin. He currently works at the Cato Institute in Washington, DC.

Not a single political project was implemented without them: the election of Putin and Unity[29] is not an exception.

When he came to power, Putin *abolished this model* and put the oligarchs at arm's length from each other. He *not only replaced* some oligarchs with others, he *denied them the continuation of their functional involvement in the political system*. Two oligarchs, who were the fullest embodiment of the integrity of the oligarchs' role — control over the media, the economy and politics; strength of will, strategising, corruption in the secret service — were forced out of the country. The rest of them sought a compromise with the President.

What did Putin offer *in place of oligarchy*? An oligarch was the sum of several components: his economic role was delegated to *tycoons* (oligarchs whose powers were limited to the purely economic sphere — see the list of the Russian Union of Industralists and Entrepreneurs' (RUIE)[30] management board members); the oligarchs' political role was delegated to *the presidential administration* (Voloshin, Surkov, Sechin,[31] Medvedev); and the role of oligarchs in the media was delegated to *'clean' mediacrats* (Lesin,[32] followed by Kulistikov,[33] Ernst,[34] Dobrodeev).[35] The expert functions of the oligarchs were assigned to the *expert community* (Pavlovsky,

---

[29] In 1999, the Unity party was formed by the Yeltsin administration to fight the popular Fatherland — All Russia party in the 2000 elections, and assisted the rise of Putin. In 2001 it merged into the United Russia party.

[30] The Russian Union of Industrialists and Entrepreneurs is a lobby that works on behalf of big business.

[31] Igor Sechin (b. 1960) has been a close advisor of Putin since his initial election as President. He is the leader of the *siloviki* lobby, which represents those veterans of Russia's secret service agencies who have gone into politics.

[32] Mikhail Lesin (b. 1958) was the creator of the Russia Today network.

[33] Vladimir Kulistikov (b. 1952) has been the head of the NTV network since 2004.

[34] Konstantin Ernst (b. 1961) is the Director General of the Channel One network. He was also the director of the opening ceremony of the 2014 Winter Olympics.

[35] Oleg Dobrodeev (b. 1959) has been the director of the All-Russia State Television and Radio Broadcasting Company since 2000.

Markov,[36] Nikonov,[37] and the expert councils of the presidential administration and TV). The enforcement officers were *left to their own devices*. It was especially evident during the period when the Security Council was headed by Sergei Ivanov[38] — the alleged 'new hey-day of the secret service' was simply the removal of the secret service from the oligarchs' control.

In separating the oligarchs' functions Putin created five separate 'departments of the political will': the *administration, the economic tycoons, the mediacrats, law enforcement, and the experts*. Theoretically they were supposed to be linked to the President while bypassing all intermediaries, who would otherwise try to further their own interests.

Putin as the Gatherer of Russian Lands[39] and Builder of Eurasia

With the advent of Putin, Moscow's relations with the Russian territories and the CIS also changed and followed the route of *'enlightened geopolitics'*. Consistent and logical geopolitics required that Putin strengthened the unity of Russia, revitalised the integration processes in the CIS and waged bold initiatives to create strategic, political and economic blocs with Europe and Asia. But Putin realised only *part of the elements of this Eurasian geopolitical scenario,* which was exemplified by: *harsh opposition to the disintegration* of Russia in Dagestan and Chechnya, *reduction of the importance of the Federation Council* as a regional lobby, the introduction of the *federal district system*, the *creation of EurAsEC*, and the signing of a *collective security agreement* with the CIS states. One can also include here closer

---

36 Sergei Markov (b. 1958) is a political scientist who works as a consultant to the Russian government.

37 Vyacheslav Nikonov (b. 1956) is a political scientist who has worked in the Russian government since the Gorbachev administration. He is currently in the State Duma.

38 Sergei Ivanov (b. 1953) was Minister of Defence between 2001 and 2007, and is currently Chief of Staff of the Presidential Administration. He was appointed secretary of the Security Council between 1999 and 2001, following Putin in the role.

39 A reference to Ivan III (1440–1505), who ended Mongol rule over Russia and tripled the size of Russia's territory. He was called 'the gatherer of the Russian lands'.

diplomatic relations with the EU and the renewal of relations with Asian states, especially China, North Korea, Japan, Iran, and India.

All these steps were aimed at enhancing Eurasian geopolitics, conducted with a certain hesitation. Basically, *it is an active foreign policy, aimed at enhancing Russia's strategic status in combination with domestic patriotism, that must compensate* (in terms of populism) *for the unpopularity of liberal reforms in the economy.* From the outset Putin started consistently, albeit cautiously, to move in that direction.

As for the territorial structure of Russia, Putin started a *genuine revolution*. Its point is to restrict to the fullest extent the geopolitical independence of the regions, *to deprive the territorial subdivisions of any traces of sovereignty and national identity*. This is an example of another (domestically oriented) aspect of Putin's patriotism, his domestic geopolitical strategy. Immediately after coming to power Putin introduced federal districts for the purpose of achieving direct strategic control over the governors, and reformed the Federation Council in order to deprive the representatives of the regions of their full-scale political representation, which had granted them broad political and legislative powers.[40] The establishment of the State Council[41] along with the Federation Council transformed the status of the heads of the territorial subdivisions *from the political to the consultative.*

The First Setback: The Atlanticist Challenge — a Loyalty Test

The setback occurred in the wake of 9/11. The US offered Russia, almost as an ultimatum, a *loyalty test*, and Putin did not resolve to answer it in a strictly Eurasian fashion. His Eurasian tendencies weakened, which led to the es-

---

40 Prior to 2000, a loophole in the Constitution made it possible for the regional governors to both occupy both their regional offices and a seat on the Federation Council simultaneously. In 2000 Putin changed the law so that the governors could only designate representatives to sit on the Council but not do so themselves. The governors, recognising that this would greatly reduce their power and influence, were furious, but under pressure from the State Duma and threats from Putin to conduct legal investigations, they finally relented.

41 Putin established the State Council in 2000 as an advisory body to the President.

tablishment of Western military bases in the CIS and Georgia, a deterioration in relations with Lukashenko,[42] and so forth. Putin's advisor Sergei Yastrzhembsky[43] then directly opposed Eurasianism. All of the above significantly *weakened the integrity and credibility* of Putin's initial formula *and reduced the patriotic potential* of his political status.

Soon after 9/11 a Civil Forum was organised which discussed Gleb Pavlovsky's proposal to move from the 'Putin majority' to a 'Right majority', which was, in effect, *a return to Yeltsin's politological model*. It did not lead to a catastrophe, but the balance shifted significantly. The Putin formula implied unconditional *Eurasianism* and *enlightened nationalism* in foreign and domestic policy as a compensation for economic liberalism. *When things shifted towards Occidentalism, the integrity of the formula was affected,* which led to fluctuating moods among the masses and *reduced ratings for Putin.*

As a result, the balance shifted away from the stable centre. The Putin formula (liberalism + patriotism) was significantly weakened by the *impairment of the national component.* This was manifested by *the reduction of the Eurasian potential in foreign policy* (a shift towards the West, yielding to the pressure of the US, and the slowing down of the integration process in the CIS); in the relative connivance to *the new wave of rebellions among some national leaders*; and in the absence of an explicit and consistent *patriotic ideology in the media, education and culture.* That said, consistency was maintained in the liberal realm: the economy was managed by the ultraliberal German Gräf and Andrei Illarionov, the Land Code[44] was adopted, and the RAO UES[45] has been forced to restructure under the formula of Chubais, among other examples.

---

42   Alexander Lukashenko (b. 1954) has been President of Belarus since 1994. He is known for having preserved the Soviet structure of government in his country.

43   Sergei Yastrzhembsky (b. 1953), after working as a press spokesman for the Kremlin, was appointed the presidential envoy to the EU in 2004.

44   The Land Code adopted in 2001 provided for the private development of land without government intervention, which was the first time this had been done in Russia.

45   Unified Energy Systems of Russia was a holding company for the power industry. In the mid-2000s it was broken up into several companies in an effort to privatise the industry.

All of the above manifests itself on several levels. As a result, at that point one could have expressly stated the following: the beginning of the fluctuations in popularity characterised by *a reduction in President Putin's rating*, the slowing down of centralisation, *poor efficiency*, the centrality and discipline of the 'departments of the political will'; *poor performance of the presidential envoys* and, as a consequence, the beginning of a new stage of regional intrigue among the heads of the territorial subdivisions who sensed the weakness of the centre; in other words, *the dead end of the political evolution of United Russia*, which had to follow the President and veered from an initially clear position as a result of the weakening of the nationalist component and the inconsistency of the pro-Western course.

Putin's Ideological Risks

Weakening the nationalist element of his formula, Putin returned to the political model of the Yeltsin era: the idea of liberal-democratic pro-Western authority opposed to the non-liberal, anti-Western patriotic masses, the latter of which will always be hostile towards the liberalisation of energy tariffs, the reform of housing and the public utilities system, and the raising of the public transport tariffs, none of which could any longer be offset by any ethical patriotic rhetoric.

One should add to this a *change in the Western attitude towards Putin*. A number of Atlanticist politicians (Paul Wolfowitz, Zbigniew Brzezinski, etc.) believed that the geopolitical self-liquidation of Russia as a potentially independent pole, capable of geopolitical competition with the unipolar realm of the US, was *too slow* with Putin in power and therefore thought that this process should have been given *a new impetus*. This impetus was and continues to be realised in the form of *a plot to remove Putin* (this scenario is favoured by American analysts as well as by exiled Russian oligarchs). This same scenario was partially behind the tragic events in Moscow relating to the taking of hostages in Dubrovka, in Beslan, the Moscow metro bombings, Domodedovo and even in the unhealthy activities of Medvedev's entourage. Washington has enough instruments to actively encourage regime change in Russia. Add to this the fact that after the military operations in Iraq and Libya, oil prices plummeted, which had an immediate negative impact on the Russian economy. And there are yet other ways they have attempted to disrupt Putin's power.

One of them is *changing the nature of the Communist opposition*. All these years it has been ineffectual because it has not been connected with *the real actors* — the oligarchs and the Western secret services. Even with the support of the majority of the population this opposition remains *politically harmless*, simply due to the *total inadequacy of its leaders, the absence of a genuine political will and of economic resources, and the incompetent behaviour of the party apparatus*. Providing this opposition with a political will, coupled with support from some anti-Russian forces in the American political establishment, is something that could *drastically change the very status of this opposition*. Zyuganov as number one on the list (negative image, an unstable temperament, a repulsive appearance) should be replaced by Glazyev[46] (a neutral image, resilient temperament, decent appearance) — and it would be possible to observe a shift *in the entire electoral mood*. That such a small factor could have that significant an influence is not a demonstration of any particular merits of Glazjev, *but of the compliance of the 'non-liberalism + nationalism' formula with the expectations of the overwhelming majority of the Russian people.*

If transforming United Russia into something more adequate requires massive efforts, a sharp rise in CPRF's status requires pointed attacks, which could easily be devised, polished and realised by hostile oligarchs, or such as were actually attempted by Khodorkovsky (especially with the consent of the US secret service). Or by Vladimir Putin himself, if he wanted to put his own men in charge of the party.

Therefore, although the Putin formula during his first two presidential terms demonstrated its *credibility*, it has little *stability margin*. Liberalism as a component of the formula gives rise to a lot of objections. With every year the real essence of liberalism in Russia is becoming ever more evident. Much more suitable for the mood of the electorate are the formulas located *within national non-liberalism* (nationalism in this case is a common denominator). The Putin formula was proclaimed, played and fixed *at the*

---

46 Sergei Glazyev (b. 1961) was one of the co-founders of the Rodina party. He currently works as an aide to Putin for the development of the Customs Union.

outset of his presidency, and due to strict compliance with this formula Putin *was entirely successful*. Today this formula is no longer sufficient. In fact, it never has been. It had to be lived with, but it was seen as an unpleasant compromise. In a country with 70 years of socialism behind it, with the means of production placed in public ownership, with free education and the guaranteed right to labour, liberalism does not yet have a chance to be a successful political slogan.

A Digression on Liberalism

Liberalism does not have roots in Russian history or culture. Although at first glance the word 'liberalism' might conjure up the idea of liberty, *libertas* in Latin (which is soothing to the Russian ear because the Russian spirit loves liberty, and maybe that is why our land is so boundless), 'freedom/liberty' in liberalism is understood in a way totally alien to Russians: it is a negative freedom. To understand its roots, we must refer to the renowned theorist of liberalism, the British philosopher John Stuart Mill. Mill distinguishes between two types of freedom, expressed by two different English words: liberty and freedom. These are completely different notions. 'Liberty' is a notion that gave birth to 'liberalism'. According to Mill, liberty is a negative freedom — a 'liberty from' something.

Mill further specifies: the mission of the liberal is freedom from sociopolitical, religious, social and mutual obligations. 'Liberty from' is the liberty of an individual from society, social ties, interdependence and judgement by others. Liberalism stresses that the measure of all things is an individual businessman: he is the meaning of existence and the centre of life. Don't stand in his way, let him do what he wants — buy and sell — and we will live in the best of all possible worlds. A businessman, propelled by egotism and greed — which are considered to be virtues in liberal philosophy — must be selected as the universal model. All legal, administrative, moral, religious, and social restrictions must be removed; his arbitrary whims, interests, calculations and benefits are to be the basis of the new value system.

The concept of liberalism was a novelty in the nineteenth century: there would be no more religious and moral standards, no class restrictions, and no governmental or social controls over economic activity. Eventually, there would be no state or society at all, just a chaotic jumble of businessmen with no homeland, faith, ethics, or culture, uncontrolled and unrestricted in every respect. Everyone would strive to satisfy their own fancies, and only one irrational force, 'the invisible hand of the market', would direct this process towards the desired goal: the fat cats will get fatter, the rich will get richer, the fortunate will prosper and the prosperous will rejoice. This is the 'liberty from', and the negation here is quite pointed: the things that we should break free from are real and palpable. Yes, it is true that man is restricted by a lot of things in society and the process of liberating oneself from these obstacles, such as ethical standards and social responsibilities, is quite transparent: fewer taxes, fewer taboos, less responsibility. But a question arises: what is this liberty for? 'What from' is clear, but what for?

Here Mill comes up with a new word: 'freedom', which he interprets as 'freedom for' and which he considers empty of substance. It scares Mill and the liberals because it refers to the deeply metaphysical, to the essence of the human spirit, to depths that are difficult to cope with. The 'freedom for' requires a higher purpose and a more fundamental understanding of mankind. It poses difficult questions: what is the positive meaning of life? Why does man work, live, breathe, love and create? 'Freedom for' tugs at the heartstrings; it is a new, life-giving darkness to which the philosophical search brings us... it is a risk, a challenge, a distant call from our last, deeply hidden depths...

John Stuart Mill pales before this question; he is oppressed by the sheer, horrifying amount of positive freedom being revealed and does not know how to handle it. He avoids the answer.

And this is where the brilliant, merciless Friedrich Wilhelm Nietzsche comes in:

> You call yourself free? Your dominating thought I want to hear, and not that you escaped from a yoke.
>
> Are you the kind of person who had a *right* to escape from a yoke? There are some who threw away their last value when they threw away their servitude.
>
> Free from what? What does Zarathustra care! But brightly your eyes should signal to me: free *for what*? [...]

Thus spoke Zarathustra.[47]

'Liberty from' is an aspiration of the eternal slave; a free spirit must choose 'freedom for'. He must begin and end with it.

Liberalism is a political platform that is alien to the Russian man. We are a proud Slavic people, powerful and brave. 'Why then have you been on your knees for centuries?' a sarcastic Anglo-Saxon will ask, waving a piece of paper with market quotations in his hand. It is because we cannot get rid of this secret, difficult, crystal-clear and lie-hating 'for'. We love true freedom too much to trade it in for the vulgar, slave-like, ugly liberal 'from'. We'd rather stay on our knees, summoning courage... And finally speak our great Russian word, the world's last word: 'Revolution'. It will be a word of ultimate freedom, positive and sun-soaked.

Freedom for...

Liberalism as an Ideology of Globalisation

The principal ideologies of the twentieth century were liberalism (Left-wing and Right-wing), Communism (including both Marxism and socialism/social democracy), and fascism (including National Socialism and other varieties of the 'Third Way' — Franco's National Syndicalism, Perón's justicialism, Salazar's regime, etc.). They fought to the death, shaping the entire dramatic and blood-soaked history of the twentieth century.

The first political theory is liberalism. It was the first to appear (as far back as the eighteenth century) and proved to be the most stable and successful, ultimately winning over its opponents in the battle of history. This victory was proof, inter alia, of the validity of liberalism's claims to be the successor of the entire legacy of the Enlightenment. Although it had been disputed earlier (in a dramatic, energetic and sometimes convincing manner) by another political theory, Communism, it has become evident that it was liberalism that was perfectly suited to the modern era. Having won the battle against all other ideologies, liberalism as an ideology is being 'de-ideologised' during the postmodern era. It has ceased to be an ideology, and

---

47   Friedrich Nietzsche, *Thus Spoke Zarathustra* (Cambridge: Cambridge University Press, 2006), p. 46.

has been transformed from a subject into an object and becomes natural state of affairs, an 'objective' state of things. In the postmodern era, liberalism 'virtualises' reality, merges with it, and ceases to be a political theory, becoming the only post-political practice. 'The end of history'[48] approaches, politics is replaced by economics (a global market), and states and nations are fused together in the melting pot of globalisation. Liberalism is becoming a global programme for humanity, although it was born out of the historical experience of specific parts of humanity living in specific, geographically restricted areas. Liberalism is not merely a technical principle oriented in a free market, with competition, freedom of enterprise, private initiative, and so forth. Liberalism is an anti-national ideology that is destructive for Russia: an ideology that proclaims money and material welfare to be the measure of all things, destroying the moral and spiritual fabric of human society. Liberalism forms a specific mentality, a system of humanitarian values, an image of humans and humanity grounded in the premise that the economy, the market, production and consumption must morph from a subsidiary sphere of our life into an end in and of itself, serving as the single measure of all social processes. Private property is proclaimed to be the ultimate truth, disrupting the social basis of human community, separating natural collectives — peoples, ethnic groups, communities, religious groups — and exacerbating alienation between people, nature and the spiritual world.

The individual is the cornerstone of liberalism as an ideology — namely, an individual stripped of any collective identity (be it class, national, communal or religious). Liberalism calls to overcome national statehood and refuses religious identity, treating religion as a private matter, and opposes any attempts at giving religion a social or public, let alone political, dimension.

---

48 The American neoconservative theorist Francis Fukuyama famously postulated in a 1989 article and a subsequent 1992 book, *The End of History and the Last Man*, that the development of Western-style liberal democracy and capitalism represents the end-point in the development of human civilisation, and that it was only a matter of time before this system spread to and was adopted in every corner of the globe. More recently, Fukuyama has considerably revised this view.

Liberalism is completely out of sync with our national tradition. Nevertheless, liberal ideology *de facto* determines many aspects of social and political life in Russia.

Liberalism is a product of the New Times, of modernity. It originated, as I already noted, out of the 'liberty from' principle, which seeks to liberate the individual from all forms of collective identity: state, class, morality, race, religion, authority, and so on. Then there is 'freedom for' — freedom to do something. But in liberal terms this is non-freedom. The liberals say: 'We only fight for 'freedom from' (liberty), not for 'freedom for.'

Today, another form of collective identity is in conflict with the liberal dogma — gender. In terms of liberalism, people are divided into men and women not because this dichotomy expresses their individual specificity, but because they share with other men and women a certain collective identity. This is why a fight for the rights of sexual minorities — perverts, transgender products of transgenic operations, homosexuals, and freaks of all sorts — is the crucial ideological platform of liberalism. Many may think that this is just an arbitrary element of liberal freedom. This is absolutely not the case — this fight is at the very core of liberal policy. Making sexual minorities, transgender marriages and other perversions *the* social norm is the principal aspect, the pivotal point and the staple of liberal ideology. There is no type of liberalism today that does not defend the rights of gays, lesbians, transsexuals, and so on. This is a very important point. Therefore, consistently destroying all forms of collective identity, liberals arrive at the necessity to free the individual from all such forms, including one's own gender and language, which is a collective phenomenon (hence the idea of an individual language). Gradually, liberalism, having lost its opponents and reaching its logical conclusion, resolves to free an individual from all other individuals, because a human being also belongs to the collective identity. From there we can jump directly to transhumanism — a notion that it is necessary to create hybrids of man and other species with the help of genetic engineering. An example of an attempt to break with human identity is 'A Cyborg Manifesto' by Donna J. Haraway,[49] and the ideas of the transhumanist programme.

Thus, liberty from gender is followed by liberty from the human.

Contemporary liberal or post-liberal ideology amends the democratic model. If classical democracy defends a decision of the majority against the minority, liberal democracy is seen as the protection of the minority from the majority. This reveals aspects of liberal ideology that we had not known before, because previously liberals had waged battles for freedom from fascism, nationalism and Communism. It was assumed that fascism was restrictive, nationalism was restrictive too, and that liberals were the liberators. That was enough for liberalism to win. Today, liberals do not have any opponents. They are left alone at the top and are free to say whatever they want. And when they do, they reveal the demonic, nihilistic essence of liberalism.

A declaration of individual freedom in effect means total dependence of the common man on the oligarchy. Individual freedom abolishes all forms of collective identity. One is not allowed to be a supporter of a national state or a religious institution, because this is not politically correct. As a result, a demand for freedom in economics, in ideology and in society in general leads to a new form of totalitarianism: the ideology of human rights as the rights of the individual is, in effect, directed against humans, against social values, traditions, language and, most of all, against freedom itself.

Today, in realising the 'liberty from', we understand ever better that this nihilistic agenda is leading us to an abyss.

It should be noted that the words 'liberalism' and 'capitalism' are rarely used in contemporary Russian politics because they are taboo. They come up mostly in Left-wing politology, which has been pushed to the margin of politological discourse. In a former socialist country, where a capitalist

---

49 'A Cyborg Manifesto', originally published in 1983, uses the cyborg as a means to demonstrate problems in feminist theory — namely, the blurring of barriers between humans, animals, and machines, which allegedly parallel the blurring of barriers between genders in the twentieth century. It is available at www.egs.edu/faculty/donna-haraway/articles/donna-haraway-a-cyborg-manifesto/.

coup was implemented on short notice, state and public property ended up in private hands and social guarantees, along with workers' rights, were done away with; such notions are provocative, controversial, scandalous and incendiary. The new ruling elite is monitoring carefully to ensure that the use of such terms is limited or, even better, used in contexts totally devoid of substance. For example, Zhirinovsky's Liberal-Democratic Party is neither liberal nor democratic. If Russians found out the true meaning of 'liberalism', as it is professed by theorists like Hayek[50] or Ayn Rand, they would lose their minds. After finding out that liberalism opposes the state, the nation, the church, the Orthodox faith, collectivism, gender, and ultimately democracy itself, the Russian electorate would permanently refute the balancing formula of 'patriotism plus liberalism' that allowed Putin to curb and accommodate the two opposing poles of the Russian community during the first eight years of his presidency. For this reason, liberalism is proliferating throughout Russian political life gradually, in small doses, and is camouflaged. Liberalism is a product of the West, so unacceptable to the Russian consumer that one must change the label before trying to sell it to us. It must always be served slathered in some sort of edible sauce. Liberalism is imported into the country disguised as 'perestroika', 'democracy', 'efficiency', 'modernisation', humanitarian values', or something of the kind. In other words, liberalism is alien to Russia, is not accepted by the population, threatens the Russian national identity, and calls the very existence of Russian civilisation into question. The second ingredient of the Putin formula, liberalism, is a challenge and a stumbling block for Russian politics; it will become ever more problematic in the coming years.

---

50 Friedrich Hayek (1899–1992) was an economist who was crucial to the development of the Austrian school of economics. He opposed collectivism and state control of the economy in favour of classical liberalism, holding that the free market and limited government were the only effective methods of organising societies.

On Putin's Responsibility before Christ and on Elite Rotation

Many perceive Russia as an Orthodox country, headed by an Orthodox leader. That being said, a lot of absurd and unfortunate events are happening in Russia, and somebody must be held accountable for this. Some people are held accountable by the legal system, others by corporations, be it the RUIE corporate ethics commission or an ecclesiastical court. But since we stress more and more that Russia is an Orthodox country, why not contemplate who will be held accountable before Christ — the people or the President? I am not in favour of splitting up Orthodox Christians into the strictly observant and the unchurched, and I think that everybody who associates himself with the Orthodox faith is an Orthodox Christian. I am personally a strictly observant Orthodox Christian and wish you to be the same. At the same time, Russia has a partially autonomous system of government, which has its own ideology and its own logic and structure that are very different from the religious and Orthodox paradigm. But there are also *the people*. 'The people' is a remarkable phenomenon that is both separate and independent. 'The people' is a phenomenon with an independent essence. It seems to me that there is a complicated relationship between these three forms — Orthodoxy (the Church), the Russian state and the Russian people — and this relationship has been constantly changing throughout the entire course of Russian history. In Russia, every politician or every man professing any kind of political philosophy has to decide how to combine these notions — the Church, the state and the people, and has to decide which one to prioritise.

My political philosophy is based on the assumption that the Russian people are the most important historical, spiritual and political category. The people above all. The Russian people are *an absolute* for me, an inherent value, and an end in itself. These people are deeply suffused with the light of the Orthodox culture and have been chosen by Divine Providence for a special mission. I do not draw a clear distinction between Orthodox messianism and the spirit of the Russian people; they are two sides of the same coin. A spiritual and careful reading of Russian history reveals that at a specific point in the middle of the fifteenth century — the collapse of Tsargrad (Constantinople)[51] the future of Universal Orthodoxy became completely fused with the future of the Russian people.

The state is something completely different. Over the past few centuries, it inevitably took lower priority than both the national spirit and the Orthodox Church. During the Muscovy era[52] the state was suffused in the light of the Church from above and in the national ethos from below, creating a certain harmony and never standing in the way of universal salvation. When the state is transparent, when it is an instrument of a pull process toward spiritual and universal salvation, everything goes well: the state naturally participates in the spiritual rhythm of holy history. But over the past few centuries this has not been the case. The state is an artificial construction, alienated both from the Church and the people. It presents itself as an entity that possesses its own ontology. This ontology, it must be noted, is quite dry, alienated and dark. From a spiritual point of view, during the Romanov era after the Schism,[53] the Russian state played a largely negative role. Any appeals to populism and Orthodoxy were superficial, imposturous and artificial. The spirit of the masses revealed itself during the October Revolution (as seen by Klyuev[54] and Platonov),[55] but during the Khrushchev and especially the Brezhnev eras the state again ended up becoming alienated from both the masses and religion. All of Russia's misfortunes can be attributed to the contemporary state, which is an artificial carbon copy of the secular European model. In its correct form,

---

51   Constantinople was the capitol of the Byzantine Empire and thus the center of Orthodox Christianity until its conquest by the Ottoman Empire in 1453. Tsargrad is the old Russian name for it.

52   The era of the Grand Duchy of Muscovy lasted from the early fourteenth century until the beginning of the Russian Empire under Ivan the Terrible in 1547.

53   This refers to the split between the established Russian Orthodox Church and the Old Believers in the seventeenth century.

54   Nikolai Klyuev (1884–1937) was a Symbolist poet who initially supported the Russian Revolution and joined the Communist Party. By the 1920s, however, he became increasingly critical of the Soviet regime, and he was shot in 1937 for his opposition.

55   Andrei Platonov (1899–1951) was a writer who initially supported the Communists but became increasingly critical of them as time went on, earning the ire of the Communist establishment.

the state should be subordinate and transparent, permeable, 'anagogic', a 'pull process', elevating; it must serve the people and the Church instead of forcing them serve the state. This is why I tend to blame the state for all the negative aspects of our history. Government 'fascism' and autonomous statism in Russian history are repulsive to me. I think that the best course would be to eradicate the state and replace it with the Holy Empire, a *basileus*,[56] a comprehensive katechonic[57] Tsardom, where the divine rays directly fuse with the great God-bearing people and make all other mechanisms and historical realities serve the higher aim, which is embodied in the secret inner existence of the God-bearing people. Therefore I am a strong opponent of the contemporary autonomous state and I tend to blame it for all absurdities and confusion. At the same time, I am an equally strong supporter of the Empire.

An Empire in Place of a National State

I want to stress that, since the beginning of the fifteenth century, the state and the empire were seen as opposite extremes in Europe. Bodin,[58] Machiavelli and Hobbes developed their theories of the 'state' in opposition to the ontology of the empire; the concept of the state is a product of the repudiation of the concept of an empire. The state is an artificial pragmatic construction, desacralised and devoid of *telos*,[59] purpose and substance. On the contrary, the empire is something alive, sacred, and replete with purpose and essence: something that has a higher destiny. In an empire, the administrative apparatus is not separate from the religious mission, or from the people's spirit. The empire *is* a universal embodiment of this mission, illuminating the elastic energy of people and culture.

---

56 Greek: 'king'.

57 The katechon is a concept derived from *Thessalonians* which refers to that which prevents the Antichrist from manifesting in the world. Carl Schmitt believed that the katechon was the justification of the Church's role in politics and society and was the ultimate meaning of Christianity in the world, as he wrote in *The Nomos of the Earth*.

58 Jean Bodin (1530–1596) was a French political philosopher.

59 Classical Greek: 'purpose' or 'goal'.

There is a concept of 'organic democracy' which implies, in the words of Arthur Moeller van den Bruck,[60] 'a people's involvement in their own destiny'. 'Organic democracy' is when a person acting in a certain cultural field actually becomes the subject of history. In this regard, I think that both the people and the President share responsibility before God for everything that happens in the country. This is my deepest political *credo*. He who creates is to blame. The question is: the people or the President? In my opinion, history is created by people. Responsibility lies with the people. The people set the limits of historical development via their own ideas about what is possible and admissible. The people *en masse* establish these parameters because they are the bearers of culture, spirituality, religion, and ideology, not their particular representatives — not even the topmost officials. The people propose certain solutions, but life tends to be a harsh critic when it comes to projects created by people. The events around us limit our possibilities when it comes to changing the parameters of our civilisation and distorting the vector of development. This self-regulating historical development is a kind of compromise between the spiritual aspirations of the people and the realities they have to face. Such pressure from our surroundings often forces changes in vector — points in history where quite palpable, personified characters, instead of 'the people' as a collective, come into play. This is an understanding of statehood and the people's role in terms of 'organic democracy'. It would be perfect if the people were involved in their own destiny and were the subject of history. This is what we are fighting for. This is the right way. It must be a moral imperative for all political forces in Russia and for the people themselves. But this is not the *status quo* — it is an aim and a wish.

The people delegate responsibility to the ruler or the ruling group, the power elite. Ideally, this is a harmonised and natural process: the people externalise in power the most intense exertion of their will, the best part of their soul. In this case, the system can be referred to as the 'people's rule', whether it is a democratic community, autocracy or even 'the people's dic-

---

60 Arthur Moeller van den Bruck (1876–1925) was one of the principal authors of the German Conservative Revolution. He is best known for his 1923 book, *Das Dritte Reich* (translated as *Germany's Third Empire*, reissued by Arktos in 2012).

tatorship'. Historically, however, the ruler and the ruling elite are not of the people. There is a rather interesting politological model describing and explaining this fact. This model says that the political elite are radically different from their people: an 'anti-people', not only in a social and functional sense, but also racially. The Polish-Jewish writer Ludwig Gumplowicz,[61] undeservingly forgotten and not widely known today, proves in his books (especially in *The Struggle of the Races*)[62] that the elites of almost all historically important states — Russia, France, Austria, Germany, India, Egypt, Greece — were initially newcomers, conquerors or representatives of ethnic, religious or cultural minorities. All political elites are a result of the introduction of an alien *ethnos*,[63] which back in the day subdued the local population and created a distinct ruling strata, or a 'political class' (R. Michels).[64] Subsequently, this group anchored its victory in the governmental system, creating a system of privileges for its protégés and establishing its own acquisitive welfare in spite of the people. Under such circumstances, power is not an expression of the spirit of the people or of religious ideas; it is a xenomorphic and alienated organisation.

If we look at today's Russia or at Russia during the Romanov dynasty, we can easily spot all the characteristics of a xenomorphic political elite, alienated from a people which they despise, hate and fail to understand. The pro-Western elite of the eighteenth century regarded the Russian people as 'savages' and 'Papuans', just as the Americans looked at Indians. Take

---

61 Ludwig Gumplowicz (1838–1909) is considered one of the founders of sociology. He was particularly concerned with the role of minorities in states.

62 *La Lutte des races: Recherches sociologiques* (Paris: Guillaumin, 1893). No English translation exists.

63 Greek: 'nation', in the sense of a community of people who all share a common heritage.

64 Robert Michels (1876–1936) was a German sociologist and student of Max Weber. His principal work is *Political Parties: A Sociological Study of the Oligarchical Tendencies of Modern Democracy* (New York: Hearst's International Library Co., 1915)

Biron,[65] for instance. My ancestor, Savva Dugin, a Dashkov[66] follower, was beheaded for demanding that the Patriarchate[67] be restored. His so-called 'Dugin papers', which survived until the twentieth century, condemned secular power and the autonomous state, and were circulated mostly among the Old Believers.

The Patriarchate is the most important element of the Orthodox tradition. It is inextricably connected with awareness of Russians as the chosen people. Savva Dugin demanded to restore the Patriarchate and dissolve the Synod in spite of the secularity and Westernism of the effectively Russophobic elite: a position that eventually cost him his life. During the cruel times of the eighteenth century, Russian men with beards, or who wore traditional Russian shirts, straw shoes and girdles, were not allowed into the capital. Before entering Saint Petersburg, they were required first to put on shakos,[68] pantaloons or tights and to shave their faces. This pro-Western group, absolutely alien to Russia, ruled the country for a century. In pre-Schism Russia, the absence of a beard was a sure sign of a 'loss of masculinity'. Aspects of a national identity weren't reestablished until the end of the eighteenth century, and the nineteenth century became a century of getting back to the national ethos. Likewise, the nobility gradually started to go back to its roots, and to recall the good ole' days.

'Organic democracy' is only wishful thinking. As it stands, the Russian state is something entirely different: something alienated, formal, mechani-

---

65 Ernest Johann Biron was the German lover of Tsarina Anna during her reign in mid-eighteenth century. Biron is thought to have exercised a great deal of influence over Anna in terms of inspiring Western-style reforms. This period is sometimes referred to as the Age of Biron due to the fact that Anna's court was made up largely of Germans, and since she exhibited a strong prejudice in favour of Germans.

66 Dmitri Dashkov (1784–1839) was an advisor at the Tsarist embassy in Constantinople from 1817–1823. An Old Believer, he favoured the restoration of the Patriarchate.

67 The highest office in the Orthodox Church,

68 A type of military cap that was modelled after that of the Hungarian hussars.

cal, aimless and pointless, a new edition of *Leviathan*.[69] To make things the way they should be, a genuine revolution is necessary, a revolution in a national and spiritual sense. A 'people's Putin', a 'people's government', a 'people's state' and a 'people's rule' must appear. So far, the xenomorphic elite still speak in the name of the state. This 'liberal' elite replaced the Bolshevik elite, which were also effectively opposed to the people. The latter, in its turn, had replaced the Romanov elite. And the cycle of alienation is sadly continuing. Our history has an example of an objectively ingenious combination of 'the peoples' and 'the autocratic', 'the imperial', the elite and the national — *Muscovy between the liberation from the Mongol-Tatar Yoke and the Schism*. This period, as I see it, is the optimal period: democratic, Orthodox and national at the same time. *The people's elite disappeared after the Schism.*

The Purpose of Orthodoxy and Political *Symphonia*

It is important to understand that Orthodoxy is not just a religion. It is also a political doctrine and a political theology. We often disregard this fact. A genuine Orthodoxy is tightly connected with political *symphonia*.[70] It can be said that Orthodoxy as a political philosophy had existed in Russia before the Schism, up to the second half of the seventeenth century. After the Schism, Russia's religious and political ideologies separated, leaving the balance between the national and the elite in the general structure of the state and society in a condition of flux.

In the seventeenth century, for a certain period of time, the Church was no longer free from the state. Why? Because *the state was no longer Orthodox, it was no longer an empire*. Note that the term 'Russian Empire' was introduced as a substitute for 'Rus' precisely when Russia ceased to be an empire in the sacral, katechontic sense. The state was 'Orthodox' only nominally. In

---

69   *Leviathan* is the principal work of the English political theorist Thomas Hobbes, first published in 1651. Hobbes argued that the natural state of humanity is 'the war of all against all', and that it is only through strong government that order can be maintained. It is considered one of the seminal texts of liberal democracy.

70   In the Eastern Orthodox tradition, *symphonia* refers to the idea that the state and the Church authorities should remain independent, but work in tandem with each other.

terms of political philosophy, it ceased to be Orthodox after the Schism. We know that Nikon[71] first took the title of 'Orthodox pope', but then Aleksey Mikhailovich[72] responded by diminishing the Patriarch's functions. Then came the council of 1666–67, when Holy Russia was abused by impostors of all sorts: Paisius Ligarides,[73] the Gaidars and Chubaises of the seventeenth century. Then 'The Horn of Antichrist', Peter the Great, abolished the Patriarchate as well as monasticism, leaving genuine Orthodoxy and *the genuine Church to become the opposition: the 'Old Believers'.* The Church, in its philosophical, religious and political aspects, started to oppose the Romanovs and continued to adhere to its roots: to the Moscow model under the global Old Belief movement. In the nineteenth century, one out of every three Russians was an Old Believer. Given that the elite did not practice Old Belief at all, this actually meant that every other Russian (of the people) was an Old Believer (sometimes referred to as a 'sectarian', 'a spiritual Christian', a Khlyst, a Skoptsy man or a Molokan),[74] but not a conformist, and not a 'tool'. Thus, we have not known genuine Orthodoxy for over three hundred years.

Incredible as it may seem, some elements of a free church emerged for a short period in 1917. Why had it not been possible to restore the Patriarchate before then? It was because the entire system of Russian statehood was devised to prevent its return. The whole system was built on the premise of an anti-Orthodox, anti-Eastern political and religious philosophy. Orthodoxy was seen merely as a moral instrument equivalent to Protestantism. Everything else was suppressed. In 1917, Russia was freed from the Romanov statehood and the Patriarchate was soon restored: the concept of 'single faith' was reestablished and a process of reassessment and reconsid-

---

71 Patriarch Nikon (1605–1681) was the seventh Patriarch of the Russian Orthodox Church. He initiated reforms which were later to culminate in the Schism.

72 Tsar Alexis (1629–1676) reigned from 1645 to 1676.

73 Paisius Ligarides was a Greek prelate who presided over an ecclesiastical council which resulted in the exile of Patriarch Nikon in 1666. Nikon believed that spiritual authority should take precedence over the political authority; the council, favouring the absolute authority of the Tsar, disagreed.

74 Various sects of Old Believers within the Russian Orthodox Church.

eration of the Old Belief began. It was a 'quantum of freedom', and it would have ended on a very positive note if the Bolsheviks had not suppressed it.

The second quantum came after the collapse of the Soviet system. The first quantum was utilised immediately because Church traditions were still alive. But after the fundamental abuse of our Church and our national idea during the period of totalitarian Marxism, we are still not able to use the second quantum. Two hundred years of atrocious 'Romanovism' and almost one hundred years of genocide of the Russian people during Communist rule have left us in critical condition. We were given freedom, but the time to use it has only come now; we are just now coming to our senses. When we start to truly ponder the nature of our 'freedom', we will also be thinking about our Russian political doctrine. This will inevitably lead us to the idea of the empire, *symphonia*, and the katechon. I think that the previous Patriarch, the late Alexei II,[75] was absolutely justified in vetoing the clergy's participation in the election process. Had he not done so, today's bewildered priests, a little drunk with freedom, might have steered us blindly toward any random idea: some toward Communism and Zyuganov, others toward liberalism, and the rest toward fascism. We, as people of the Church, must understand how to use this freedom correctly. I think that the model of the Church's relation to politics should be built around the roots of our tradition and embodied in some sort of religious-political project. But the right time for such a project has only come now, and requires some time to mature fully.

Globalisation as an Incentive for Archaisation

Globalisation and the postmodern era associated with it can be perceived by Russian society, by the core of the Russian people, as a new incentive for even further fundamental archaisation. If we reach the paradigmatic depths of our people's collective unconscious, they will be better equipped to use the models of globalisation and the postmodern era as an efficient instrument for awakening, just as they were able to find an efficient anti-Western instrument in Western Bolshevism. This does not mean that postmodern-

---

75   Alexei II (1929–2008) was the fifteenth Patriarch of the Russian Orthodox Church, from 1990 until his death.

ism and globalisation are good at their core. They are not good; they are the worst of all evils. But if we look closely at the structure of this evil, almost absolute and immaculate, we will be able to formulate the most radical and decisive antithesis, to reach the very depths of our national soul. The Russian people and our Orthodox tradition must be restored by an act of will to its initial pure form.

Have the Russian people disappeared or not? This is an almost ontological question. If we look at *people* as a collective assembly of various tendencies — historical, cultural, ethnic, religious, philosophical and conceptual — then, of course, they have become invisible. 'There is no people' is as metaphysical a statement as 'there is a people'; it follows the same formula. We cannot make a reasonable argument here. If we assume that *'there is no people',* then there is only society, and therefore globalism is a more advanced and modernised form of the social structure, which means that it will inevitably win. There will only be passive resistance to it, and therefore our gradual dissolution into globalism is inevitable. This is what globalists and liberals themselves think. But the belief that there is no people is an evil belief; it wishes for the concept of 'a people' to be non-existent, and it kills the concept by its very existence. This is wishful thinking...

There is a more hopeful belief — a belief that there *is* a people. This belief gives rise to a *new historical subject* — the *demos*,[76] which we possibly just cannot see. The people is an 'infinitely big atom' which we do not see. But it is there, and it occasionally makes itself known. If we stick to the hypothesis of the fixed existence of an *ethnos*, the *hypothesis of the permanence of the Russian people* with its own stable system of paradigms, which reacts to everything as a *uniform living being* — retracts, attacks, calms down, shouts — then we will be able to draft a project of *the permanent people's* participation in contemporary history, as well as in postmodern and global history. In this case, the contemporary influences that Russians have definitely already absorbed will not necessarily stand in the way of *archaisation*. We can try and assimilate modernity, globalisation and postmodernism for our national ethnical purposes and build a system of civilisation, government and religion that would meet our core interests, the interests of our

---

76 Classical Greek: 'the people', in the sense of the common people in a Greek city-state.

people. This project can be dubbed a Eurasian Empire, a new multipolar world, and a qualitative mutation of the substance of postmodernism. We should think, search for and make attempts in this direction...

The xenomorphic entity whose representatives have interpreted globalisation not only as an objective phenomenon and challenge, but as an *ethical positive* they were prepared to serve and obey and which they were going to make the basis of the country and its statehood, and which had been largely in their control for some time, has lost the fight for power. They were not merely 'reformers', they were '*globalist reformers*', they *shaped Russia into a country that fit into globalism*. Khodorkosvky directly stated this, Voloshin supported it, and Pavlovsky repeatedly declared it as an ideology. Chubais stressed it in economic and political terms. That said, the 'progressives' of the globalist type have a fundamental base not only overseas, which is obvious, but in Russian society as well. This base is an alienated Russian statehood, which has been dubbed 'tools' by the Old Believers. These are totally Russian, slightly alcoholic and slightly anti-Semitic *civil servants*, who feed the decision-making xenomorphic elite *with their own blood*. The basis for the rise of Khodorkovsky, Voloshin, Chubais and their successors is the huge vested interests of the 'tool' Russian officials of the state, who, in fact, had given birth to the oligarch system and set the scene for the globalist system, for the implementation of the 'global' corruption of the state and of the social fabric. In reality, the huge government apparatus of 'tools' is the principal source, creator and patron of the socially functional existence of the representatives from the liberal oligarchy, the cosmopolitan intelligentsia and the 'Family' clan of corruptors and lobbyists of the Yeltsin breed. Therefore, when we speak of the 'rotation of the elite' we must be clear: the front ranks have merely been filled by scapegoats and clowns. The scriptwriters and giants of decay and degeneration lurk in the shadows. If new henchmen of this meaningless state corruption machine replace them, we will be even worse off than we are today. It will be a faux substitution, not a genuine rotation. The forces of alienation and degradation will place new people who will, in turn, be removed and replaced by others, all of the same mentality.

We have the Russian people: they must be legally and politically acknowledged as *the supreme authority* with *enduring value,* and their *God-bearing* status must be confirmed. Then we must not only use their will and existence to oppose the withering and already partially imprisoned xenomorphic elite, but also to challenge the alienated bureaucratic government machine that gave rise to this elite class by engineering it, advancing it, and backing it with property and social leverage. This is not an easy task. Russians are living in an imaginary world, and it is highly probable that we will again be deceived and betrayed by an intermediate caste of state 'tools'. And we will fall for their tricks again, unless we recruit fundamentally *new people* to serve for the good of the nation. Let them be Armenian, Jewish, Georgian, or Chechen, but they should be bright personalities and energetic activists. Creative people are needed, no matter their origin, to be sworn supporters of the immense, great, eternal, holy and universal principle represented by the Russian people. Let 'small people' who are able to work efficiently help to realise the aspirations of the 'great people'.

Putin on His Own: Without the Elites

Putin, for the first time in a long era of history, has created the possibility of and the foundation for a genuine revival of the Russian people. Currently, Vladimir Putin is alone; he is surrounded by a massive bureaucratic apparatus which will undoubtedly nominate a new elite force who will only worsen the current state of affairs. Under the right circumstances, it is easier to convert people like Khodorkovsky and make them genuine *narodniks* — true advocates of the state — than to expect any help from the 'new predators' and the 'new greedy' officials, even if they are ethnic Russians. This, to me, is the only way to initiate a genuine rotation of the elite: to make the 'small people' serve the Great Eurasian cause. We are less interested in individuals, and much more concerned with the *ideological paradigm*. Khodorkovsky had the good sense to request *books on Russian history* while serving his prison sentence. He was ripe for a proposal of *a systemic plan to join Eurasianism.* He could not be bothered with trifles or monetary threats, to which he responded honourably, plainly and clearly — 'no'. He knew how to converse with law enforcement officers, beggars and bandits.

But if one were to approach him with a system, complete with logistics and a model, he would probably be the first to support another version of globalisation — not in the American, unipolar way, but in a Eurasian and multipolar one. Khodorkovsky was wrong, but he made a systemic error, not a chance error; replace the plus in his philosophy with a minus and he, along with Yukos,[77] would be invaluable. With specific types of people, inducing such a shift is much easier than it might seem. I would suggest that the 'democrats' and 'liberals' who are starting to feel the beginnings of a political backlash not take it to heart, but focus instead on *studying the history of the Russian people* and trying to understand the logic behind it.

The Anti-American Consensus

The American invasion of Iraq in the spring of 2003 had serious repercussions for the domestic political environment in Russia, yielding quite a few electoral surprises on the eve of the upcoming parliamentary and presidential elections. Russian society is ideologically divided along completely different lines than party affiliations might suggest. Our party system was created hurriedly; it is constantly inundated with immature players, and some forces who genuinely represented the people have been forcefully excluded. This system does not reflect our society and therefore raises eyebrows and evokes disgust. Russians think, feel and believe in a way that is entirely different from the people who have been offered up by the Russian party system and its political strategists. Remove these parties and there won't be any fundamental changes — new parties can easily be created, or even forgotten altogether as a useless and insignificant concept. But this does not mean that the people are apolitical and indifferent, only that they have opted to choose what to care about from a completely different set of categories.

After the onset of American aggression in Iraq, the overwhelming majority of Russians made one such choice: *anti-Americanism*. Saddam was not an especially sympathetic character, but George W. Bush was particu-

---

77 Yukos was an oil and gas company owned by Khodorkovsky. It went bankrupt in 2006 as a result of being unable to pay taxes levied by the Russian government, following accusations of tax evasion.

larly disliked. This was not just an idle reaction to global problems confined to a few sign-waving protests. It was, and continues to be, *a living, vibrant social factor.* The people feel what is going on with their hearts, their very skin. It is a deeply emotional position. Anti-Americanism and increased attention to the US as a threat to Russia is a recurrent social motif. In order to change it radically, an event of a similar scale needs to occur, and it is hard to imagine what event this could possibly be.

The Russian government, represented by Putin, took *an anti-American stance* on Iraq. Then Putin entered into a coalition with two European states, France and Germany, which also refused to support the unlawful US invasion of Iraq. He asserted Russia's sovereignty in terms of foreign policy, and maintained his strategic interests in Iraq. 'The invasion of Iraq is a mistake', Putin said,[78] pitting himself against the Russian community of experts, which, in late 2002 and early 2003, unanimously claimed that Russia must join the coalition against Iraq (today Putin's refusal to make concessions to the US is seen by the same experts as a logical foreign policy strategy).

At the time, Putin's difficult decision was not influenced by public sentiment alone. In fact, Putin has repeatedly proven that he can have his way even when the masses disagree with him (his support of the ultra-liberal economic bloc of the Russian government is a good example). In joining the 'peaceful coalition' (France, Germany, China, some Islamic states, etc.), Putin was driven primarily by *geopolitical considerations.* The people, relying primarily on their emotions and intuition, might use different arguments and logical processes to explain his actions, but anti-Americanism was the primary focus no matter which way you look at it. This is already a social fact.

The fact that the Russian government began to resonate with the public's anti-American sentiments *added legitimacy* to the authorities, giving rise to a new consensus structure. This consensus has clear ideological parameters: a national idea, a statehood, rejection of American as the ultimate standard, and the strengthening of Russia's sovereignty and status as a

---

78 On 20 March 2003, shortly after the American invasion of Iraq began, Putin demanded that the US cease hostilities, referring to the war as 'a big political mistake'.

world power. Many sceptics call this 'the phantom pain of the lost empire', a nostalgia of sorts. Be that as it may, this sentiment is, at the same time, a kind of remission: social myths have power and might become truly mobilising factors. The Treaty of Versailles, for instance, resulted in the Third Reich by creating large-scale national frustration in Germany. Putin, acting quite correctly in his relations with the US, obtained a brand new social resource for his domestic policy. He obtained additional sanctions. And since the US acted outside the boundaries set by the international legal framework, repeating its transgressions against Iraq in Libya and ultimately destroying the old world order that had been agreed upon in Yalta, Putin received *a special historical mandate* that allowed him to move confidently and energetically through the complex international playing field: he was backed by *the social consensus of anti-Americanism*.

What is anti-Americanism? Naturally, it isn't directly related to the US and its political and economic system. The resentment is directed, first of all, at American aggression toward other countries (grounded in the expectation that Russia 'may be next'), and not at the US itself. This is defensive, conservative anti-Americanism, a sentiment grounded in survival and preservation. In this sense, it is a *mass* phenomenon. This characteristic sets it apart from other forms of anti-Americanism, which are common in either Right-wing conservative Orthodox-patriotic movements or, on the other end, in Communist circles that reject the US *in principle*. But, in the face of the events in Iraq, these differences were washed away and became negligible: ideological and radical forms of anti-Americanism became assimilated into the more passive anti-Americanism of the masses. The definite focus of this general phenomenon is Putin. Putin has effectively become the driving force behind social integration, the axis of sociopolitical life, and the direct spokesman for the hopes and expectations of the majority, even to a greater extent than necessary.

How can Vladimir Putin use the anti-Americanism of the masses for his benefit? One should take into account that Putin's positions will contrast greatly with that of the political elite, who traditionally rely on transnational projects, support marginal liberal politicians, and in some way or the other have ties to the US. Changes in the balance of this sphere require the development of *new rules regarding cooperation between the oligarchs and the authorities, with allowance for geopolitical (military-industrial) indexes and social projects.* Putin can implement a *covert renationalisation* of the country's largest companies, not in terms of changing their legal or property status, but in terms of establishing a new system based on the direct and transparent consideration of national and social interests. *Putin and the nation happen to be on the same side of the fence*, and the oligarchs' chance to use the 'blind masses' in their own interests is almost non-existent. Simultaneously, the functional role of the CPRF as a supporter of nationalisation would also be called into question, and its mission would be delegated directly to the authorities.

Putin's Munich Speech — a Turning Point in Russian History

Vladimir Putin's speech in Munich[79] became a turning point in contemporary Russian history. It would be a mistake to think that the Cold War ended in 1991. Rather, one should say that the Soviet Union unilaterally withdrew from the war. In doing so, it did not sign any documents and did not negotiate any terms. This withdrawal was presented to the Russian people as the end of the war. Imagine the following situation: two powers are fighting with each other. Suddenly one of them proclaims: 'I am out of the war,' without specifying whether it considers itself the winner or the loser. A dubious situation arises: one of the sides withdraws from the conflict, thinking that the other will withdraw as well. Except the other side doesn't. Notably, the former, who has already dismissed its army (the Warsaw treaty),[80] tore down its bases (both in Eastern Europe and in the USSR) and began to concern itself with internal affairs, in effect finds itself

---

79   At the Munich Conference on Security Policy on 12 February 2007, Putin condemned the order represented by the unipolar world, calling for multipolarity, and accused the US of overstepping its bounds. The complete text is available at www.washingtonpost.com/wp-dyn/content/article/2007/02/12/AR2007021200555.html.

80   The Treaty of Warsaw established the Warsaw Pact in 1955, which was the Soviet answer to NATO by providing a treaty of mutual defence among the Communist states in Europe that were under Soviet domination.

in the position of the loser. 'The winner', in turn, starts to treat its opponent as the loser. But the political elite of the losing country does not tell its people that their country has lost, and continues to act like nothing happened. It makes it seem like the Cold War is over and it's a tie.

This situation had persisted since Gorbachev and continued until Putin's speech in Munich. The Americans have never stopped fighting the Cold War. They keep on advancing, expanding the NATO bloc and, at the same time, claiming everything that we aren't keeping an eye on: first in Eastern Europe and the Baltic states, then in the CIS itself. In other words, the US always has, and always will be waging a Cold War against Russia. This is why Putin, by and large, didn't really say anything new in his Munich speech. Conversely, the Russian government during the Gorbachev and Yeltsin eras acted like a colonial administration, pretending that the US was not waging a Cold War against us, glossing over US occupations, and not allowing the people to mobilise themselves in order to obtain freedom and sovereignty. These leaders destroyed the people's drive for resistance and victory by dulling their sense of awareness. During Yeltsin's presidency, a completely opposite model was promoted: Russia was acting in line with NATO's policy and betraying its own geopolitical essence. When Putin came to power, many of his statements and actions gave rise to speculations that he was more inclined to side with the Eurasian model and the multipolar world than with Yeltsin's political course...

From the 'Cool War' to a 'Hot Phase'

During his first presidency, Putin, under the guise of obedience to the occupation forces, pursued a policy of internal mobilisation. In other words, he was preparing an uprising. He was merely waiting for the right moment when he would be able to openly say to the world and his own people that the Cold War against Russia had never ended in the first place, and that, in kind, our country was still at war. He started off talking about the concept of *'sovereign democracy'*, and finally called a spade a spade in his Munich speech in 2007.

The concept of *'sovereign democracy'*[81] became common in 2005–2006 and was one of the principal ideologemes during the presidential and Duma elections in 2007–2008.

At the time, I was contemplating the deconstruction of democracy and thought that this strange concept of *'sovereign democracy'* should serve to remind us that democracy is not something that should be taken for granted. Its dogmatic status and refusal to acknowledge alternatives prevents the very possibility of a free philosophical discourse.

Democracy can be accepted, as well as rejected. It can be established, as well as disposed of. History has known perfect societies with no democracy and dreadful societies which had democracy, and vice versa. Democracy is a man-made project, a construct, a plan, but not a destiny. It can be rejected or accepted. It needs validation, an *apologia*. Without an *apologia*, democracy will have no sense. An undemocratic form of government should not be considered as the worst possible form of government. The 'lesser of two evils' formula is a propaganda ploy. Democracy is not the lesser of evils… it may be evil and may not be evil at all. Everything requires philosophical consideration. Only on the basis of the above assumptions is it possible to analyse democracy thoughtfully.

Let us consider the etymology of the word *demos*, since democracy means 'rule of the *demos*'. Usually, this word is translated as 'people'. But there were many synonyms of the word 'people' in use in the Greek language: *ethnos, laos, phule*, and so on. *Demos* was one of them, and it described a population: that is, people living on a specific territory.

Julius Pokorny's[82] Indo-European etymological dictionary[83] states that the Greek word *demos* is derived from the Indo-European root * dā (*də-), which means 'to share', 'to divide'. Therefore, the very etymology of *demos* refers to something divided, sliced into separate fragments and placed on a certain territory. The Russian word with the closest meaning

---

[81] This term has been widely used with several different meanings starting from the eighteenth century. Rousseau for example used the words *démocratie souveraine* to denote the sovereign power of the people; in America in the nineteenth century the 'party of sovereign democracy' was called the Democratic Party.—AD

[82] Julius Pokorny (1887–1970) was an Austrian linguist.

[83] *Indogermanisches etymologisches Wörterbuch*, 4 vols. (Bern: Francke, 1951–1969).

is «население», 'population', but not 'people', because 'people' implies a cultural and linguistic unity, as well as a common historical existence and a certain destiny (predestination). A population can (theoretically) do without the above. A 'population' is everyone who has settled or has been settled on a particular territory, but not necessarily people who have roots or citizenship in that land.

Aristotle, who introduced the notion of democracy, had a somewhat negative attitude to it in its 'Greek' meaning. According to Aristotle, 'democracy' is equivalent to 'rule of the masses' and 'ochlocracy' (mob rule). As an alternative to democracy, the worst form of government, Aristotle discussed not only monarchy and aristocracy ('the rule of one' or 'the rule of the best', which he viewed positively), but also *politeia* (from the Greek 'city-state'). *Politeia*, much like 'democracy', is the rule of many, although not on an indiscriminate basis. It is the rule of qualified, conscientious citizens, who stand out as a result of their significant cultural, genealogical, social and economic characteristics. *Politeia* is the self-rule of citizens on the basis of traditions and customs. Democracy is a chaotic agitation of rebellious masses. *Politeia* involves cultural unity: a common historical and religious base for citizens. Democracy can be established by an arbitrary set of atomised individuals, 'divided' into random sectors. Aristotle, in fact, mentions other forms of unjust rule — tyranny (the rule of a usurper) and oligarchy (the rule of a small group of rich scoundrels and corruptors). All negative forms of government are connected with each other: tyrants often draw upon democracy, just as oligarchs often appeal to it. Integrity, which is so important for Aristotle, lies within monarchy, aristocracy and *politeia*. Division, fragmentation, and atomisation are on the side of democracy.

The idea of division and atomisation was employed by modern philosophers to describe human societies and the state of man himself. With the concept of an 'individual', the indivisible, an 'atom', modern history was freed from metaphysics, authority, the rule of the Church and from morals. It freed humans from the divine care of theocentrism.

The modern era has established itself on the cult of 'methodological individualism', as opposed to 'methodological holism'. It is the negation of the Only (God) and the recognition of the priority of the Many (individuals) that is the principal dogma of modernity and the main hypothesis of the modern era. In the postmodernism of our times this thesis remains undisputed.

In this context, the concept of 'sovereign democracy' in Russian politics circa 2005–2007 meant roughly the following: the Western world distributes and insists on democracy, referring to a very specific model that was established in Europe in the modern era. It is built around the principles of individualism and 'liberty from' — principles that have guided Western civilisation for almost three hundred years, since the modern era began. Russia is a non-individualistic country; its history and culture have always been based on integrity, being united, the common, and the collective (be it the people, communities, the Church, God, the state, or the Empire). Western democracy does not suit Russia because it is individualistic and is based on a rational, goal-oriented and assertive individual subject. We must have our own democracy — one that takes into account the peculiarities of our national pattern and national history. This is what the sovereignty of our choice and of our democracy is about.

It is interesting to note the way these arguments by Russian political commentators had touched upon the topic of a multipolar world before Vladimir Putin officially spoke of it in his 2007 Munich speech.

This speech was a turning point in Russian history. Its content was a direct reflection of the world as it really is: America is waging a 'cool war' on us. Even Western political scientists have said the same thing. The fact is that a Cold War is possible only in the case of a fully symmetrical weapons system, meaning that the adversaries must control equivalent spaces. For now, Russia is left with asymmetrical answers only. There is a possibility that this war can become a 'warm war' or even a 'hot war' at any moment. And the anticipated attack on Iraq, which was in direct opposition to Russia's strategic interests, was a step toward shifting the 'cool war' into a hot phase. If the US attacks Syria or Iran, America is actually threatening Russia.

Putin said it all in his Munich speech, thereby evoking a shift in Russian self-awareness. Prior to the speech in Munich, we had spent 15 years living under the impression that there was no 'cool war', thanks to our corrupt colonial government. They had convinced us that there was no unipolar world and that everybody was working toward a multipolar world. So, after this period of intellectual frenzy in which Russia found itself after Gorbachev and Yeltsin, the country started to come to its senses. People started to see things as they really are. The 'period of confusion' was over. In and of itself, this understanding of reality was actually quite sad: if we look at what we had been doing for two decades in light of Putin's speech, we should be ashamed of ourselves. We had put ourselves in the hands of the occupation's elite, which consisted of oligarchs, pro-Westerners and liberals who intentionally destroyed our strategic positions and tried to strip our country of its sovereignty.

The Munich Speech: A Foundation for Geopolitics

It would not be an overstatement to call Putin's Munich speech a historic one. It had been decades since a Russian leader spoke so clearly and categorically about the future of international politics. In Munich, Vladimir Putin declared Russia's principal stance as that of a world geopolitical force in the future world order. The theses voiced by Putin briefly covered, succinctly and decisively, the conclusions that I had drawn as far back as the mid-1990s in my book *The Foundations of Geopolitics*. The book was devoted to the fundamental conflict between the 'land civilisation' and the 'sea civilisation',[84] and to the infeasibility of a unipolar world. The book stressed that Russia should lead the forces which would oppose unipolar globalisation and the spreading of Atlanticism embodied in the North Atlantic treaty (NATO). In Munich the President combined these fragmented statements into a concise and clear statement. In essence, Putin expressed his readiness to oppose US international policy.

During the 1980s, when the Soviet Union was still intact, and during the 1990s, when the Soviet Union disappeared (and, in fact, long before that, since Woodrow Wilson and Theodore Roosevelt), America was tak-

---

84 This is a key dichotomy in geopolitical thought, as first established by Sir Halford Mackinder. Carl Schmitt wrote, 'World history is the history of the wars waged by maritime powers against land or continental powers and by land powers against sea or maritime powers', in *Land and Sea* (Washington, DC: Plutarch Press, 1997).

ing strategic steps toward creating a unipolar world. The only question was whether it would share this global sovereignty with other countries or not. Putin challenged the contemporary state of affairs and the entire course of international politics. When such statements were made by Hugo Chávez, Kim Jong-il, or Ahmadinejad, they were easily brushed off (although Ahmadinejad stood apart). When they are made by Russia, they are a game-changer.

When a country that possesses the second-largest nuclear arsenal in the world, occupies a huge territory, controls energy resources, and has a lengthy history of a national mission and opposition — essentially a 'country-continent', a civilisation — challenges the United States, NATO, the Energy Charter[85] and the entire world order, it means that all masks come off. Putin stated that the unipolar world was absolutely inadmissible, and that the ballistic missile defence system that is being created in Europe by the US, cannot be directed at North Korea — it is directed at us. Russia strongly opposes the construction of the BMD system and cannot ignore it. Putin said that NATO is not a partner but an enemy who is destabilising the political environment throughout its entire sphere of influence, and that the Energy Charter that Europe is forcing upon us, intending to ensure access to Russian energy resources without giving Russia access to European energy resources in return, is a humiliating, occupation-style agreement: 'You give us everything and we give you nothing.' That's the way people negotiate with losers, who are expected to submit to the winner's will. Putin essentially declared that Russia would be challenging the world order and paving the way for a geopolitical revolution — no more, no less.

Putin's Mandate for a Revolution in Consciousness

The results of the 2001 all-Russian poll conducted by the Sociology Department at Lomonosov Moscow State Linguistic University established, among other things, that Vladimir Putin had higher approval ratings than

---

85   The Energy Charter Treaty was signed at the end of 1991 with the intention of integrating the energy resources of the former Eastern bloc territories into the global marketplace. Russia has refused to ratify it, which it sees as unfairly balanced against its national interests.

any other Russian decision-maker. This was not extraordinary at all. Its main peculiarity was the fact that it was conducted at the initiative of academic sociologists and not in any way connected with political circles, nor rigged by the government or the opposition.

I would like to focus on an interpretation of several items in the poll. Let me start by saying that this interpretation is subjective and can easily be disputed by other commentators.

My conclusion may seem radical: there is no democracy in Russia, I don't see it coming, and it cannot be and should not exist in Russia. What is the basis of such an opinion? The basis is the profile of the average Russian, which was obtained during the poll and which fully confirms the conclusions of my long-term analysis of the society we live in from an insider's perspective. The results show that a significant percentage of Russians still trust the authorities, and that the majority of Russians associate 'the authorities' with Vladimir Putin. This is a stable monarchic trend, reflecting the fact that a powerful authoritarian figure is in high demand. Does Putin comply with these expectations? I am more inclined to say 'yes' than 'no', and Russian society fills in the missing gaps, not in accordance with any serious analysis but rather on the basis of an inherent, deeply-rooted belief system.

Putin is seen through the prism of a family metaphor: a state is subconsciously perceived as a 'big family', and its head as 'the father'. In a family structure, the father possesses a stable authoritarian status, which means the rest of the family is submissive and complicit in enhancing the father's authority instead of undermining it. When the personality of the head of state or a national leader makes this dynamic possible, demonstrating at least some of the required virtues, the public consciousness fills in all of the missing elements until the model of patriarchal authoritarianism is complete. The initiative comes from the people — an expression of stable and traditionally established 'monarchic' attitudes. It is this monarchic tendency of the masses that creates conditions for authoritarian rule, thus liquidating the substance of democracy via a democratic process and giving power back to the authorities represented by the father figure. This is a striking characteristic of a traditional society which shines through a democratic façade. And this, as has been repeatedly stated by the scientists conducting the poll, does not diminish the legitimacy or legality of the democratic procedure. Monarchy in Russia can easily be legal and legitimate within the framework of a democratic procedure which would function as a kind of *zemsky sobor*.[86] Thus we are dealing with a sort of 'plebiscitary authoritarianism' — a monarchy that is a voluntary legacy of the masses.

This poll clearly demonstrates that Russians remain quite critical as well. For instance, the assessment of government activity was three times lower than the assessment of its head (Putin was Prime Minister at the time). Here we see a conscious scepticism toward the actual deeds of the government, which are assessed realistically and critically and then acknowledged to be ineffective, poorly managed, and generally wrong. Concern about economic development, unemployment, safety, corruption, and deteriorating ecology are common sentiments among a significant share of the respondents. In other words, the people fully understand what is happening and do not approve (at least, substantially) of the prevailing course. Yet, there are a large percentage of people who are happy with everything. Given that the scientists who conducted the poll were not politically motivated, this 'happiness' is likely a genuine reflection of public sentiment. The bottom line is that, according to the poll, the people trust Putin, recognise his right to take decisive action, and demand that he exercise this right.

Putin is on the threshold of a new role — as a 'man of destiny.' Such were de Gaulle, Churchill, and Stalin. The new Putin draws his power from society, is guided by geopolitics, defends national interests, rises to the challenges of history, and lives and acts under the formula 'I am the state, the people and the society.' This role is reinforced by another existing tendency to establish a monarchy, a legitimised trend that is emanating from the people, from below. Will the new Putin comply with legislative regulations? This is possible but not essential, because up to this point he has very carefully employed even the powers legally granted to him under the auspices of a presidential republic. Given that 'the people' are the most important category, the state must be 'dissolved' in the people and then reconstructed from the bottom up. And it must be done with the help of *our* Putin, who

---

86 'Assembly of the land'.

can even be deified (we should not spare anything for the sake of a great cause) so that he can perform great deeds calmly and steadily, without bothering himself with petty 'elections'. We must grant Putin the status of the 'Sun King'[87] and strengthen his rule in tandem with a reformed and flexible xenomorphic elite, who will swear allegiance to the great Russian people. And only then will we be able to revive the great empire.

---

87 Louis XIV of France was called the 'Sun King', since he made France the most powerful country in Europe in his day.

CHAPTER 3

Putin's Test

Putin against the 'Sisters'

The *Nord-Ost* events[1] became yet another serious test for Vladimir Putin, on par with the 9/11 terrorist attacks. On 22 October 2002, the terrorists, holding hostages, challenged the future of Russia, the political regime and Vladimir Putin. For two days, the future of the Russian state was uncertain. This was not simply a terrorist attack, it was a genuine attempt at a coup. Not an ideological one, as was the case with the Civil Forum, but a genuine one — hot and brutal. At that point, Putin's credibility was based on his political and 'strong-arm' reaction against the Moscow attacks and guerrilla actions in Dagestan during 1999. The Russian people accepted and elected Putin precisely for the way he acted in that particular situation; it became the basis of the national consensus regarding his legitimacy. In his response to the challenge from the Chechen separatists, Putin outlined a new 'agenda' for post-Yeltsin Russian politics. This agenda, to put it briefly, was the following: 'The inherent value and integrity of the Russian state must not be questioned.' Putin backed this premise with his first steps as President, and Russian society — the intelligentsia, the media, the Chechens, Tatar-

---

1   On 22 October 2002, Chechen terrorists attacked the Dubrovka theatre in Moscow during a performance of the musical *Nord-Ost* and took the entire audience as well as the performers and crew captive, numbering approximately 850 people. After two and a half days, Russian security services pumped gas into the building and then stormed the theatre. All of the terrorists and over 130 hostages died in the attack.

stan, the governors, the Duma — had to follow it. However, after implementing its first radical measures (the introduction of the federal districts, the Federation Council reform, the expulsions, as well as the restraining of the geopolitically scheming oligarchs), Putin did not immediately back his early endeavours with decisive action. His hesitation led all the players in the political process to believe that we were retreating back to the late Yeltsin period, especially since the delay in implementing reforms was accompanied by geopolitical concessions to the US (which became especially evident after the events of 9/11). It seemed that Putin's reforms had been rolled back.

It appears that certain geopolitical forces, as well as domestic opposition — separatists, Islamists, several oligarchs, and so on — thought that *the time had come to seriously destabilise Putin's Russia*. They resolved to challenge Putin and Russia, which led to the tragic events at the Dubrovka theatre. Curiously enough, it is obvious that *everyone but the Chechens themselves had political interests in this terrorist attack*. For some period of time leading up to the tragedy at Dubrovka, Chechnya had accepted Putin's rules of the game. The Chechens and their leaders had been actively and almost enthusiastically cooperating with the authorities and law enforcement. Northern Chechnya had fully recognised the legitimacy of federal rule, and even the majority of field commanders had entered into a kind of symbiosis with the Russian Army, in one way or another, which sometimes seemed almost paradoxical. A political solution to the Chechen issue was a priority on the national agenda, and the majority of Chechens had found the solutions to be agreeable. This attack put an end to all of this in the blink of an eye. From then on, Chechens could no longer aspire, even in theory, to obtain the status of a 'political subject'. They no longer had rights as a people, and only their citizens' rights remained. Chechens no longer exist as an *ethnos* in the political sense, and this will remain the case for a long time. As for Islam, the forces that challenged Vladimir Putin and Russia *cannot have stemmed directly from the Islamic realm*. Islam as a civilisation is very weak in certain aspects; it urgently needs partners to realise its geopolitical ambitions — Russia, Europe, the Asian countries, and other prospective participants of the multipolar world. Islamism, Islamic radicalism, Wahhabism, and Al Qaeda all act against Muslims' interests and against the *Ummah*,[2] in the name of the ideals of their own heretical sect (the so-called 'pure Islam', which could be dubbed Islamic Protestantism) and for the benefit of the Atlanticist unipolar world. The mission carried out by Islamic terrorists is not a Muslim one, but rather that of their opponents, advancing the interests of those against whom their struggle is supposedly directed. Islamists and their institutions — various 'international' organisations and 'Islamic committees' — must be wiped out. This is in the best interests both of humanity in general and of Muslims themselves. By attacking Moscow, these forces acted against the interests of Islam. In the West, especially in the US, opinions about the Putin regime at the outset of his presidency were divided. Some experts thought that Putin was acceptable for the West and sufficiently loyal to the US. The other camp — Brzezinski, Wolfowitz, and so on — were convinced that Putin was merely appeasing the West in order to give Russia a break it desperately needed, and that the country would soon rise again. Backed by some anti-Putin circles comprised of former and current Russian citizens, this second camp decided to cynically test the condition of Putin's system, which had, judging by certain external characteristics, started to crack. The *Nord-Ost* attack became a reality check of sorts, much like the Georgian attack on South Ossetia in August 2008.

It is obvious that the Dubrovka attack was instigated by these geopolitical forces. The Chechen Islamists (note that Movsar Barayev[3] had been spawned by the Islamist al-Khattab[4] and his assistant, who were, as is well-known today, working for the CIA) played into the hands of the Atlanticists. The TV channels showed the 'sisters', wrapped in black cloth with only their eyes visible: they were Arabic, not Chechen. It later emerged that the supporting infrastructure for the terrorists in Moscow was not the Chechen diaspora at all. When the terrorists implemented the first part of

---

2   In Islam, this refers to the entire community of Muslims around the world.

3   Movsar Barayev (1979–2002) was the leader of the Chechens who attacked the theatre.

4   Ibn al-Khattab (1969–2002) was a Saudi-born jihadi who fought against the Russians in Afghanistan during the 1980s, and later received training in Al Qaeda camps there. He went to Chechnya in 1995 and fought against the Russians in both wars, and also in the Dagestan War. He was assassinated by the FSB in March 2002.

their plan, many things became evident. Again, as during Yeltsin's last years, the so-called 'democratic' politicians — Khakamada,[5] Nemtsov, Yavlinsky, Kobzon, even old Primakov — popped up, reanimated by the residual media influence of the exiled oligarchs. The forgotten slogans of the human rights activists, such as 'No to the war in Chechnya', reappeared. Had this campaign been allowed to continue, Putin's political legitimacy would have been lost forever, and we would now be living in an entirely different kind of country. This is what the wicked plot was about: to expose Putin as indecisive when it came to key issues and to make Russia irrelevant again, just like in the Yeltsin era.

The grave reality of this challenge was marked by another complication as well: had the hostages died during the attack, Putin would most likely have had to make his case by employing measures he was psychologically unprepared for. Besides, it could have provoked an uncontrollable upsurge of unbridled national anger and ethnic tensions, which would have brought the country to the verge of a civil war. The attack's organisers had planned everything perfectly: this kind of challenge would be too much for the system set up by Putin, which was clearly unable to cope with much easier tasks in more favourable situations and appeared to have been altogether stagnant for several years. Vladimir Putin would have been forced to back his radical decision with a series of political measures so drastic that they would have been crippling to the country and the Russian people. There was only one thing to do: to walk through a dangerous passage, a decision reminiscent of the Symplegades.[6]

During the *Nord-Ost* incident, Putin, the political regime and Russia as a whole were rescued by the secret service. At the time, law enforcement managed to resolve a seemingly unmanageable situation. On 26 October 2002, 700 hostages were saved. But they weren't the only ones: Russia was saved too.

---

5   Irina Khakamada (b. 1955) ran against Putin in the 2004 election.

6   In Greek mythology, the Symplegades were two 'clashing rocks' that stood at the entrance of the Bosporus to the Black Sea, preventing travelers from passing through. They stopped clashing after Jason and the Argonauts succeeded in passing through them.

During the tragic events at Dubrovka, the best coverage by the TV channels (who helped Vladimir Putin, the people and law enforcement) turned out to be Channel One and Russia. They stood up to the challenge and demonstrated that they truly were national media. TVC, on the other hand, did not. It seemed that the then-mayor Luzhkov had been waiting all along for Kremlin to lose its footing. Overall, it became evident that we, together with Putin, had come a long way since Yeltsin. Until 1999, the terrorists would have been allowed to hold press conferences on all the Russian channels, to talk with 'Kasyanov' and 'Putin' on the phone, and to shoot hostages... *Nord-Ost* also served as a test for Putin because it demonstrated yet again that the North Caucasus issue and security in general did not depend solely on law enforcement agencies or the international community. It was also bogged down by the corruption of the political class, including the military. Resolving this issue is impossible without a *concrete and substantial revolution in the political cadres*. Today, this revolution is inevitable.

Temptation by the Void

Aside from the immediate external and domestic challenges and emergencies, Putin also had to cope with the 'illusion of peace': a challenge in mentality. The liberal, nationalist and Communist forces were so marginalised and dispersed that they no longer posed a threat to anyone, and Russian society exhibited all the signs of a political consensus. This illusory political reconciliation had mostly been fabricated by spin doctors. The Kremlin spin doctors, primarily Vladislav Surkov, had exploited the fact that Russian partisan and political life in the 1990s was in itself artificial, 'theatrical' and manipulative to elevate this farce to the point of absurdity.

De-politisation became the foundation of the 'new policy'. It is worth noting that Russian political parties do not exhibit so much as a trace of a consistent political philosophy, and are comprised mostly of arbitrary conglomerates and populist slogans. Russian political parties do not have ideological magazines, institutions, proper expert centres, or funds for intellectual projects. De-politisation had rendered Putin virtually the single most important political object, providing him with limitless political freedom. Much like Louis XIV,[7] Putin can easily claim: 'I am the state.' This situation, in turn, begs yet another question: 'If Putin IS the state, what is the political substance of Putin himself?' Of course, the majority of Russians implicitly understand Putin: Putin is for Russia, Putin is not Yeltsin, Putin is against oligarchy, Putin supports Gross Domestic Product (GDP) growth, Putin is against violations, terrorism and extremism, Putin supports modernisation, Putin is independent and self-sufficient, Putin is powerful — sometimes cruel, sometimes tolerant.

The dismantling of the political constructs that were subject to demolition as a result of this process was now over. It was tactful to inform the public about the second, positive half of the programme in small doses during the previous stage. This tactic demoralised Putin's opponents. But the situation had changed, significantly and profoundly. That which constituted an achievement during the previous stage — de-politisation — had turned into a threat, an obstacle, and a challenge.

In other words, the main subject of Russian politics, Vladimir Vladimirovich Putin, was faced with a dilemma: to build a new and substantial political structure from scratch, delegating the development of an organic, consistent ideology, national strategy, and political philosophy to his supporters (United Russia, the government, the Parliament and the Federation Council), or to leave everything as it was, suspending the status quo and merely pulling the strings of obedient and effectively powerless puppets. This choice was not self-evident, and either choice carried with it a certain amount of risk. If Putin resolved to build a meaningful policy — a proper strategy with ideological backing — he would invest his personal capital in a political system that would be able to function and develop on its own. In this case, Putin would share his concentrated political power with others: not only with his followers, but also with the oppositional forces who would obtain ideological legitimacy and the possibility of a succinct ideological and political dialogue. The risks for Putin are evident but such is the

---

7   Louis XIV (1638–1715) was the King of France from 1643 until his death. He made France the leading power in Europe and consolidated political power over the country in the monarchy.

price for a place in history, for the creation of something bigger than one's individual personality and for the most fantastic career.

There was another option: the 'conservation of a void'. Putin could have left the current techniques that imitate politics and the opposition intact, continuing to substitute a show for reality: a nervous show of the manifestation of social and economic interests, and a repulsive imitation of genuine democracy. This would ultimately have disappointed his supporters, the intellectual class and the greater public. Putin would have had to make his way toward political meanings, and to uncover the secret nature of real substance.

During his first eight years in office, Putin totally dismantled Yeltsin's political system. He didn't transform or modify the system: he totally demolished it. He broke down all aspects of the farce, unravelled all the intrigue created by the opposition, and stopped everything that was moving in a suspicious direction, and he was successful in all respects. The unruly oligarchs were exiled and imprisoned. The national patriotic camp that the Yeltsin authorities had only grappled with was crushed. The governors and members of the Federation Council were reined in. Alexander Voloshin, the all-powerful master of political visions, disappeared without a trace. He was followed by the Yeltsin negotiator Kasyanov, who was dismissed along with his cabinet. Khodorkovsky went to jail, and the rest of Yeltsin's cronies followed suit. The SPS and Yabloko vanished from the Duma. Kudrin's government, an epitome of the liberal bloc, was deposed. Vladislav Surkov was dismissed. Anatoly Chubais alone awaits his share of thanks.

Putin is now free from adversaries, competitors, enemies, and opponents. There is an empty *void* around him. And it is this void that is his principal enemy, the subject of dialogue, the chief adversary and his primary opponent. Putin is destined to fight the void.

'A big country' is a viable alternative to the void: not as an adversary, but as Putin's support system that would serve to accompany Putin as a testament, a mission, and a higher aim. The country hates the government, the officials, and the people who have effectively gotten rid of politics, transforming the bureaucracy into a single ruling class and destroying our culture, the economy, and the entire social sphere. If it came to pass that the

President shot the government dead, the people would be happy. Putin is only now morphing into the 'real' Putin, having confirmed the decisiveness of his transformation with very concrete and convincing steps that are clear to the people and to the political elites. We will try and observe the Putin who has emerged out of these decisions — a hero, who has overcome the void. The Putin beyond the void. Our Eurasian Putin.

Putin and the Void II: Political Solitude

In the months leading up to the 2012 elections, everyone knew that President Putin would be re-elected. And it was evident to everybody that the process would not be an election per se, but rather a nationwide confirmation of Putin's mandate as the national leader. Putin did not have genuine opponents or a viable opposition. Putin was alone. He was countered by a nothing — a void. And while this was undoubtedly a good thing, this void carried with it hidden risks and dangers, posing an invisible, and therefore all the more fearsome, threat.

He Slightly Gathered Russia[8]

As I noted above, Putin did not obtain his landslide win in the blink of an eye. He gained his first wave of supporters by taking a tough stance on Chechnya — a move that contrasted sharply with the slack and disjointed management style that characterised Yeltsin's presidency. The people realised that Putin intended to 'put Russia back together', assuming that he would retain our new liberal economy, continue carrying out market reforms, and maintain cordial relations with the West. This strategy was accepted by virtually all of the top politicians in Russia. His tough superpower style struck a chord with the patriots, and even with the Communists. At the same time, his liberalism and his moderate policies oriented toward the West impressed the liberals. *At the time, Putin embodied a consensus between the elites.* But the Putin of that time was different from today's Putin, the one who emerged after the start of his second presidency.

---

8   Again, a reference to Ivan III.

The Structure of Non-Void

How did Vladimir Putin arrive at this pre-election void? Consider that at the beginning of his presidency, he was surrounded by the following actors: 'the Family', a group of people with immense influence who ruled Yeltsin's Russia; the regional barons, who were united structurally under a single influential organisation, the Federation Council, and politically under the moderately oppositional party Fatherland — All Russia; national republics that were steadily gaining independence from the central government, such as Tatarstan, Bashkiria, Chuvashia, Sakha, and others; the unquenchable (as it seemed at the time) hotbed of separatism and terror that was Chechnya; powerful media owners who could distort the truth to serve their own ends; large clans of oligarchs who were backed by international interests and corporations and had all but complete independence from the national administration, acting as 'transnational' and 'extraterritorial' entities; and the influential political opposition parties, which were aspiring to establish a dialogue both with the Right (the SPS, Yabloko) and the Left (the CPRF). Vladimir Putin spent his first two terms methodically reducing the number of these independent actors. Today, this mission has been largely accomplished: government independence from 'the Family' has been achieved; the Federation Council has been reformed; Fatherland — All Russia has been fused into the pro-Putin United Russia party that obeys Putin without question; the national republics, inch by inch, are giving up on claims of sovereignty and have stopped trying to engage in confrontations with the centre; Chechnya has been won back and is generally subdued and restored; the most notorious oligarchs have been driven out of the country or imprisoned; the SPS does not exist anymore, Yabloko is not represented in the Parliament, and the CPRF has been silenced both organisationally and morally. Putin is left to face no one but himself.

What Next?

The question that is especially pressing today is not the question the West keeps asking — 'Who is Mr Putin?' — but the Russian one: 'What next, Vladimir Vladimirovich?' In order to find an answer, let us take a closer look at the uniting factor behind all of the forces that have disappeared from the forefront of Russian politics, and whose absence has created a new threat: the threat of the void. The forces that had been active during the first eight years of Putin's presidency as 'independent actors' can generally be referred to as 'the forces of disintegration'. They emerged from the ruins of the empire, having contributed to its disappearance, and exploited the social momentum created by its disappearance (including that of the economy, state, culture, society, and nation) and planned to foster even greater destructive forces in the future. They positioned themselves as 'strangers' to Russia, as opportunists. Metaphorically speaking, the oligarchs, the liberals, the separatists, and the pro-Western democrats and media tycoons all bet on the downfall of Russia as a corporation, and sold her shares at well below the market price, preparing the ground for a 'total liquidation'. They acted as various departments working together on a single operation: the 'selling out' of our nation. They were influential precisely because the people who could pay up were abroad during those dark days, and the order to sell out the motherland in an ideological, economic, cultural and territorial sense ultimately came from them.

Let us dispense with all illusions: the sell-outs agreed to put Putin in charge as a temporary measure, assuming that they would remain in control of the government and, together with their foreign clients, retain the management structure.

But their calculations fell through. Putin started methodically and steadily eradicating the main actors of 'management from outside' from Russian politics, reducing their influence to a critically low point.

The 'Worms That Dieth Not'[9] and Putin's New Men

The fact that Vladimir Putin has completed the introductory part of his programme is undeniable. The first presidential cycle was devoted to making a clean slate of Russian politics, completely eradicating the marked-up 'rough draft' we had inherited from his predecessor. Putin passed with flying colours, and today, before the elections, he finds himself in a curious

---

9   From Mark 9:48, where Hell is described as a place where 'the worms that eat them do not die, and the fire is not quenched'.

situation: the forces of evil (in their most vivid and aggressive forms) have been defeated, but the future of Russia is completely up in the air.

Therefore, the void described in this text is a very complex phenomenon. First of all, this void could be harbouring the seeds of new oppositional forces, and the oligarchs have already tried to harness its force to 'boycott the elections' in 2004.[10] They argued that the fact that there was no viable alternative to Putin meant he was a dictatorial figure, demonising him and turning him into a *persona non grata* in the eyes of the West. In other words, by failing to provide a legitimate competitor for the election, the entire band of losers could unify under a single excuse in an attempt to sabotage Putin, taking advantage of any pitfalls in his presidential strategy and tactics. But today, there is even less of a possibility of an alternative to Putin then there had been back then.

Putin was able to cope with the 'election boycott' of 2012:[11] nominal and harmless figures were put forth as 'candidates' from the ranks of the principal political forces, and the façade of pluralism was successfully maintained. But, knowing the forces that are trying to suppress Russia and its revival, there can be no doubt that the boycott tactic was merely the first step in a fully-fledged sabotage programme. Since it failed to work, we can be sure that another strategy will emerge from the void, and the next move might prove to be a lot more difficult to manage.

Secondly, the void is a draft of Putin's new presidential programme — the new Putin, the Putin of the second presidential cycle, the Putin of the future. If a concrete programme exists, it indeed must be hidden for the time being. Pretending that it is non-existent — 'a blank space', so to speak — is the best political strategy. Either during the election period or immediately after, Putin will have to remove this disguise, revealing a wonderful, ingenious model of our great motherland's revival, sparkling like gold in the morning sunlight. This second aspect of the void is merely a secret plan, a Russian x-file covering up a leap towards national greatness. I think this

---

10 Before the 2004 election, Garry Kasparov led a coalition which urged Russians to boycott it, claiming that the election would be a farce of democracy.

11 Kasparov and others who opposed Putin attempted another boycott during the 2012 elections.

kind of plan most likely exists, and I think it is a project to build a Eurasian empire. Otherwise, what would be the point of it all?

Third, the void may be a curtain, behind which Putin's new men are hiding. Not just the 'Peter Guys', who only helped the President to clean the territory of old rubble. Putin's new men are the grapevine of a secret national elite, cultivated in a laboratory far away from the oligarchs, political clowns, cynical spin doctors, and corrupt puppets of the Yeltsin system. Putin's new men will (possibly) be the biggest surprise to emerge from the void. I know some things about them, but I am too cautious to talk about them just yet.

Putin's Grey Zone

Two days after Vladimir Putin's inauguration into his second term, the ill-omened explosion in Grozny that took the life of Akhmad Kadyrov[12] took place. It was a bad sign, and I involuntarily thought to myself, 'What if Putin's luck has run out?' In fact, everything had panned out in his favour during his first term: Putin managed to escape the 9/11 crisis and the events at Dubrovka in the autumn of 2002 mostly unscathed. The stable oil market climate, political stabilisation, the taming of the governors, the dispersal of his political opponents and tight control of the media had all put Putin in the *'white zone'*, a time when he was completely unmarked by problems or opponents. It seemed that everything was just right for Putin, and, propelled by a steady tailwind, all he had to do was slightly adjust the course. Another important factor — *contrast* — was also working in Putin's favour. The previous presidents, Gorbachev and Yeltsin, were seen by the wider public as a *national catastrophe, an absurdity bordering on insanity*. The entire history of Putin's closest predecessors was a history of never-ending losses, concessions, disgrace and deterioration. Before he came to power, the state and its geopolitical influence had been shrinking before our very eyes. During Yeltsin's presidency, the Kremlin turned into a hotbed of drunken frenzy, an oligarch rat race marked by the total deteriora-

---

12   Akhmad Kadyrov (1951–2004) was the Russian-backed President of the Chechen Republic. On 9 May 2004, he was killed in a bomb blast set by Chechen rebels while attending a victory parade celebrating the USSR's victory in the Second World War.

tion of the strong values of the state. In light of all this, Putin had been received by our nation as *a deliverance*, a turning point, a chance. The Russians *delighted* in Putin, regardless of what he may have been doing. He was everything we could ever dream of: a self-disciplined, sober, young, serious leader who took care of our country.

Putin's political formula during his first presidency was a combination of patriotism and liberalism. This combination suited the expectations of the vast majority of Russians perfectly. The patriots applauded the steps he took to revive Russia as a superpower. Meanwhile, the liberals (at least the moderate ones) were satisfied with the fact that the majority of 'their own men' remained in the government's economic sector, upholding a mostly pro-Western style of foreign policy. The Duma elections went smoothly, and Putin won the presidential elections by a landslide. Putin's inauguration on 7 May 2004 was the apogee of the 'white zone' of Putin's rule. But then history's plans were disrupted and took a wrong turn. Something went wrong.

The assassination of Kadyrov — symbolically, on 9 May[13] — was an *absolute* disaster. Shortly before the event, if media sources were to be trusted, the opponents of the new regime 'were almost gone', and the guerrilla forces had surrendered *en masse*. According to the victor's reports, everything in Chechnya was going smoothly. And suddenly, like thunder rolling across the sky, Akhmad Kadyrov was no more. Since bad news has a tendency to come in threes, these 'non-existent', 'eliminated' and 'decisively defeated' guerrilla forces started an uprising in Ingushetia on 22 June, attacking federal institutions. Simultaneously, Mikhail Saakashvili,[14] who was hell-bent on removing Russia's principal trump cards in the South Caucasus, began his bloody Caucasian spree in Georgia.[15] This was followed by the challenge of Aslan

---

13 The date that Russia and the other former Soviet republics celebrate their victory over Germany in the Second World War, when Germany's unconditional surrender to the Allies went into effect, Moscow time.

14 Mikhail Saakashvili (b. 1967) was President of Georgia from 2004 until 2013.

15 Throughout Saakashvili's first term, there were many clashes between the Georgian military and pro-Russian separatists in South Ossetia.

Abashidze,[16] which was completely inexplicable in light of Putin's courageous policy. In July, for the first time during Saakashvili's presidency, a dark cloud of uncertainty hung over South Ossetia's and Abkhazia's[17] future.

At the same time, the monetisation of social benefits was not well-received by Russian society: the initiative could not even have been saved by Kremlin spin doctors orchestrating processions of homeless people holding banners saying 'Deprive us of benefits! We don't want them!' Although control over electronic media sources and a tamed Duma prevented the reaction to this series of unfortunate events *to be expressed politically* (unfunny comedians tried to offset the cries of the people on TV programmes, and outrage in the Duma was quickly suppressed by United Russia), it all led to an unfortunate outcome: *the 'white zone' of Putin's rule was over.* We stood on the threshold of a 'grey zone'. *The 'grey zone' meant that the same political moves, formulas, tricks and manoeuvres that had previously yielded positive results would from then on be perceived differently.* The 'grey zone' *is the first step toward the erosion of our expectations*, the first twilight of disappointment, and the beginning of dissatisfaction, apathy, and exhaustion. These very dangerous symptoms had a significant influence on the overall style of Putin's second term. They also constitute the challenges and risks of the new third term. We will now analyse the signs that we were entering the 'grey zone' in detail.

First, let's analyse the element of contrast. The fact that Yeltsin (not to mention Gorbachev) was slipping from memory had previously worked *in Putin's favour,* but *was now working against him.* All of Putin's strong points — his age, sober attitude, toughness, pragmatism, and so on, looked especially appealing in contrast with his predecessors. During his second term, however, critics were comparing Putin to Putin himself (or to his own, still inarticulated, political programme). The contrast factor wore off, and the bar for warding off complaints, questions, quandaries, and critique

---

16 Aslan Abashidze (b. 1938) was the leader of the Ajarian Autonomous Republic in Georgia between 1991 and 2004. Following the Rose Revolution, tensions arose between Abashidze and the Georgian government when it asserted its authority over the separatist regions. After Abashidze accused the Georgian government of attempting to overthrow him and mobilised his armed forces, he resigned when they refused to fight against Georgian forces that entered the republic.

17 Another region claimed by Georgia that has declared its autonomy.

had been raised. Whereas it had previously been sufficient to say 'Putin!' and have everyone understand that it meant 'non-Yeltsin', entering the 'grey zone' meant that public reaction had shifted: 'Putin? What has Putin done, what is he doing now and what is he going to do next?' At this point we, as his supporters, had to retreat and really think about it.

Second: the team. The Putin of the earlier era had pushed the hateful oligarchs aside, taking power away from 'the Family' and introducing the humble and invisible 'Peter Guys' from his team into the Russian government. These changes were met with applause *via contradiction*: a reaction propelled largely by 'contrast logic'. Putin moved cautiously but consistently. The very act of removing some of the most notorious Yeltsin-era figures had been sufficient during the 'white period'. But after the tipping point — Putin's inauguration — it suddenly became evident that a contrast play would *not be enough*. A huge segment of spin doctors from 'the Family' had retained their positions of power, maintaining their pro-American, Russophobe outlook; the majority of the oligarchs were still around; the quiet Peter Guys proved to be politically weak aside from the occasional interjection into internal quarrels and behind-the-curtain battles for the division of influence over finances. No significant political rotation took place, a solid team was never formed, and political development came to a halt.

Third: Chechnya. After the death of Kadyrov, it turned out that the decision to reign in Chechnya by force had not been followed up with any significant political measures. There were only 'virtual' policies, which proved to be extremely fragile. The way the triumvirate — the confused metropolitan youth Sergei Abramov,[18] the awkward Kadyrov Jr.,[19] and the old hand Alu Alkhanov[20] — appeared to the public sent a strong message: something was

---

18   Sergei Abramov (b. 1972) was Minister of Finance when Kadyrov's assassination, and temporarily took his place in the aftermath.

19   Ramzan Kadyrov (b. 1976) was appointed Deputy Prime Minister in the wake of his father's assassination. Putin appointed him President of Chechnya in 2007, following Alkhanov's dismissal.

20   Alu Alkhanov (b. 1957) was a former soldier who was Minister of the Interior at the time of Kadyrov's assassination. He was elected President of Chechnya in August 2004. Putin dismissed him in February 2007 and appointed him a Deputy Justice Minister in Russia.

wrong with Chechnya. It's a sore subject, but the overt displacement of a concrete political decision by a PR surrogate made the 'grey zone' even more grey.

Fourth: Georgia. Saakashvili did not come to power out of the blue. He was coached and brought to power from overseas to fulfil a mission: *to drive Russia away from the Caucasus either peacefully or by military means.* The Rose Revolution[21] was presented as an ultimatum to Russia. We did not take any practical steps to affect an alternative scenario that would have been more suitable for us. The expulsion of Aslan Abashidze was unacceptable. It was a flashback to the Gorbachev and Yeltsin era, when Moscow betrayed our friends and allies, surrendering our geopolitical positions without a fight. The beginning of a fully-fledged war in the form of constant conflicts in this region in August 2004 was the logical extension of our fundamental errors. This problem, quite obviously, would not be easily remedied.

An important point is the priorities of our foreign policy. Russia did not get a chance to sort them out during Putin's first term. We did not ultimately choose which Western power we wanted to support: was Russia with the US or the European Union? Which forces in the US should we support: the Republicans (imperialists) or the Democrats (globalists)? Did we even have any partners in the US at all? There was also no clear solution as to how to handle relations with Asian countries. We made some advances, but then strayed in the pro-American direction again. The initiative to combat 'international terrorism' also ended in failure, along with the American occupation of Iraq and the start of military assaults against the civilian population (especially in southern Iraq), which had nothing to do with either Al Qaeda or Saddam Hussein.

After Yeltsin's squeamish attitude toward the CIS states, everyone expected a faster integration of the post-Soviet space from Putin. Initially, these expectations seemed to be justified: the initiatives of Nursultan Nazarbayev[22] were finally supported by the Kremlin, the EurAsEC was created, followed by the Collective Security Treaty Organisation, and the creation of

---

21 The Rose Revolution was a peaceful, Western-backed mass protest movement that brought about regime change in Georgia in November 2003. It was seen in part as an attempt by the US to weaken Russia's influence over the country.

22 Nursultan Nazarbayev (b. 1940) has been the President of Kazakhstan since 1989.

the Union State of Russia and Belarus.[23] But the process gradually came to a halt as actual measures were replaced by declarations, and tedious details and private differences weakened the push toward integration. And yet again, via 'contrast logic', everything seemed to be going a lot better than before Putin.

Vladimir Putin's main achievements were in the field of mass media. He put an end to anti-state broadcasting, which gave rise to patriotism and the revival of national traditions and covered up the crude reality of the oligarch wars. Respect for the state and government policy was generally restored, and the compliance of the media was evident. During Putin's 'white zone' presidency, watching TV was an absolute pleasure. But gradually we forgot how it had been before Putin came to power: good things are easy to get used to, and public attention shifted to other things. Television became overrun by completely mindless channels which were overtly biased and had a strictly managed model of political process coverage (which led to its utter emaciation). Programming was marked by a deliberate disregard for important and serious social, historical and cultural topics. The focus on spectacles, unbridled voyeurism, vulgarity, shamelessness and cynicism in contemporary Russian media is objectionable beyond criticism. And since these media sources are now under the control of a 'managed democracy', our complaints about these developments are directed toward the Russian authorities. Unfunny TV humour is a disturbing feature of the 'grey zone'. If the thick-lipped wannabe Galkin[24] is the 'face of Russia', then something must be very wrong with Russia.

In terms of economic development, Putin had noticeably relieved social tension by challenging the oligarchs. In light of his policies toward them, the fact that the national government was overrun by liberal economists appeared to be one of Putin's temporary concessions. But Gräf, Chubais, Kudrin, Khristenko[25] and their opponent Illarionov continued to press

---

23   The Union State is a commonwealth that was formed between Russia and Belarus in 1996. While Russia has attempted to strengthen the Union, Belarus has remained resistant, fearing for its independence. Discussion of the Union State has been subsumed into Russia's larger project of a Eurasian Union for the region.

24   Maxim Galkin (b. 1976) is a Russian comedian.

25   Viktor Kristenko (b. 1957) was the Minister of Industry from 2004 until 2012.

on with radical Gaidar-style shock therapy tactics that even the latter-day Yeltsin tried to distance himself from. The only thing that saved the Russian people from drastic Western 'adjustments' to public utility rates, transport tariffs, and electricity and fuel prices was the fact that oil prices on the global market continued to grow. In the future, even competent stabilisation measures coupled with a favourable economic environment will not be able to preserve the current order of social spending and the corresponding income indexation. The liberal concept of monetising social benefits is only the first step toward a new wave of liberal reforms and privatisation cycles. Indeed, the 'grey zone' was marked by a gloomy outlook.

The patriotism + liberalism formula was initially quite satisfactory: everybody interpreted it in his own way and was generally pleased with it. The liberals, such as Pavlovsky, Chubais or Surkov perceived 'patriotism' as a mere disguise — a 'façade' created to relieve social pressure. The patriots — the Peter Guys and the *siloviki*[26] — prioritised the restoration of a strong state and a vertical power[27] structure over Russia's economic structure, agreeing to make concessions so long as Russia could regain its geopolitical influence and independence. At some point, however, the combination patriotism + liberalism stopped working: the liberals were constantly striving to push their agenda, attempting to guide Putin *from economic liberalism towards geopolitical Atlanticism* in order to finalise the liberal course; the patriots, in turn, *realised the negative social impact of liberal reforms in the economy* and kept insisting on implementing market mechanisms to meet the national and social needs of the state. After employing Putin's political formula to establish their initial positions, both forces gradually *raised their expectations*. There is no more room for compromise, and *Putin will need another formula* in order to find a way out.

During Putin's 'white zone', the issue of presidential elections was simple: the key challenge was to frame the re-election in the most organic and

---

26   The *siloviki* lobby represents those veterans of Russia's secret service agencies who have gone into politics.

27   Putin coined the term 'vertical power' to describe his intent to bring about the centralisation of political power in Russia within the federal government, and in particular within the presidency.

elegant light possible, as nobody questioned Putin's success per se. Putin was Putin's ideal successor. The election of 2008 (the end of the second term constitutionally barred Putin from running for President again) meant that the entire system was running the risk of total collapse. Putin's successor could not have been worse than Putin, but he could not have been better either. He could not systematically inherit Putin's line, since his most successful accomplishments were concentrated in the 'white zone' and were based on its contrast with the previous, strictly negative power models. The 'grey zone' successor did not have this advantage. Besides, to continue with the zones analogy, an altogether more sinister 'black zone' waited on the end of the 'grey zone', and it was inescapably connected with the fatal date: 2008. I have already listed the alarming symptoms of the 'grey zone' in my analysis above. I am convinced that once we had entered it, there was no way back. My personal political position is to support Vladimir Putin, as before. I *positively* assessed (and still do) his overall presidency, his main strategies and his potential. But this does not mean that one should underestimate or deny the seriousness of Russia's current predicament.

Unexpected Visitors

Putin's 2007 Munich speech, in which he clearly demonstrated that he intended to build and strengthen Russia's sovereignty, marked his triumphant exit out of the 'grey zone'. Sovereignty is a very profound notion. On the one hand, it is simply a nominal, legal concept. On the other hand, though, it implies geopolitical power. Many countries have legal sovereignty, but real geopolitical sovereignty is possessed only by a select few. The concept of sovereignty, which had been thrust into the spotlight of the Russian political community, is one of actual geopolitical sovereignty. Russia has always possessed it, and it had been the subject of discussion during the entire term of Putin's presidency. After Putin's speech in Munich, the actual substance of this political sovereignty was called into question, and it requires serious consideration and reassessment.

Essentially, Vladimir Putin's Munich speech changed the entire world order. Previously nobody dared to challenge the hegemony of the US as the principal political subject. Nobody, apart from some marginal forces, talked about the unfairness of a unipolar world. In his Munich speech, the President of a great nuclear power decisively rejected the unipolar model of the world. When uttered by the President of a democratic, powerful country, this statement was not a simple declaration void of political substance: it was a declaration of a new political course. Putin established a path to a multipolar world, which was a fundamental achievement that became the most important event in recent history. After this speech, Russia regained its status as a great world power that plays an active role in setting the world's policy agenda.

After this historical turning point, Putin was finally able to gain ground in terms of domestic policy, effectively pushing Russia's ultra-liberals to the sidelines of the political playing field. The parliamentary election results were particularly telling in this regard: Kasyanov, Kasparov, and Right Cause are seen today as a political embarrassment rather than as a viable alternative. The Kremlin followed suit, because such anti-sovereignty forces had become entirely redundant and out-of-place in a sovereign democracy. This shift might be cruel to the people who were once in power, but it is nonetheless a kind of salvation and a necessity, and is absolutely the right move for Russia.

Patriotic rhetoric has finally come to dominate the media, although themes pertaining to the empire and the greatness of our national achievements still exist side-by-side with mindless entertainment that has become even more dominant. This can be considered a negative trend. But all political and all meaningful programmes are designed in terms of promoting the Russian singularity, highlighting the greatness and dignity of the Russian state and Russian history. This is a fundamental turning point, because in the 1990s such vulgarity as was being presented at the time was accompanied by the endless Russophobic derision of our people and history. Russophobia is finally in the past, and although our media sources remain far from ideal, they are fairly patriotically oriented, and this is certainly a positive development.

In 2007, the *sovereign democracy* doctrine was finally formulated. The ideological formula of sovereign democracy was fully supported by Russian society because such concepts are normally in high demand with our people. But what was the purpose of this? Unfortunately, the authorities failed to develop this ideological trend any further and, although much was said about sovereign democracy and Putin's plan, these discussions proved to be vague and diffuse, and though all very good and proper, they were ultimately never clarified.

Medvedev's appointment essentially nullified the expectations of the supporters of Russia's geopolitical revival. Yes, there was the lingering hope that it would all turn out to be an astounding special operation by Putin to preserve continuity. Unfortunately, preserving political continuity in Russia has always been a problem. The logic behind Russia's structure of political elites mechanically followed the example set by the political agenda of the 1990s, when this structure swarmed with notorious crooks, scoundrels, corruptors and Western agents. This same group of people remained largely intact while Putin was in power as a mere parody of a legitimate political structure. This is why I was extremely worried about the destiny of my country and the legacy of Putin's achievements. After all, in spite of steering the country's course away from the rampant liberalism of the 1990s, Putin retained a fairly liberal stance in terms of the economy. His liberalism was largely patriotic, but Putin had not completely parted with liberal dogmatism. So far as making the choice between Atlanticism or Eurasianism in the geopolitical space, Putin had clearly and unambiguously opted for Eurasianism. His stance was clear: Russia's only choice is to be a great country, Russia respects herself and her dignity, Russia is integrating the post-Soviet space. Sovereignty was the primary national focus that would become the driving force behind Russia's political value system. But, in spite of all these positive developments, Putin's departure in 2008 seemed to be the end of the 'golden age' of his rule. A new era had begun: the era of Medvedev.

Putin is unquestionably the chief protagonist of Russian politics, as well as a worldwide leader: a fact that has been rightfully recognised by *Time* magazine.[28] Putin is the man who revived Russia, infusing her with power and might. Putin should have ended his triumphant rule with a third term, and then Russia's 'golden age' would have continued on, uninterrupted.

---

28 Putin was named *Time*'s 'Person of the Year' in 2007.

Unfortunately, this was not the case. At the peak of his power, in spite of being the sole and absolute sovereign and autocratic subject in Russia's political reality, Putin allowed himself the extravagant gesture of obeying the Constitution that had been illegitimately adopted in the '90s. The disruption served as a test for Putin and for the entire country, and I never understood this gesture.

No Time to Relax: New Network Challenges

With four dangerous years of Medvedev's presidency finally behind us, it seems that nothing is threatening Vladimir Putin any longer. His ratings are fairly high, and United Russia's performance does not matter anymore. This shouldn't come as a surprise. The notion of 'Putin' in people's minds is associated with the aspiration to establish Russia's sovereignty, which, as history tells us, has always been a priority for the Russian people. It is clear now: Putin is not 'sovereign democracy'. Putin is simply 'sovereignty', and the concept of democracy is just a product thrown in for appearances. Putin may indeed believe in democracy, but this is irrelevant because a lot of people sincerely believe in democracy, but this belief is not enough to become Putin. In most cases, sincere supporters of democracy evolve into something quite the opposite of Putin, into 'orange revolutionaries',[29] the enemies of Russia and the Russian people. As for Putin, he is the embodiment of Russian sovereignty. This is what 'Putin' is all about. All other aspects of Putin that are not related to sovereignty are subsidiary and insignificant. The point of Putin's actions is to strengthen and defend Russia's sovereignty in the face of globalisation. This is also precisely the point of continuity.

So, what threats is Putin's search for sovereignty facing, and who is the 'enemy' of Putin's plan?

---

[29] In late 2004 and early 2005, large Western-backed protests in Ukraine following the national elections, which resulted in Viktor Yushchenko becoming President instead of Viktor Yanukovich, who was the more pro-Russian candidate. Orange was the colour of Yushchenko's campaign, hence the name. As with the Rose Revolution in Georgia the previous year, in Russia this was seen as another attempt by the Western powers to weaken Russia's power within its sphere of influence.

The principal enemy is not internal, but external. The United States of America is quickly changing its manner and methods of interaction with other states and polishing the so-called 'network wars' technology. Network wars are wars conducted mostly in the sphere of information. These wars are based on the resonance effect, meaning that various and otherwise unrelated ideological, social, civil, economic, ethnological and migratory processes are manipulated by external agents to achieve a specific final purpose. The main goal of a network war is to strip opponents of their sovereignty. This is the basis of the new model of relations between all countries, primarily Russia and the US, and it cannot be reduced to a simple logic. Concepts like 'friends vs enemies', 'competition vs partnership', and 'confrontation vs cooperation' are no longer applicable. The logic of 'network wars' is of an entirely different breed. Currently, the authorities (and Putin in particular) are helpless in the face of the network challenges coming from the US. They are not prepared to adequately react to them due to stark differences in historical traditions, and also because they are overwhelmed by an enormous amount of technical and economic problems. But it is the global 'network war' that is the driving force of international politics, and neither Vladimir Putin nor our authorities in general are adequately prepared to realise the severity of this new problem. Our men are of a different breed altogether, and the 'network', along with the postmodern values that spawned it, is a dangerous blind spot that poses the biggest threat to Russia's sovereignty and to Putin personally.

The Chaord and Its Strategies

The contemporary US is a unique type of empire. It is a thalassocracy: a maritime, decentralised, polycentric and eccentric empire. The post-Marxist American philosophers Negri and Hardt talk about this phenomenon extensively in their book *Empire*.[30] An empire has always been perceived as a logical, regulating, intelligible entity, and the concept of an 'empire' has always implied order over chaos. But in the contemporary world, empires acquire a paradoxical character that mimics order, and contemporary em-

---

30   Michael Hardt & Antonio Negri, *Empire* (Cambridge, Massachusetts: Harvard University Press, 2000).

pires tend to breed chaos instead of reining it in. There have been two types of empires throughout the course of history: land-based and sea-based. As opposed to centralised land-based empires like the Roman or the Eurasian empires, which favour vertical power structures, the American thalassocratic (sea-based) empire is horizontal, network-based, rhizomatic,[31] tuberous: the empire's centre is simultaneously everywhere and nowhere. In this kind of empire, order is fused with chaos, creating what Negri and Hardt called 'chaord' — a synthesis of chaos and order.

The main thesis, argument, political goal, means and weapon of America in the contemporary world is democracy as a self-sustaining virus. In the global world, the promotion of democracy is an effective method of extending US influence. The Western world is based on the principle of developed individual initiative. When Western democracy is projected on societies marked by a tradition of individualism, it creates a system in which democracy propels social development. It worked with the projection of democratic principles onto Japanese society, because the concept of individualism is extremely developed in Japan. But if democracy is imported into societies with weak individualistic principles — societies of a holistic type — it destroys whole ensembles and creates chaos. Democracy in such a system performs a creative and a genocidal function at the same time. The formula of order simultaneously opposes and provokes chaos. The contemporary American empire actively employs the chaos strategy, transferring this discourse into a space of non-linear processes, giving new nature and proportions to international relations, creating paradoxical paradigms of decision-making, and constructing a new geometry of power, projects, planning, and confrontation. Russia will not be able to confront globalism through obsolete anti-globalism or an alternative globalism without employing the laws of the network and the radically new proportions of this dynamic, eccentric chaos strategy.

---

31 The philosophers Gilles Deleuze and Félix Guattari used the term 'rhizome' and 'rhizomatic' to describe concepts that allow for multiple, non-hierarchical entry and exit points in their interpretation.

The Objective and Subjective in Putin's Course

After examining some of the challenges Vladimir Putin has to tackle, it is important to consider the outline of the new course that he has set out to implement. The global geopolitical processes, the subjective state of Russian society and its psychological reactions to the events of the 1990s all led to the inevitable replacement of the Yeltsin power model by an alternative. Otherwise, the new external administrative force and the creation of a vacuum in the balance of power would have ensured Russia's demise. During Yeltsin's presidency, Russia was beginning to withdraw from the global arena, and the global environment was rapidly changing. Russian citizens, of course, intuitively sensed the catastrophic nature of these changes, which meant that Yeltsin's legacy, represented by political figures like Gaidar, Chernomyrdin,[32] Nemtsov, Satarov,[33] Yumashev, Yavlinsky, SPS and Yabloko, didn't stand a chance.

Russia's new political course was closely intertwined with Vladimir Putin's personality. At the time Russia had two alternatives: it could simply cease to exist as we know it, or be revived by a series of reforms proposed by Putin. In a sense, Putin had no choice but to implement these reforms: if he did not want the country to disintegrate, he had to do it. As a competent and dependable man, he began to implement the only viable political programme that was available to him. Putin's political course is an objective phenomenon, and, being a cautious and prudent leader, he simply carried out an order: an order given by the people, by Russia's history, and by the state of global geopolitics. Objectively, this was a fairly easy political course to choose. Subjectively, however, it was very difficult. Day after day, he was confronted by a swarm of scum who did not want a Russian revival, who acted in the interests of the American hyperpower and who tried to sabotage this objective and natural course of events.

---

32 Viktor Chernomyrdin (1938–2010) founded Gazprom, which is the state-owned natural gas company, and was Deputy Prime Minister for energy resources from 1992 until 1998.

33 Georgy Satarov (b. 1947) was an advisor to Yeltsin. Since then he has been involved in political groups opposed to Putin.

To Putin's personal credit, he ignored the historically anti-national political elites, especially during the first term of his presidency. He did not listen to the various groups which pushed him toward Western policies, towards Russophobia, and toward a 'civil society' that would essentially mean a surrender of Russia and Putin's personal suicide, as well as the suicide of his course of action, his country and his people. He did not listen to these elites and listened instead to the voice of history, the people and geopolitics. The continuity of Putin's course is the continuity of common sense and the preservation of Russia as a nation. If we want Russia *to stay alive*, we must follow in Putin's footsteps. If we do not want that, we may think about the alternatives. Putin's course is an objective and in fact the only possible course, and we can only discuss how fast we should move along it. In the end, this course will be followed on the strength of its objective merits.

But this objectivity has a weak point: Vladimir Putin did not create a new elite to succeed himself; he did not create the prerequisites for a continuity of his course of action in the subjective consciousness of the political elite of contemporary Russia. At some point a personal successor emerged, but there is no collective successor in the form of a new elite. The political elites in Russia are still arbitrary, much like they were in the 1990s, and Putin did not eliminate this arbitrariness and the resulting transient nature and ephemeral mentality of the political and economic elites. He did not limit their lust for power, as well as for business, as he did with corruption. This is a weak point in his personal continuity, and *a weak point in the continuity scheme*.

Our current political elites are marked by total inadequacy and subjectivism. This includes the people brought to power by Putin, because they, like everything in Russia, were also brought in at random. They did not reverse the negative tendencies of the Yeltsin period's political elites, but blended with them instead. They are better than the previous ones only because they follow Putin's orders, and Putin follows the orders of history and of the Russian people, but subjectively they are the same. Subjectively, they have not woken up; they are unaware of the historical significance of their mission, and fail to understand the geopolitical goal, nor do they feel any civic responsibility. Putin did not create new, adequate politicians; he hasn't even started the process of forming this elite group. Formally, not a single person aspiring to play an important role in Russia would argue against the continuation of the current course, but the subjective inadequacy of the political elite will result in power struggles in Russia throughout Putin's rule.

We know that the chances of the liberals gaining ground are practically negligible, because everybody rejects the alternative to Putin's course: both the masses and the elite. The people who dare challenge this course don't stand a chance. But in terms of ensuring the continuity of Putin's rule, some catastrophic developments that are being propelled by the intellectual inadequacy of Russia's political elite have already begun to take shape.

Contrary to popular expectations, the threat is not coming from the 'orange revolutionaries'. In fact, they have even been somewhat helpful, as the unpopularity of their position forces Russia's competent, healthy forces to gravitate toward Putin. It is possible that the existence of fringe forces that are openly supported by the West or the oligarchs (and which the majority of Russia's population treats with suspicion) is the sole reason behind some semblance of cohesion among Putin's elite, but the subjective state of the pro-Putin forces in power forebodes a catastrophe. The current state of affairs could have been changed, but instead turned into a merry make-believe of disinformation games, and it will only get worse. Since Putin has decided to retain responsibility for the country, this is the first problem that he will have to resolve.

If Spring Comes Tomorrow

Currently, politics is almost non-existent in Russia. It is especially non-existent during the winter holidays and the New Year's break. This is not only because the ruling class relaxes during this period between the Catholic Christmas and the Old Style New Year, trying to extend the holidays to the Eastern style New Year, but because there is no politics in Russia at all. Political discourse is absent because nobody has any use for it. The elite does not need it because having a defined political platform would inevitably restrict government authority and force them to explain how their actions, results or declarations match their stated political goals, guidelines, and ideals. The absence of political goals, guidelines, or ideals means that there is nothing to explain. When there is no political discourse, the authorities are completely free from responsibility. As long as they are tolerated, they can do anything they please.

The absence of political discourse doesn't seem to concern the masses either. There are several reasons for this. First, the people became completely disillusioned with politics during the 1990s. They grew tired of the scandalous alcoholic loon Yeltsin, his stupid daughter and the 'Family', the mighty scheming oligarchs, the obscure media assassins dropping subtle hints, the whining of populist politicians, and meetings that always seemed to be directed 'against' something (nobody could figure out what). The absence of politics and a political discourse meant the absence of neurosis.

Secondly, the people were enjoying their lives during Putin's presidency. They enjoyed the fact that Putin provided a mix of sternness and tolerance. They liked Putin's alpha policies and the partially demoted liberals in the government. They relished in the balance between a strong, fatherly care and a soothing democratic discourse. Everyone could pick what he liked best. Putin's discourse was like therapy, a Buddhist *kōan* that contained irreconcilable oppositions but spared listeners from making intellectual efforts.

Third, the Russian people do not understand politics: it confuses them. Communism as a political model fell apart in the 1990s, and its disintegration, aided by Zyuganov's inadequate management of the Communist Party, continued during the 2000s. Liberalism didn't sit well with Russians either. Nationalism frightens us with its ecstatic energy. Given these three inadequate options, a serious effort would be required in order to become interested in politics. Even the ready-made political recipes are not very easy to understand, let alone creative thinking in terms of political theory (beyond liberalism, Communism, and fascism). Spare us, please. Maybe some other time.

This dynamic is how the authorities and the people arrived at the 'forget politics' consensus. This is how the structure of the current state of *apo-*

liteia[34] was constructed. Its symbol is the ruling party of the 'party-less majority' that avoids political discussions (and for a good reason, if you ask me). In a sense, this is democracy at work: if the majority doesn't want to deal with politics, then it shouldn't have to deal with politics. The question is, how long will this *dolce vita*[35] last? For how long will we be able to forget about politics? When will this vacation come to an end?

The Strategy of Medvedev's Prospective Party: The Network

What is a possible scenario for the return of politics? This is difficult to predict. Putin has an undeniable advantage when it comes to the 2018 elections, but his victory is not guaranteed. If Medvedev plays his cards right, he might stand a chance. Intellectual superiority (liberal PR specialists and spin doctors) and international support (which means American PR-specialists and spin doctors too) will be on his side. In order to respond, Putin will have to add more substance to his 'party' (which has yet to be created, and will possibly be based on the All-Russian People's Front) and to himself. And this begs the following question: will he figure out whose support to seek in 2018, and does he have such a support system (he was never especially kind towards intellectuals)? Will he choose the easiest route, bribing the competitor's staff and using force or subversive methods? Will he attempt to suppress political discourse altogether instead of outlining an alternative to Medvedev's policies (which will require a political formulation of the consensus which already exists between Putin and the people *de facto*, but not ideologically)? These questions have yet to be answered.

I want to say a few words about the international context. Imagine how impatient the West (primarily the US) must feel with respect to the return of 'politics' to Russia. This is a great opportunity for Washington, and the Americans will undoubtedly activate all of their agents of influence in Russia in order to create the perfect conditions to radicalise our nation. 2018 is the year of the 2008 Orange Revolution, initially postponed due to Med-

---

34 Latin, denoting those who refuse to engage with politics.

35 Italian: 'good life'.

vedev's appointment. This is the most favourable historical moment for the West to disrupt the emerging process of Russia's return to international politics as a sovereign power. The West will most likely use any available means.

First of all, the liberal layer within Russia will be activated: the numerous Non-governmental Organisations (NGOs), funds and radical opposition forces. They will be delegated with the task to create a social atmosphere — in the media, the community of experts and among young people — which will be favourable to Medvedev and detrimental to Putin. Medvedev's network will be activated: not the nominal pool of the average Russian civil servants (the President's thousand)[36] but the invisible network developed outside of Russia. In the 1990s such networks were extremely effective in their support of Yeltsin and the young reformers. Then a new upsurge of destabilisation in the North Caucasus will follow. The disruptions happening in that region now are only child's play. Ingushetia, Dagestan, Kabardino-Balkaria and at some point Chechnya itself will turn into a theatre of military operations. Here the networks operated from outside Russia will carefully play up to Medvedev. Finally, on the diplomatic level, the West will express strong support for Medvedev the Prime Minister and will defend him fiercely and in unison, using measures demonstrating the alleged successes and great results of his policies (as opposed to Putin's).

The Strategy of Putin's Party: Ideology

What is the ultimate strategy for Putin in such a situation? Politicisation will prompt him to do what he had always postponed 'for later' and what he wanted to avoid in the future: to elaborate a comprehensive development strategy for Russia and to create his own political programme. The desires of the masses and history with respect to the content of this strategy are obvious. The people expect order and centralisation from Putin: strong 'fatherly' (paternalistic) rule, full reestablishment of Russia's international position, protection of Russia's sovereignty, and a return to patriotic imperialism. All

---

36   In 2008, during Medvedev's administration, he declared a programme to train of a reserve of administrative personnel for all the levels of government. The most successful administrators, he said, would be included in a database called the 'President's thousand' so that they could be made available for recruiting when needed.

of these elements are already in place, but are not clearly defined, nor implemented in a consistent programme. Now is the time to do it.

But there is one thing that everyone had been expecting from Putin: a full-scale persecution of the oligarchs. The exile of Gusinsky, Berezovsky, Nevzlin,[37] and so forth was a priceless gift for the people. The imprisonment of Khodorkovsky and Lebedev[38] was even better. But those were isolated actions and the people need a programme for the eradication of oligarchy as a political and economic phenomenon. It should be declarative, exemplary and systemic. Until all 'iconic' figures (from Abramovich to Deripaska)[39] go to jail or go away, the people's happiness will be tarnished by doubt. Besides, the imprisonment itself is not as important as Putin's heartfelt criticism of the oligarchy: simple and clear human words. They will mean more than the imprisonment. The Russians are not bloodthirsty: we simply love righteous, morally sane speech.

Finally, Putin will have to clearly outline Russia's future plans. He must reinforce his Munich speech with further commentary: explain what the multipolar world means and why Russia needs it, explain the perils of the liberal 'end of history', outline the prospects for the revival of the Russian economy, and draft the ideal boundaries of our influence in the world. He must reinforce the conservative values that are deeply rooted in Russian culture (family, morals, communalism, sacrifice, the awareness of a universal mission). He will have to describe a future that is dear to him personally.

The continuing influence of Putin on the civil servants, the *siloviki*, and those who came to Moscow from Saint Petersburg with him is a very important factor. But these people cannot immediately be transformed into politics. The civil servants and the *siloviki* are depoliticised to an even greater degree than the masses. They have something to lose and, therefore,

---

37   Leonid Nevzlin (b. 1959) was a senior executive at Yukos who has since left Russia for Israel. In 2008 he was found guilty on several counts of murder in Russia, and the Russian government continues to seek his extradition.

38   Alexander Lebedev (b. 1959), a former KGB agent, was one of the richest oligarchs in Russia in the late 1990s and 2000s, although his businesses have suffered many setbacks recently and since 2012 he has declined considerably.

39   Oleg Deripaska (b. 1968) is a successful businessman and one of the richest individuals in Russia.

the majority of them are bound to join the winning side in the case of a real fight. As people, they are mostly garbage not worthy of our high hopes. Before securing their support, one must politicise them. And in order to politicise the supporters, one must have politics.

In order to win the 2018 election, Putin, against his own will and, to an extent, against the state of the masses, will have to enter politics and liquidate (or suspend for a time) depolitisation, the oh-so-convenient-and-pleasing state of *apoliteia*. If the circumstances prompt Putin to do it, he will, among other things, have to finalise the development of a *substantial political and ideological project*. This would be just great if the threat were not so serious: if politics returns to Russia, it will bring all of its inherent risks along for the ride. At this point, the inconclusive nature of all of Putin's previous reforms may have a very negative impact: separatism will undoubtedly resurface, as well as the residual fifth column (a mediator of external influence), the cynicism of the oligarchs, our crumbling industry, the unsolved social problems, and the extremely inadequate moral education of the younger generation. In short, we can, in fact, slide back into the 1990s.

CHAPTER 4

Putin's Geopolitics

Shift in Foreign Policy

Vladimir Putin's presidency was marked by drastic changes not only in the domestic policy structure, but also in Russia's foreign policy course in the early 2000s. The new Eurasian politics course began with Putin's visits to countries in the Far East. The fact that Russian politics gravitated toward the East became a logical and very reasonable extension of the government's awareness of Russian geopolitical challenges in terms of their new historical context. The key dilemma in world politics had been outlined: will we live in a unipolar world that caters to the US as its only historical subject, or will it be possible to establish a multipolar world? Neither Russia nor any other large regional power is able to singlehandedly counter-balance the geopolitical power of the US. Russia's only chance to remain a subject of history is to build a long-term strategic alliance with great Eurasian powers that have strong demographic, economic, military and cultural potential. The new President's tour was devoted precisely to the implementation of this Eurasian foreign policy course, which was gradually becoming the fundamental idea behind Russian politics. Putin proposed and implemented bold geopolitical initiatives, such as the revitalisation of relations between Berlin and Moscow, Moscow and Tehran, Moscow and Delhi, Moscow and Beijing, and Moscow and Tokyo (though they were not all equally important). All of these initiatives are part of the Eurasian geopolitical strategy — the only strategy suitable for Russia — and we are ready to do our best to support and help Putin throughout the course of his mission.

In the process of establishing close links with Asian countries, Russia acquired long-term partners in economic and strategic development, constructing the basic framework for a multipolar world and reminding the West that its aspirations to international hegemony are invalid and suit neither Russia nor a large number of the leading world powers. The substantive part of Vladimir Putin's Asian tour in the early 2000s and an analysis of the declarations and assessments made by the various regional media sources indicated that those were not simply routine courtesy visits, but the beginning of a new Eurasian course.

Territorial Thinking

For a long time, geopolitics was thought to be a flawed, 'bourgeois' science in Russia. Let me remind you that this discipline frames world history as a confrontation between two types of civilisations: sea civilisations and land civilisations. The field of geopolitics portrays geographical space as a kind of reality — not only geographical, but qualitative, capable of affecting the way a civilisation on that space develops, and shaping the psychological makeup of the people who live within a given territory. It is the connection that culture, tradition and civilisation has with qualitative territory that underlies the field of geopolitics.

This method was initially proposed by Friedrich Ratzel,[1] the German founder of political geography (the precursor of geopolitics), and Rudolf Kjellén,[2] a Swedish scientist who first coined the term 'geopolitics'. But the foundations of geopolitics were laid out in a small article, 'The Geographi-

---

1   Friedrich Ratzel (1844–1904) was a German geographer and ethnologist who attempted to merge the two disciplines, and is regarded as the first German geopolitical thinker.
2   Rudolf Kjellén (1864–1922) was a political scientist and also served in the Swedish Parliament as a conservative. A student of Ratzel, he further developed the latter's ideas, and his conception of geopolitics was to be very influential on Haushofer and the German geopolitical theorists.

cal Pivot of History', by the English scientist Sir Halford Mackinder.[3] The article introduced the idea of a conflict between civilisations based on the land and on the sea. Mackinder argues that land civilisations possess certain characteristics: hierarchy, authoritarianism, the prevalence of idealistic values over mercantilism, and prioritise collective and social values over the individual. Sea civilisations, by contrast, are marked by individualism, plutocracy, materialism and the idea that it is possible to boil different value systems down to their financial basis. As examples, the author cites Rome as a land civilisation and Carthage as a sea civilisation, as well as England — the queen of the sea — and her continental opponents France and Germany. The stronghold of land civilisations is what geopolitical thinkers call the 'heartland' or 'middle land'. This is the massive part of the Eurasian continent lying in its Northern and Western regions, which geographically and historically overlays the territory of Russia: the Russian Empire, the Soviet Union, and the Russian Federation.

This historical approach leads the author to a conclusion about the natural, predetermined confrontation of these two types of civilisations, based not on an ideology or on national interests (which may differ even between states belonging to the same political system), but on a fundamental civilisational opposition — a principle as basic and absolute as class struggle and as the confrontation of labour and capital in Marxism. Geopolitics outlines the dialectical struggle of the land and the sea, which influences the process of historical development in countries and civilisations.

As applied to Russia, geopolitical analysis is a method for identifying strategic interests based on an understanding of the natural and organic confrontation between Russia (irrespective of the regime, whether democratic, Communist or Tsarist) and the Western world (mainly embodied by the English-speaking countries such as the US and its principal European ally, Great Britain). Therefore, the application of geopolitical theory to history demonstrates that the confrontation between the Russian Empire and the British Crown had been pre-determined by fundamental geopolitical

---

3   Sir Halford Mackinder (1861–1947) was an English geographer, and also Director of the London School of Economics. A pioneer who established geography as an academic discipline, he is also regarded as the father of geopolitics.

parameters. All principal conflicts of the second half of the nineteenth and the early twentieth century took place within the framework of this confrontation. These conflicts included the Crimean War, the Balkan wars, the clashes in Afghanistan and Central Asia, the intervention in China in 1900 and even the Russo-Japanese War in which the Brits took part. On the sociopolitical level, all of these wars were part of a confrontation between two monarchies. At that time, this greater conflict was passed off as the clash between imperial (colonial and imperialist) interests. Subsequently, when the Bolsheviks came to power in Russia, this same conflict grew into an ideological confrontation between socialism and capitalism, but the geopolitical essence remained the same. The geopolitical analysis also explains why the transition to new ideological models in Russia, which has officially accepted liberal democratic values, has not muted previous geopolitical confrontations with the liberal, democratic America.

Geopolitics makes the ideological factors behind the Cold War less relevant by tying them to the geopolitical model. It does not mean that ideology does not play an important role — it does, and will continue to do so. But the ideology itself should be viewed as a kind of sublimation of geopolitics in the first place. Time has shown that, in spite of our rejection of the ideology that allegedly led to the confrontation between the USSR and the US, the relations between Russia and the West have not improved. Russia is still treated with distrust, misunderstanding and suspicion. NATO is expanding towards the East and bombs our allies, the Serbs. We continue to make concessions, but are told that Russia has 'a criminal oligarchic regime', that 'Russians have the wrong model of democracy' and so on. It means that the West will always find excuses for viewing Russia as an enemy, and such behaviour has geopolitical implications.

The geopolitical method is important because it is replacing ideological gimmickry. The West has nothing to justify its continuing confrontation with Russia besides geopolitics, which explains the success of Zbigniew Brzezinski's ideas and his book *The Grand Chessboard*.[4] On the surface, they don't have any arguments to explain this situation, and neither do we.

---

4   Zbigniew Brzezinski, *The Grand Chessboard: American Primacy and its Geostrategic Imperatives* (New York: BasicBooks, 1997).

Russia has become a democratic state: there is a party system and a nationally elected President, which means that a value system formally similar to the Western one now exists. But the substantive part of our civilisation has turned out to be fundamentally different. In order to establish Russia's place in the contemporary world, we need geopolitics. This is not a short-lived fad: it is our destiny.

Taking into consideration the fundamental dualism of a world civilisation that consists of two opposing systems, geopolitics today consists of two global centres where theory coincides with practice, with the decision-making, and with global influence — the US and Russia. In the US the most influential organisation in the geopolitical sphere is the Council on Foreign Relations (CFR).[5] Its main theorists, Zbigniew Brzezinski and Henry Kissinger, also influence international organisations that make important geopolitical decisions: the Trilateral Commission and the Bilderberg Club. In the CFR, geopolitics determines the positions of the majority of US Congressmen, both Republicans and Democrats, on key strategic issues. This demonstrates the universal nature of geopolitics. It is the baseline of American strategic thinking! Their main values are formulated on the basis of geopolitical principles, foundations and imperatives, and the only subject up for discussion is how to implement them. Take, for instance, Francis Fukuyama's theory of 'the end of history' and Samuel Huntington's 'clash of civilisations'.[6] These are the two forecasts of the general 'West-centric' course of events in the geopolitical sphere. Fukuyama proposes the creation of a world power 'here and now', while Huntington argues that this project must be delayed because there are still many contradictions in the international arena. Both authors agree on the purpose they

---

5   The Council on Foreign Relations is a privately-owned political think tank in the United States, which has its origins in the peace process at the end of the First World War. The CFR claims that it seeks to influence global politics in a direction that provides peaceful conflict resolutions and multilateralism.

6   Samuel Huntington (1927–2008) was an American political scientist who was well-known for his 1993 essay 'The Clash of Civilizations' published in *Foreign Affairs*, which was later expanded into a book of the same name, in which he theorised that the changing world order following the collapse of Communism would be defined by conflicts between cultural blocs, such as the West and the Islamic world.

have in mind, unanimously arguing that it is necessary to build a single, global Western-oriented state under American control and to establish a world government. Moreover, Fukuyama argues that now, after the collapse of the Soviet Union and the socialist system, is the best time to do it, but Huntington believes that the civilisations of the world still have to undergo a complex process of creation and disintegration into new political blocs. This is a serious dispute, but it remains strictly within the limits of a single geopolitical model.

Since the confrontation is taking place between the Atlanticist world and the East (Eurasia), the second largest pivot of geopolitical thought is Russia. The Russian and American worlds are still comparable in terms of their geopolitical weight. American strategists do the thinking for the entire Western world and for the entire sea civilisation, while Russian geopoliticians are forced to think in terms of the rest of the continental world: the land civilisation of Eurasia.

The chief geopolitical centre in Russia is the Centre for Geopolitical Expertise (CGE). The CGE works with parliamentary organs, as well as the Security Council, law enforcement agencies and the presidential administration. It develops large-scale components of the Russian geopolitical strategy. In terms of its functions, the CGE is the Eurasian equivalent of the Council on Foreign Relations, but, sadly, it operates on a much more modest scale, because the vital necessity for geopolitical strategy has not yet been fully understood by national leaders. But this is merely a technical issue and a question of time. Besides, there are a number of other institutions that claim to also be 'geopolitical centres'. The majority of them, however, are only interested in dealing with geopolitics because it is the trendy thing to do. There are relevant subdivisions in most law enforcement enforcement agencies bearing other names, but, in fact, they are closely related to geopolitical research. Overall, Russia is undergoing the formation of a geopolitical school and of geopolitics as a science. This is why there are organisations boasting proud names, but lacking substance, and vice versa.

If Western geopolitics cannot help but be Atlanticist, Russian geopolitics cannot help but be Eurasian. This is not a matter of choice, but a question of national survival. Either our strategy will be aimed at sustaining

Russia as an alternative to the West, or Russia will simply cease to exist and will become an Eastern appendix, of sorts, to the West. It should also be noted that between the two global geopolitical poles there are intermediate zones, the so-called 'rimland' or the coastal zones. They have their own versions of geopolitics, as for example the European school, whose outstanding representative, Yves Lacoste,[7] was an advisor to the former French President Mitterrand and is the editor of an interesting geopolitical magazine, *Herodotus*. His is a version of small-scale geopolitics that steers clear of the generalisations which are typical of American or Russian geopolitics and were typical of Karl Haushofer's[8] German geopolitics. At the same time, the works of Pierre Béhar, such as *Une géopolitique pour l'Europe: Vers une nouvelle Eurasie?*[9] and Pierre Gallois'[10] *Géopolitique*[11] are fairly unbiased. In its turn, the German geopolitical school operated on a global scale. Haushofer was a strong opponent of the war on two fronts. He argued that, in terms of the laws of geopolitics, Germany is not an independent pole but the 'rimland', an intermediate space between Atlanticism and Eurasianism, and therefore it must choose whether to be allied with the Soviet Union or England. In joining the USSR, it would oppose England, and in joining England it would oppose the USSR. As we all know, Hitler remained indifferent to these warnings and pursued a foolhardy geopolitical policy. It was not simply a mistake, it was a colossal crime against the German and the Russian peoples, in fact against the whole world. This is what a wrongly chosen geopolitical model may lead to! In geopolitical terms, incompetent

---

7   Yves Lacoste (b. 1929) has written many works pertaining to geopolitics, and is the head of the French Institute for Geopolitics.

8   Karl Haushofer (1869–1946) was a German General who helped to establish geopolitics as a discipline in Germany.

9   Pierre Béhar, *Une géopolitique pour l'Europe: Vers une nouvelle Eurasie?* (Paris: Editions Desjonqueres, 1992).

10 Pierre Gallois (1911–2010) was a Brigadier General in the French Air Force. After serving in the Second World War as a bomber crewman in the Royal Air Force, he worked in the French Ministry of Defence, and was instrumental in France's decision to develop its own nuclear arsenal. He later became known for his geopolitics, and strongly opposed NATO's intervention in Serbia during the 1990s.

11 Pierre Gallois, *Géopolitique: Les voies de la puissance* (Paris: Plon, 1990).

advisors or analysts can screw things up. In general, however, the European geopolitical school does exist and, as Europe moves toward the status of an independent political subject, it will actively develop. But for now, it is only an emerging phenomenon. There are not yet any large government centres. All research is conducted by individual specialists, such as the Austrian Jordi von Lochhausen; Lacoste, Behar and Gallois in France; and the Belgian, Steuckers.

As a scientific field, geopolitics has many adversaries. As a rule, such adversaries are either pure Marxists or pure liberals, like Soros.[12] They strive to apply universality to their own, rather totalitarian ideologies and deny the influence of geographical space on history and politics. Nevertheless, this science is becoming a new way of thinking and a new political language of the twenty-first century, without which it is impossible to understand any of Russia's domestic or external problems. Today any top leader or manager must think territorially and operate within geopolitical categories. If Putin is going to regain Russia's status as a geopolitical subject in earnest, he should also be thinking in terms of geopolitics.

Patriotic Enlightenment

The US is systematically moving towards world domination. This is the official project of their foreign policy, irrespective of who has the power, the neoconservatives or the Democrats. Strategically speaking, they control the world by holding power over the coastal zone of the Eurasian continent, which must constantly expand further into the continent. For Russia and the post-Soviet space, this Grand Chess game can mean only one thing: the unipolar world dominated by the US will be established at our expense, and it is being brought about by means of forces from abroad. The scenario is the same for the entire post-Soviet space: pro-American forces, backed by local nationalists, overthrow the indecisive Moscow-leaning regimes and

---

12 George Soros (b. 1930) is an American billionaire who uses his wealth to promote liberal causes around the world. He funded many dissident groups in Eastern Europe and the USSR during the Cold War, and continues to support democratic causes there. Critics have said that Soros is merely acting as an agent of American foreign policy interests.

initiate cycles of instability in Russia's periphery, especially where the ethnic makeup leaves nations prone to internal conflict. The strategic plan of the US for the next decade is to ultimately strip Moscow of control over the CIS states and to begin the disintegration of the RF itself.

In particular, the situation in the Caucasus is a direct consequence of Western plans to enhance American hegemony. This plan is in effect now and is called the 'Project for the New American Century'.[13] The Rose revolution in Tbilisi was a key part of the plan. As Shevardnadze[14] was torn between Washington and Moscow, the young pro-American nationalist Saakashvili was brought to power, thus implementing the plan to destabilise the weak point of the entire Eurasian geopolitical construction. It was followed by the treacherous invasion of South Ossetia, which halted the implementation of the plan but did not annul it: the US has continued to rearm Georgia after a short respite. In a recent interview, Vladimir Putin unambiguously expressed his attitude towards the forthcoming upsurge in violence in the Caucasus: 'I can see that the intentions of today's American administration are clearly evident. But there is another point to be made. For example, further rearmament of Georgia is currently in effect. What for? This is reality — it is something we can see with our own eyes. If there had been no rearmament two years ago, there would have been no aggressions and no blood would have been spilled. By the way, our partners were well aware that this was taking place, including our European allies. But nobody responded. And what do we have now? They have escalated the situation to the point of war. And now the rearmament continues.'[15]

---

13 The Project for the New American Century was a private institute established in 1997 which served as a mouthpiece for neoconservative thought until it was disbanded in 2006. The Project sought to develop ways to maintain and extend American supremacy into the twenty-first century, and many of its members were either part of or influential upon the administration of President George W. Bush.

14 Eduard Shevardnadze (1928–2014) was the President of Georgia from 1992 until 2003, when he was deposed during the Rose Revolution.

15 Interview in *Kommersant*, 30 August 2010.—AD

Gorbachev's and Yeltsin's Atlanticist Heritage among Putin's Entourage

Under Gorbachev and Yeltsin, Moscow was overtly playing up to Washington, unilaterally removing all the obstacles that stood in the way of the American domination of the world: the Warsaw treaty and the USSR. Moscow sided with the US (in other words, against itself). Such behaviour is best described as 'geopolitical betrayal', pure and simple. Vladimir Putin came to power as Russia was trying hard to shrug off the self-destructive strategy of the 1990s. Putin was elected for his brawn — for his intent to put an end to the surrender of Russian interests in domestic and foreign policy. Putin responded adequately to Basayev's[16] invasion of Dagestan and he was granted geopolitical legitimacy and the people's support, but he failed to reach a geopolitical turning point during his first term. The pro-Western Atlanticist experts inherited from the Yeltsin era steered Putin toward Atlanticism during crucial moments, and any compromise with Atlanticism was equivalent to the rejection of Moscow's own strategic interests. Moscow's solidarity with Washington on the issue of so-called 'international terrorism' did not and could not yield any concrete results: the West still puts pressure on the Kremlin in terms of the North Caucasus issue, and American military bases in Central Asia don't do much for Russia's national security.

Due to the efforts of the Atlanticist group in the President's entourage, Putin's patriotic strategy during his first term failed to reach a point where it could become irreversible, preventing Russia from finally establishing its path towards a geopolitical revival.

South Ossetia: A Critical Point for Russian Geopolitics

The contradictory nature of Putin's geopolitical stance revealed itself in his relations with Saakashvili, who was brought to power precisely to intensify

---

16 Shamil Basayev (1965–2006) was the leader of the radical Islamist faction of the Chechen guerrillas. He fought in both Chechen wars, and also fought against the Georgian government in the early 1990s.

conflict with Russia, to ultimately remove Russian influence from Georgia and to create the conditions necessary for the deployment of American forces in the Caucasus. This plan was part of Bush's 'Greater Middle East Initiative'[17] and involved attempts to further destabilise the North Caucasus area. This strategy included the key elements of the murder of Akhmat Kadyrov and an uprising in Ingushetia, with a subsequent permanent destabilisation and guerrilla insurgency in Kizlyar. Riots in Kabarda and a new tension cycle in Karachay-Cherkessia are on the agenda as well. His Atlanticist advisors and direct pressure from Washington convinced the Russian President that Saakashvili would be content with Ajara alone and thus the problem would be solved. This was a serious political error. Saakashvili will always act in strict accordance with the nationalistic agenda devised in Washington: the more Russia follows Georgia's lead, the better. The US does not see Russia as an equal partner, but rather as a force to negotiate with. Having coerced Russia into ousting Abashidze, Saakashvili started to insist on the 'eviction' of Kokoity[18] and Bagapsh.[19] When Moscow tried to resist, Washington, as usual, decided to aggravate the situation.

The tragedy in South Ossetia in August 2008 became a kind of test for Vladimir Putin: would he actually step back and delegate his real powers to the more liberal and West-oriented Dmitry Medvedev, or would he remain in control of principal strategic issues related to the preservation of Russian sovereignty?

---

17   The Bush administration unveiled this plan in 2004 before the G8 summit as a 40-year plan to democratise the Middle East. It drew widespread criticism, not least because none of the nations it sought to transform were consulted.

18   Eduard Kokoity (b. 1964) was the President of South Ossetia from 2001 until 2011. He strongly opposed reunification of South Ossetia with Georgia, believing it should end up as part of Russia.

19   Sergei Bagapsh (1949–2011) was the President of the Republic of Abkhazia from 2005 until his death. Previously he had been Prime Minister.

South Ossetia: President Putin's Geopolitical Choice

In August 2008 Vladimir Putin found himself at a point of fundamental bifurcation: his geopolitical legitimacy (patriotism and Eurasianism) obliged him to actively support South Ossetia. The situation was particularly crucial because the force Saakashvili was up against was not a rebellious clan, but the ancient, militant Ossetian *ethnos* who had joined Russia voluntarily back in the day and had historically functioned as a Russian outpost in the Caucasus. North Ossetia, too, will never agree to the radical separation of the South Ossetian lands from Russia. If he had done in South Ossetia what he had done to Adzharia, Vladimir Putin would have permanently lost his legitimacy with the patriotically-inclined segment of the Russian society that acts as the basis of his political support, and he understood this perfectly. The surrender of South Ossetia would have been a personal catastrophe for him: the end of his political legitimacy and the denunciation of his mission to revive statehood. But a drastic measure in relation to Tskhinvali was not easy either: it meant a drastic falling out with Washington, as well as possible direct sabotage by the pro-American agents of influence controlling many strategic issues in the Russian economy, the community of experts and the media.

With every new step the US took to undermine Russia, the compromise between patriotism and Westernism that had served as the basis of Putin's geopolitical formula during his first eight years in office became less plausible. One can only imagine how difficult Putin's choice was: to be on the side of his country and its people meant to challenge the overseas colossus; to surrender to pressure from the Atlanticist colossus meant the betrayal of Russia and its national history.

Today, Putin faces yet another dilemma: to loosen his grip on the country, which is what the newly rising liberal-Atlanticist lobby in Medvedev's entourage wants him to do, or to assume responsibility for Russia and the destiny of its people, starting a new cycle of patriotic history and rebuilding Russia's status as a great world power. The Munich speech that startled the Western community has become Putin's genuine political platform: 'In fact, it was the truth. I told the truth', Putin said several years after making that speech. 'I simply had not realised its importance at the time... They told us one thing, and would do the complete opposite. In fact, they have duped us in every sense of the word! During the withdrawal of our troops from Eastern Europe, the NATO Secretary General told us that the USSR could at least be sure that NATO would not expand beyond its current borders. So what happened to that promise? I asked them directly, but they have nothing to say. They cheated us in the most primitive way. By the way, I have to say it, unfortunately, and I will say it out loud right away, without hesitation: tactics like cheating are very common in politics when it comes to global issues, and we have to move forward with this in mind.'[20]

Vladimir Putin's Munich speech became the programme of his return as a political figure who had finally embarked on a path toward Russia's revival. In this respect, 2012 should be considered a turning point. Vladimir Putin may return only as a historical figure who has finally accepted the mission to revive Russia as a great power. Otherwise, everything that he had said and done before would be pointless. Russia is waiting for a leader to help her regain her previous greatness.

Putin: I Renounce the Devil

Lately, the principal aspects of Vladimir Putin's statements regarding Russia's new foreign policy, which stem from his decisive intent to raise Russia to the status of a great world power and to make her an independent and influential actor on a global scale, are becoming clearer. For the first time, Vladimir Putin is letting the world know how he envisions Russia's role within the G8. And this, in turn, has shed light on the Kremlin's approach to its relations with the West and the rest of the world. 'I know that there are inveterate haters of our country. They are still living in the previous century and all of them are specialists in Sovietology. Even though the Soviet Union has ceased to exist, they are still there, because they have no other specialty... Nobody wants the G8 to turn into an assembly of 'fat cats', because the differences and imbalances in the world are growing,' declared

---

20   Interview in *Kommersant*, 30 August 2010.—AD

Vladimir Putin in response to allegations made by US Secretary of State Condoleezza Rice when she protested against Russia's chairmanship of the G8.[21]

There is, in fact, a very legitimate geopolitical concept behind Putin's 'fat cats' metaphor and the 'golden billion' reference.[22] The G7, that is, the G8 minus Russia, was a club of the most developed countries (sometimes also dubbed 'the First World'). At the opposing end there are emerging markets — the 'Third World'. Previously, the USSR had been considered the 'Second World', a specific geopolitical entity that was less developed technologically, economically and socially than the West, but more successful than Third World countries. During Yeltsin's presidency, Russia desperately tried to qualify for the 'First World' league and was ready to sacrifice everything, including its traditional areas of influence in Asia and the East, to get it. Join the West at any cost, even at the cost of Russia's disintegration — such was the course outlined by pro-Western politicians. But in trying to enter the 'golden billion', Yeltsin's Russia not only lost its global position, but lagged even more significantly behind the West. There was a great risk of the country turning into the backyard of civilisation. As a result, we almost slipped into the 'Third World'. The two-faced West actually encouraged Moscow's self-liquidation and made Russia a member of the G8 as a reward, remembering to move NATO institutions closer to our borders and to remove the post-Soviet territories on a piecemeal basis from the zones of our influence. Vladimir Putin put an end to all of this. Putin's motto was to preserve Russia's status as 'Second World' by all means, and his perseverance in conducting this independent and self-sustained policy was met with growing hostility from the West.

Putin's Russia is becoming more and more aware of her global mission — counterbalancing the unilateral domination of the 'Rich North' and building a fair world order which favours the interests and wishes of all countries and civilisations. Contemporary Russia does not have sufficient strategic potential to unilaterally balance the Western pole, like it did in the Soviet era. But it has enough energy, while remaining one of the most

---

21 Putin made this statement at a press conference at the Kremlin on 31 January 2006.

22 A Russian metaphor for those living in the wealthy nations of the West.

developed countries, to speak for all of those who have been humiliated and insulted. Putin once said, rather unambiguously, 'Firstly, we still have enough missiles, besides which, we are developing our nuclear deterrence capability. [...] Two years ago we conducted successful tests of such missiles which have never existed before and which no other country could put into operation before us. These are very advanced weapons for which it does not matter whether there are missile defence systems in place.' From here on it is clear that all attacks by the 'inveterate Sovietologists' who continue to apply a 'Cold War' mentality to our country will be fended off unceremoniously. As Putin said when talking about his adversaries in the West, 'There is no point arguing with them... What can you say to such people? They only deserve one small remark: "Screw you!" and that's it.'[23] So, in telling the so-called 'Sovietologists' to piss off, Putin symbolically rejected Atlanticist geopolitics, based as it principally is on opposition to the continental states occupying the central region of Northeast Eurasia (be it the Russian Empire, the USSR or the new, democratic Russia). This gesture is not unlike an Orthodox baptism, where the baptised person turns to the West, to the place where Lucifer was cast down, and spits three times, repeating 'I renounce the Devil.'

Let us call a spade a spade: Vladimir Putin's conduct and his statements are signs of a historical recoup, a re-establishment of our status as 'Second World', and an aspiration to be at the forefront of the complex but rightful construction of the new multipolar world.

President Putin's Liberal Reform
A Geopolitical Analysis

Geopolitics as something for the mentality of the country's leaders, and as a science about power and for power, had long been expressly prohibited by Communist ideology. The importance of geopolitics for Russia was revealed only when Vladimir Putin came to power. Geopolitics involves analysis of the world and world processes tied to geographical realities, to

---

23 'Vladimir Putin: To the Critics We Reply: Screw You', *Komsomolskaya Pravda*, 2 February 2006.—AD

a place, space, and a *topos*,[24] and each of these notions acquires a cultural and civilisational significance. For example, when we speak of democracy, nationalism, liberalism and monarchy we need to refer these notions to the places where they developed and formed. When we see that space, taken in a deep sense, in conjunction with culture and tradition, creates and produces various types of democracies, nationalisms, monarchisms, political constructions and economic systems, then we can discuss Russian, Eurasian and Western democracies separately, and talk about how 'democracy' is applied to the East.

The same goes for economic models. It is necessary to place both 'economic plans' and 'markets' in their actual geographical and historico-cultural-geographic contexts instead of treating them as separate entities. But the easiest expression of geopolitics can be summarised as in the following: there is a permanent historical and civilisational contradiction between the contemporary Eurasian model of many civilisations and the contemporary Atlanticist, Western one with its ideas about its own universality and exclusiveness, and this contradiction cannot be reduced to problems of ideology. This fundamental geopolitical contradiction has existed since Russia and Britain were empires and monarchies. When Russia became democratic, these antagonisms with the democratic West did not vanish. NATO continued to expand eastwards and bombed the Serbs (our geopolitical allies), thus only confirming the basic laws of geopolitics, which state that civilisational space and cultural geography determine the historical relations between large geopolitical blocs, people and powers.

The Eurasian Project: The Path to Superpower

Without rejecting liberalism in its absolute sense, one should nevertheless reject the recipe for Western-type liberalism that the Atlanticist geopolitical forces are forcing upon us. It is clear that some elements of liberalism in the economy must be adapted to the peculiarities of our Eurasian reality. As for Soviet and Tsarist projects, those historical forms of our common Eurasian path are now outdated in Russian history. One should not insist

---

24 Classical Greek: 'place'.

on their total rejection or refutation, but understand that historically they have run dry.

The Eurasian model is a contemplation of our current situation on the basis of a qualitative civilisational space. We must preserve the main impulse (geographical, historical, cultural, civilisational) of the previous stages in the development of our state and develop a brand new and unique mentality for twenty-first century Russia. We must move forward: not just go back into the past, but create a new synthesis. Putin's federal reforms must be assessed from this point of view.

The appointment of Vladimir Putin as acting Prime Minister represented the start of a new stage in the history of the Russian state. The substantive part of the events and transformations that had taken place in the years before the emergence of Putin represented a transition from the Communist model to a liberal democratic one. The explosive events between the late 1980s to the late 1990s developed along these lines. By Yeltsin's midterm, however, it was already evident that a direct introduction of Western liberal values into Russia is impossible because it is confronted by a profound resistance, not only from the opposition but from the basic archetypes of our national way of life.

The new course was already maturing with Yeltsin, when the introduction of patriotic and strong state values into Russian ideology began to take root, but with Yeltsin in power this process was not fully realised. His successor, Vladimir Putin, embodied this exact course — a course for the establishment of a new and strong state policy and for the consolidation of the entire Russian society during a difficult historical period, when the principal values of our state were at stake.

Putin's course, his tough stance on the brash Wahhabi attack in Dagestan, and on the seizure of Dagestani territories by the Wahhabis during the second Chechen campaign, coupled with his federal reforms, were aimed at strengthening Russian statehood.

Largely, this became a revolution from above. We progressed from Communism to democracy, and subsequently, with Putin, from a pro-Western, extremist, liberal democratic Atlanticist model to a patriotic Eurasian course. This intense process affected absolutely everyone. It caused a shift in mentality and was a lot more significant than a mere redistribution of property or of powers and authority. Putin proclaimed it and Putin started to carry it out.

The Unification Strategy of Russian Lands

Putin's policy on Chechnya can be considered the beginning of a federal reform — not a single episode in itself, but it was the beginning of something bigger. First, it was necessary to suppress the hotbeds of separatism in the Russian Federation, which stemmed not only from Chechnya and Dagestan. At that point there was an enormous threat to the territorial integrity of our state due to the abuse of power by the parochial governors' systems. The governors themselves had largely transformed into little tsars, establishing semi-criminal regimes that had very weak links not only with law but to unity with the centre.

The Yeltsin period saw the beginning of the objectionable practice of political trade between the regions and the centre: the centre put pressure on the regions, imposing its conditions, and the regional governors then bargained with the centre. There was no consistent policy between the centre and the regions with Yeltsin. The prospects for the breakup of the state were becoming more acute, and the sole legal administrative, managerial authority of the country was disrupted. Basically, the threat of disintegration was growing.

I work with a lot of materials from various Western projects and services, both secret and semi-secret, and I can honestly say that behind the governors' abuse of power in the Yeltsin period there were constant and omnipresent strategies and scenarios devised by our geopolitical enemy. Directly or indirectly, by economic, political and other structural, industrial and diplomatic methods, the Americans pushed on with their scenario for a geopolitical dismemberment of the Large Space.[25] Chechnya was the peak in the efforts of the Western secret services, via Turkey and Saudi Arabia, to explore the possibility of dismembering Russia in the most extreme form: by setting the heretical pseudo-Islamic Wahhabi sect against the Russians. Putin challenged this disintegration process, and his federal reform became the extension of this challenge. I think that it had a clear purpose: it is a consistent policy of unifying Russian lands. We can also mention his support for the creation of the Union State of Russia and Belarus and the integration of the countries of the Customs Union[26] into the CIS.

Putin was forced to take extraordinary measures in order to extinguish a fire. If, when fighting a fire, the firemen step on a crystal glass set, it is really insignificant when compared to the fact that peoples' lives and the surrounding buildings are saved. I also want to note that the regions should receive some form of compensation when the sovereign powers that they managed to acquire during the period of the 'derelict' state management of the Yeltsin era are revoked. It is not a question of reparations or payments; it is a necessity to explain again to the regions, and to the Russian people living in most of these regions, and to the other Russian ethnic groups as well, why they should actually be part of a single state.

This is where the idea of Eurasia can help. It does not reject the previous forms of Russia's mobilisation into a single state. Before 1917 Rus-

---

25 In *The Fourth Political Theory* (London: Arktos, 2012) Dugin writes: 'The "large space" is a different name for that which we understand by "civilisation" in its geopolitical, spatial and cultural senses. The "large space" differs from other existing national governments precisely in that it is built on the foundation of a common value system and historical kinship, and it also unifies a few or even a multitude of different governments, tied together by a "community of fate".'

26 The Eurasian Customs Union was established in 1995 as an attempt to unite the countries that were formerly part of the Soviet Union into an economic bloc along the lines of the European Union. It currently consists of Russia, Belarus, and Kazakhstan, but Russia hopes to eventually add many other nations. The catalyst for the Maidan revolution in Ukraine occurred when Ukrainian President Viktor Yanukovych ended efforts to integrate into the EU in favour of the Customs Union.

sia followed the *Uvarov formula:*[27] *Orthodoxy, monarchy and nationality* explained the unity of the state and the people. During the Soviet period there existed an idea of international friendship between people in a socialist state, and it was an incentive to bring them together into a unified state. Today, these principles are outdated. Saying that we must be in a unified state for the sake of democracy is absurd because our democracy is a very uncertain thing, and not yet fully formed. Practically no sane people can be mobilised by this notion into a conscious and wilful preservation of the unity of the state. In light of this, we must develop a new incentive system.

The Concept of the All-Eurasian Destiny

The Eurasian ideology that we are developing is not yet a consummate complex of ideas; it is an idea in progress. This evolving mentality is based on the 'concept of the all-Eurasian destiny'. The peoples living within the territory of Russia, and more broadly within the territory of Eurasia, are united by a certain civilisational attitude. It is especially evident when our people travel to the West. I talked in Moscow with a prominent businessman of Chechen origin. He told me that when he was in the West (even when he was in Turkey, which supposedly has a mentality similar to the Chechens for a number of historical reasons), he felt like a Russian, he spoke Russian, and he thought of himself and of any other representative of Russia — an Azerbaijani, an Armenian, an ethnic Slav — as brothers in a foreign civilisation. This is the principle of the common denominator in the face of a new civilisation — Western, Atlanticist, and based on alternative principles. The contemporary West is based on the principle of individualism: this is what unites all Atlanticist peoples and states. The Eurasian communities and peoples are used to various forms of anti-individualism, communal life and collectivism. A Russian or a Muslim community — both are formed around a collective mentality, open to the world and to nature, whether these people are Islamic, Buddhist or professing any other religion. These

---

27   I mean the formula 'Orthodoxy, autocracy and nationality', an ideological basis of the 'theory of official nationality', proclaimed in 1832. Its author was Count Sergei Semionovich Uvarov (1786–1855), Deputy Minister of Public Education, responsible for the ideological backing of the rule of Nicholas I, eradicating the Decembrists' heritage.—AD

elements of a traditional society, communal psychology, and a single geographical, civilisational unity, when properly analysed, can create a firm basis for solidarity within a state. I want to emphasise that we should not forget about it, especially at the next stage, because there is no force that can hold different people and regions together. This is not a question of force. We should use this mentality as a foundation for Vladimir Putin's federal, centralised reforms of integration so that people realise that they belong in the state as a result of their historical choices and the choices of their ancestors. We must delve deep into history in order to try to single out this common denominator. The Eurasian model, developed by our predecessors, the founders of Eurasianism in the 1920s — Count Trubetzkoy,[28] Savitsky,[29] Alexeyev[30] — provides us with an excellent starting point.

Eurasianism is not a product of an individual creative process. It is an objective tendency. Whether the leaders of our nation understand it or not, whether they think in terms of Eurasianism and geopolitics or not, actions aimed at strengthening those elements that will lead to a return of our superpower statehood, directly or indirectly, consciously or unconsciously, will steer our leaders toward Eurasian geopolitics. In his speeches, Vladimir Putin constantly uses the words 'geopolitical', 'geopolitics', and 'the geopolitical situation of Russia'. Pick up my textbook on geopolitics (which I wrote and which was accepted by the majority of higher education institutions), and

---

28 Prince Nikolai Trubetzkoy (1890–1938) was a linguist and historian who left Russia following the Russian Revolution. Trubetzkoy believed that Eurasia formed a unity, even though it was divided politically, and laid some of the theoretical groundwork for the Eurasian movement of the time. His seminal essay on Eurasianism, 'Europe and Mankind', is available in English in Nikolai Trubetzkoy, *The Legacy of Genghis Khan and Other Essays on Russia's Identity* (Ann Arbor: Michigan Slavic Publications, 1991).

29 Pyotr Nikolaevich Savitsky (1895–1968) was an economist and a philosopher who belonged to the White Russian movement. He was also one of the leading figures of the original Eurasianist movement. An excerpt from one of his Eurasianist essays is available in English at *The Soul of the East* Website, souloftheeast.org/2014/02/22/the-eurasianist-worldview/.

30 Nikolai Alexevey was an attorney associated with the Eurasianists.

you will find a clear definition of geopolitics.³¹ Putin uses the word 'geopolitics' and understands it as it is defined in my textbook.

Today, it has become trendy among senior military officers to write scientific theses and books on geopolitics. Putin was seen at the defence of a thesis by an admiral who talked about the vast oceanic geopolitical spaces of Russia. If the President is surrounded by senior military commanders who line up to defend geopolitical theses, if he constantly uses the term 'geopolitics', if he conducts actual reforms in a geopolitical, Eurasian way, can one say that this is just a coincidence? In fact, it is not at all, especially given that my book on geopolitics is almost constantly available at the bookstore in the presidential administration building.

Vladimir Putin as a Man of Destiny

My politological assessments are usually based on the assumption that politics is a continuation of spirit. If the spirit is dirty, the politics is dirty too; if the spirit is clean, the politics is also clean. We have a false impression of politics as something done by a showman, a demagogue or a civil servant. Today, politics in Russia is divorced from ideas and our politicians change their ideologies as often as they change their clothes. This approach is doomed. We need a politics of ideas and we need relevant politicians. I am convinced that a new type of person must enter politics. This is not easy, and there is enormous inertial resistance. There are relevant techniques as well. I taught a course on political philosophy and I am aware of its techniques.³² Strictly speaking, *I have been engaged in politics since the early 1980s, that is, I am one of the oldest Russian politicians.* But only today have I matured enough to assume personal responsibility. I previously thought that my role was limited to simply generating political ideas, but it turned out that they were immediately distorted beyond recognition. My almost 30-year experience in Russian politics finally motivated me speak as

---

31 Alexander Dugin, *The Fundamentals of Geopolitics* (Moscow: Arctogaia, 1997).—AD (No English translation exists.—Ed.)

32 Alexander Dugin, *The Philosophy of Politics* (Moscow: Arctogaia, 2004).—AD (No English translation exists.—Ed.)

a leader backed by a large number of convinced supporters and followers who gave me their trust.

The Revolutionary Potential of Vladimir Putin

I think that we underestimate the revolutionary potential of Vladimir Putin. Not as a personality, but as a historic figure, predetermined by time and place. He was appointed acting President of Russia on the day indicated by Nostradamus as the time of the coming of the 'great King of Terror'. Putin is a portent, and the extraction of this portent from out of his political and psychological particulars is a matter of the most sophisticated theurgical surgery.

My late friend, the great French writer Jean Parvulesco,[33] wrote a visionary book entitled *Putin and the Eurasian Empire*[34] in which he states that 'Vladimir Putin is a man of destiny'. In the last part of the book there is an interview with me, in which I stated the problem as follows: 'The political battle for Putin is a battle for the meaning of history' (*'La lutte politique pour Vladimire Poutine c'est la lutte pour le sens de l'histoire.'*). But all this is located beyond Yeltsinism, and not everybody will be able to take a step beyond it. In time new people, new political organs and new books will be required.

At some point, part of Russia's population was under the impression that we were moving towards a 'liberal dictatorship', when Gräf-style reforms would be introduced using Stalinist methods. All things liberal are bad for the Russians. The same goes for dictatorship. Stalinist methods require a relevant mobilising ideology: something that can't be achieved with liberalism, so concerns about liberalism are pointless. This is a temporary phenomenon and the entire liberal course will be gradually discarded. There's no need to panic prematurely. We had better strengthen the super-

---

33 Jean Parvulesco (1929–2010) was a Romanian writer who fled to France following the Communist takeover. He was a traditionalist and esotericist, He was close to Alain de Benoist's GRECE, In his geopolitical writings he called for an axis between Paris, Berlin and Moscow to be formed to counter Anglo-Saxon hegemony.

34 Jean Parvulesco, *Vladimir Putin and the Eurasian Empire* (St. Petersburg: Amphora, 2003).—AD (No English translation exists.—Ed.)

power statehood policy of the Russian authorities until we have passed the point of no return. So far, geopolitics in Russia is only ripening. Previous convocations of our State Duma staged a permanent farce in the form of a geopolitical committee, in which wild LDPR members tried to discredit this discipline. Today the state of geopolitics is still unsatisfactory, because instead of serious scientific work, analysis of sources, translations, and so forth, everybody prefers to copy huge chunks from my textbooks and articles, omitting references, and then dilutes them with their own 'original' rubbish. I think that the wave of Duma and non-Duma plagiarists will recede, and a properly qualified school of geopolitics will be formed based on the foundations I have already laid out. But it requires time.

There is another extremely important point to be made here. There is a significant difference between the pro-American and the pro-European course. Russia's pro-European course is part of the Eurasian geopolitical strategy. The European Union shares a common culture with the US, but it has different interests. Europe's culture is very different from Russian culture, but we sometimes share common interests, especially when it comes to the energy sector. A strategic union between Russia and Europe is important for both Europe and Russia, but unacceptable for the US. This complex picture determines the frame of Moscow's geopolitical strategy.

Putin, the Secret Service, the Army, and NATO

With respect to the secret service, the Eurasian course involves a number of dialectics. The most 'Eurasian' secret service is the GRU, or military intelligence (the Main Intelligence Directorate). Since the interests of a great power, irrespective of its current political regime, are defended primarily by the army, the GRU has traditionally performed the functions of strategic planning. The Soviet Union's KGB, just as in the present-day FSB,[35] the top priority was political issues, which are subsidiary in geopolitics. Starting with Gorbachev, the KGB began to play a negative role, losing track of the strategic interests of the country and the Eastern bloc in general, in turn permitting the disintegration of the USSR and its entire system. This

---

35   Federal Security Service, the counter-intelligence and internal security service of the Russian Federation.

was accompanied by staving off the GRU and the marginalisation of the Armed Forces. In the next stage, the KGB itself fell victim to anti-Eurasian inertia, and the Ministry of Internal Affairs dealt mostly with criminal issues, often ignoring politics altogether, let alone geopolitics. The strengthening of the Ministry of Internal Affairs began in the mid-1990s, when the prevalent mood of Russian politics and society in general was far from Eurasianist. In fact, it was exactly the opposite: the dominant attitudes favoured Atlanticism, opportunism, oligarchy, unbridled corruption, overt disgust towards one's own country, its history and people, hatred of the state, and on and on.

But as the external political situation became more pressing, the necessity of geopolitics for Russia gained growing acceptance among the establishment. The rise of Vladimir Putin, a former KGB officer, is an important sign of this. The role of the secret service was reversed. The strengthening of the KGB became, at some point, an important *Eurasian element*. It prepared the country for a gradual transition towards a fully-fledged strategic mentality and the domination of superpower interests over everything else. Naturally, after the events of 9/11, all this reasoning was somehow overshadowed by the political realities of the time. In this regard the most frightening assumptions are possible — a precedent outlined in my book *Conspirology*.[36]

There is another decision of Vladimir Putin's that is worth mentioning. He approved measures related to a gradual replacement of the conscription system by manning and equipping the Russian Armed Forces on a contractual basis. I know a thing or two about this process, because I developed the geopolitical models for reforming the Armed Forces — in particular, the part related to strategic perspectives. I understand why military reform, including its transition towards a contractual basis, has been deliberately slowed down. The truth is that military reform, as a practice, must be implemented by first adjusting the regulations of military doctrine in their theoretical aspect. Such things are closely intertwined and cannot exist separately. The current military doctrine is ambiguous because it does

---

36 Alexander Dugin, *Conspirology* (Moscow: Arctogaia, 1993).—AD (No English translation exists,—Ed.)

not answer the principal question: 'Who is our potential enemy?' And the answer to this question underlies the entire military doctrine and, correspondingly, the process of military reform, where the transition towards a contractual basis is just one of its elements. The principal aspect, the potential enemy, has been at the centre of the invisible but very active and aggressive struggle between law enforcement agencies and ministries and the political leaders of the country for many years.

The military insists that since the Americans view Russia or the so-called Eurasian bloc as one of their most likely potential enemies, we should also consider the US as our principal enemy. This is quite logical, but the Kremlin does not view it this way. As a result, Army reform is not implemented and all related issues, including the move toward a contractual basis, are markedly speculative and abstract. A certain consensus seems to have been reached while Putin was in power: a national security concept that was oriented toward the idea of a multipolar world was adopted, which makes the US our primary enemy as the builder of a unipolar world. But then the events of 9/11 threw our plans off: it was unclear once again whether the US was our principal enemy or not. If it was not, then Russia needed to build build an Army in which the strategic sector would be minimised and its main focus would be on the formation of professional, well-knit armed forces capable of combat operations along the borders of the Russian Federation. In this case, the Army would become an extension of the police or, say, the border guards. But, in reality, this idea is at odds with the logic of geopolitics.

Americans are always ready to smile and to talk about concessions, but they never change their positions when it comes to strategy. As a result, tension here escalates again, not between the supporters and the opponents of a professional Army, but between the two competing, primary definitions of Russia's geopolitical function. I think Putin himself has not yet arrived at a conclusive decision on this issue, although his position is gradually becoming more outlined.

The same goes for NATO relations, Russian membership being an occasional topic. In the event it joins it (which is quite unrealistic), Russia will destroy this organisation: our membership in the North Atlantic alliance will radically change its structure and geopolitical inclinations. If a strong

Eurasian nuclear power with its own explicit continental interests joins this bloc, it will cancel the very notion of 'Atlanticism', turning the alliance into something completely different. In this case NATO, by definition, will not be able to perform the functions for which it was created in the first place. It will be a completely different strategic union. Besides, Russia's strategic and military status is so high that the organisation will not be able to conduct the unified civilisational and geostrategic policy that NATO is currently following. Vladimir Putin has been taking concrete and persistent steps in this direction from the outset (for instance, by proposing to create an all-European missile defence system). As far as I know, such amendment to the current model of geostrategic relations with the West is one of Putin's priorities and an integral part of his entire foreign policy. But NATO also understands perfectly what this is all about. In my opinion, the US is absolutely unprepared for such transformations within the alliance, and will agree to it only if it realises its own fundamental vulnerability. This is why we should seek NATO membership, but should not be surprised if our application is rejected: we are not dealing with idiots. On the other hand, Russia is actively trying to showcase its geopolitical personality to Europe and the US. This is entirely correct, and our possible participation, in any form, in any anti-terrorist actions taken by the international community must be backed by a number of strategic conditions stipulated by Russia. Overall, our direct involvement with American anti-terrorist actions is extremely undesirable and, possibly, even disastrous. But other, more flexible forms of Russia's participation in combating international terrorism should by all means also be backed by a number of conditions, in particular by a demand to stop NATO's expansion.

The Eurasian way is the future of Russia. According to the Russian Public Opinion Research Centre, 71% of Russians believe that Russia is an independent Eurasian, Orthodox civilisation. Putin is a national leader. He cannot turn a blind eye to his people's choice. He inherited a difficult legacy and cadres which are unsuitable for the realisation of his historical mission. But we shall overcome. The leader of Russia-Eurasia cannot but be a Eurasian. This is a political axiom.

CHAPTER 5

Putin's Eurasian Revolution

Vladimir Putin and the Conservative Revolution

During his first term, President Putin desperately and persistently tried to hint at the agenda that he was going to propose to the nation. Many wanted him to speak out with more clarity and to be more concrete, but Putin's style tends to be more general: he gives us an idea and leaves a lot of room for interpretation. But gradually, everything seemed to come together. The enigmatic Putin, silent, simultaneously frowning and smiling, finally let us know that his presidential programme would be defined by one simple word: conservatism.

So, during his two terms Putin ruled in the vein of a 'conservative programme' and clearly intends to continue this policy into his third term. But what does 'conservatism' mean in modern Russia?

The Essence of Conservatism

Conservatism in its most general sense means *a positive attitude towards historical tradition*. It holds up the political and social history of a state as a role model, striving to preserve the continuity of the people's national and cultural roots. The past is viewed by all denominations of conservatism as a positive phenomenon. Not everything in the past is perceived as positive, but a consistent conservative will never deliberately tarnish any period in the history of his people and state.

Moreover, conservatism is based on the premise that the people and the state have a certain historical *mission*, which can vary from universalist religious messianism to humble awareness of the importance of their national identity. The present, the past, and the future in the eyes of a conservative are tied together in a single integral project striving toward a clear national goal. In making any political or economic decision, a conservative always turns to the past and ponders the future. A conservative thinks in terms of landmarks and epochs, disregarding quick profit. His temporal, geographical, and value-related horizon is always broad.

A conservative is a dedicated bearer of national culture and seeks to comply with its norms. A conservative always over-exerts himself: from mandatory prayer to cold showers in the morning. A conservative consistently ranks duty, honour, the public benefit, loyalty to tradition, and his good reputation over comfort, benefit, profit, or popularity.

A conservative is reserved and prefers to speak prudently and thoughtfully. A conservative is civil and always has an extra pair of glasses, even if he has perfect eyesight.

A conservative is unsettled by objective reality and carefully selects books for reading. A conservative never considers himself as such.

A conservative smiles, turning up the corners of his mouth, and never expresses himself with his hands.

Anyone who does not comply with these requirements is not a proper conservative, he is just...

Fundamental Conservatism

Conservatism has an underlying philosophy. To be a conservative means to say 'no' to what we have now and to express one's disagreement with the current state of things.

There is fundamental conservatism, which is called traditionalism.

Traditionalism is a form of conservatism that argues that everything is bad in its entirety in today's world, not just in certain aspects. 'The idea of progress, technical development, Descartes' subject-object dualism, Newton's watchmaker argument, contemporary positivistic science and the education based on it, pedagogics, and what we call modernism and post-modernism — they are all bad.' A traditionalist likes only what had existed prior to modernism. In the twentieth century, when there seemed to be no social platform left for such conservatism, a constellation of thinkers and philosophers appeared out of nowhere and started to defend, radically and consistently, the traditionalist position: René Guénon,[1] Julius Evola,[2] Titus Burckhardt,[3] Leopold Ziegler,[4] and all those known as traditionalists. They proposed a programme of fundamental conservatism, described traditional society as a timeless ideal, and the contemporary world (modernism) and its basic principles as a product of decline, degradation, the mixing of castes, the disintegration of hierarchy, representing a shift of focus from the spiritual to the material, from Heaven to Earth, and from the eternal to the transient. Fundamental conservatives exist today in both the Orthodox and Catholic milieus. They completely reject modernism and believe that religious laws are absolutely relevant, and that the contemporary world and its values are an embodiment of the Antichrist, and which cannot offer anything good in the first place. These tendencies are common among Russian Old Believers. There is still a Paraclete Union in the Urals which does not use electric lighting because it is 'the light of Lucifer', and they use only pine splinters and candles; there are also sects which strictly prohibit cof-

---

1 René Guénon (1886–1951) was a French writer who founded what has come to be known as the traditionalist school of religious thought. Traditionalism calls for a rejection of the modern world and its philosophies in favour of a return to the spirituality and ways of living of the past. His central works are *The Crisis of the Modern World* and *The Reign of Quantity and the Signs of the Times*.

2 Julius Evola (1898–1974) was the most important Italian member of the traditionalist school, which is to say that he opposed modernity in favour of an approach to life consistent with the teachings of the ancient sacred texts. His main work is *Revolt against the Modern World*.

3 Titus Burckhardt (1908–1984) was a Swiss German art historian who also participated in the traditionalist school.

4 Leopold Ziegler (1881–1958) was a German philosopher. Although not strictly part of the traditionalist school, his thought did bear similarities to theirs, and he was in contact with representatives of the school as well as with the Conservative Revolutionaries.

fee. When a group of young people in eighteenth-century Russia started to wear chequered trousers in accordance with the current fashions, the Fedosevans[5] summoned an assembly in the town of Kimry, sometimes called the 'trouser assembly', and discussed whether those wearing chequered trousers should be excommunicated. Part of the assembly insisted that they be separated from the community and the other part voted against it.

The US has its own conservative tradition that is naturally based on the priorities of America's national interests. Marked by a significant degree of messianism ('the American civilisation is the peak of human history'), American conservatism respects the past and strives to preserve and strengthen the positions of its great country in the future. American conservatives profess loyalty to patriotic values as well as to religious, political, social and cultural norms that were established throughout the course of their historical development. This is natural and, as a consequence, American conservatism is flourishing: the US has achieved incredible power internationally, which makes its citizens justifiably proud and convinced of the righteousness of their ways. In America, fundamental conservatism is professed by a significant share of the Republican electorate, and TV programmes which feature Protestant fundamentalists criticising all things modern and postmodern and tearing them to shreds are watched by millions of people...

But the direct emulation of 'Republican' American conservatism by Russia yields absurd results: it turns out that what is to be 'conserved' are values that are not only foreign to historical and traditional Russia, but which are basically absent from contemporary Russian society.

Russia is an ancient land-based empire with a strong collectivist spirit, traditionally tough administrative rule and a very specific messianism. The US is a relatively new sea-based entity, intentionally designed as a laboratory experiment for the introduction of 'progressivist' bourgeois democratic principles that matured among ultra-Protestant sects. What is valued in the American civilisation is a sin and a disgrace for the Russians. What they respect is disgusting to us, and vice versa.

---

5   A congregation of Old Believers.—AD

Russia was moving towards the East and the US was moving towards the West. Yes, they have won and we have lost. They proved to be stronger. But, according to our logic, God is not power, God is the truth. This is what a proper and consistent Russian conservatism says. Obviously, American conservatism says exactly the opposite.

Globalism can be both recognised and attacked in the US itself (this is their world domination project; some Americans agree with it and some do not). In Russia, globalism was imposed on us from the outside. We can put up with it and recognise our defeat, and join the American value system. This position is possible, as is collaborationism. But it would be the opposite of conservatism.

All peoples have their own conservatism because each nation develops its own value system, and this constitutes its national identity. The cultural outcome of American history does not have anything in common with the cultural outcome of Russian history. A conservative is always loyal to his traditions, his people and his ideals — not only in their heyday, but also when they are desecrated and despised by all.

Liberal Conservatism

The second type of conservatism is 'status quo conservatism' or liberal conservatism. It says 'yes' to modernism as today's main trend, but at each stage of the trend's implementation it tries to slow it down: 'Please, slow down, let's not do it today, let's postpone it.' The liberal conservative Fukuyama initially concluded that politics had disappeared and was about to be replaced by the 'global marketplace' where nations, states, ethnic groups, cultures and religions would vanish (this is liberalism in its purest form), but then he decided that we should slow down and introduce postmodernism quietly, without revolutions. He wrote that it was necessary to temporarily strengthen the nation-states (in this case, what he is proposing is liberal conservatism).

A liberal conservative is afraid that the accelerated dismantling of modernism, which is taking place within postmodernism, can release pre-modernism. For instance, the former Leftist turned liberal Jürgen Habermas[6] is afraid that postmodernism will destroy the subject, engulf humanity in chaos, and bring back the creepy shadows of tradition.

The bin Laden character, irrespective of whether he actually existed or was invented by Hollywood, is a caricature of postmodernism collapsing into pre-modernism.

Right-wing Conservatism

If liberal conservatism is nonsensical and just another 'refuge of a scoundrel' (Samuel Johnson),[7] Right-wing conservatism, on the contrary, is quite acceptable and natural. In contemporary Russia, a Right-wing conservative is a person who seeks the revival of his motherland's international imperial greatness, the nation's economic prosperity and the revival of the moral values and spirituality of the people. He thinks that this aim can be reached through a competent use of market mechanisms and the system of religious, monarchical, and centralist-leaning values.

Such Right-wing conservatism can focus on cultural-political issues (the consolidation of traditional denominations, the revival of national customs, the restoration of a segment of social, public and political institutions) or on economic aspects. When it comes to the economy, a Right-wing conservative project must logically develop in line with the theory of a 'national economy', summed up by the German economist Friedrich List[8] and implemented in Russia by Count Sergei Witte.[9] This project can be called 'economic nationalism'. Its extreme formula is roughly as follows: an absolutely free domestic market with a severe customs control system

---

6   Jürgen Habermas (b. 1929) is a German Marxist philosopher.

7   Samuel Johnson (1709–1784) was an English poet and essayist. According to his friend and biographer James Boswell, Johnson once said, 'Patriotism is the last refuge of the scoundrel.'

8   Friedrich von List (1789–1846) was a German philosopher and economist.

9   Sergei Witte (1849–1915) was an advisor to the last two Tsars of Russia. He oversaw the industrialisation of Russia and was the author of the 1905 October Manifesto, which was written in response to the Revolution of 1905 and the subsequent need for democratic reforms, and was the precursor to the Russian Empire's constitution.

and thorough regulation of foreign economic activity in the interests of domestic entrepreneurship.

A national economy does not involve the nationalisation of large monopolies but insists on the consolidation of large businesses around political authorities with the transparent and clear aim of finding a collective solution to facilitate the nation's mission, the strengthening of the country and the achievement of prosperity for all of the nation's people. It can be achieved via a certain 'patriotic code', which implies the assumption of moral responsibility by national businessmen before the country, people and society. This model in today's political spectrum roughly corresponds to what is usually called 'the Right-wing centre'. It seems that Putin himself prefers the 'Right-wing' centre of conservatism to any other type of conservatism.

Left-wing Conservatism

The notion 'Left wing' is usually not associated with conservatism. The Left wants change and the Right wants to conserve the existing state of things. But in Russia's political history the public sector, which is related to the 'Left-wing' value system, has always been extremely significant and developed, and the communal factor, both in the form of Orthodox conciliarism[10] and Soviet collectivism, had long become a dependable political and economic tradition. A meaningful combination of socialism and conservatism was already evident in the Russian *narodniki* (populists) of the nineteenth century, who were devoted to national problems and strove for a fair distribution of material wealth. Left-wing conservatism also existed in other countries: as social Catholicism[11] in France and Latin America, and as German National

---

10 Conciliarism in Orthodoxy refers to the belief that the Church should be governed by a council of bishops, rather by a single one.

11 Catholic social teaching addresses issues related to social justice, opposing capitalism and socialism in favour of distributism. It originated in Pope Leo XIII's *Rerum Novarum* encyclical of 1891.

Bolshevism (Niekisch,[12] Wolffheim,[13] Laufenberg,[14] etc.). A distinctive representative of social conservatism is Georges Sorel,[15] who wrote *Reflections on Violence*.[16] He argued that Leftists and Rightists (monarchists and Communists) were fighting against one common enemy: the bourgeoisie. Left-wing conservatism is close to the Russian National Bolshevism of N. Ustrialov,[17] who identified Russian national myths in Left-wing Marxist ideology.

In contemporary Russian politics, social (Left-wing) conservatism is fully legitimate. Russian Left-wing conservatives seek to preserve Russia's civilisational values, strengthen our geopolitical power and bring about a national revival. Left-wing conservatives believe that the best way to implement this mission is through the nationalisation of mineral resources and large private companies engaged in the export of natural resources, as well as by increasing

---

12 Ernst Niekisch (1889–1967) was a German politician who was initially a Communist, but by the 1920s sought to merge Communism with nationalism. He published a journal, *Widerstand* [Resistance], and applied the term National Bolshevik to himself and his followers. He rejected National Socialism as insufficiently socialist, and was imprisoned by them in 1937, and was blinded under torture. Upon his release in 1945, he supported the Soviet Union and moved to East Germany, but became disillusioned by the Soviets' treatment of workers and returned to the West in 1953.

13 Fritz Wolffheim (1888–1942), a Communist, was one of the first to develop the idea of National Bolshevism in 1919. He later became involved with a nationalist organisation called the League for the Study of German Communism, which included some National Socialists, although Wolffheim, being of Jewish descent, was unable to make much of these connections. He was imprisoned in Ravensbrück concentration camp in 1936 and died there.

14 Heinrich Laufenberg (1872–1932) was a former Communist who was one of the first politicians to formulate National Bolshevism in Germany in 1919.

15 Georges Sorel (1847–1922) was a French philosopher who began as a Marxist and later developed Revolutionary Syndicalism. He advocated the use of myth and organised violence in revolutionary movements. He was influential upon both the Communist and Fascist movements.

16 Georges Sorel, *Reflections on Violence* (Cambridge: Cambridge University Press, 1999).

17 Nikolai Ustrialov (1890–1937) was a professor and Slavophile who fled the Soviet Union following the Russian Revolution and joined the anti-Soviet White movement. Originally opposed to Communism, he later sought a fusion of elements of Soviet Communism with Russian nationalism. He returned to the Soviet Union in 1935, believing that National Bolshevik ideas were becoming more acceptable, but was charged with espionage and executed in 1937, during the Great Purge.

government control in the spheres of energy, transport, communications, and so on. Such social conservatism can insist on the legitimacy and natural character of the Soviet approach, viewing it as a part of the general national dialectics. Another trend is so-called social conservatism, which can be considered as a sub-family of the Conservative Revolution. Both Left-wing and Right-wing conservatism, by definition, must have a common ultimate aim: the revival of statehood, the preservation of national identity, the international rise of Russia, and loyalty to our cultural roots. The approaches toward achieving this common goal, however, differ between the two schools of though.

Conservative Revolution

There is yet another, and very interesting, type of conservatism. It is usually referred to as the Conservative Revolution, and it dialectically links conservatism with modernism. This trend was adopted by Martin Heidegger, Ernst and Friedrich Jünger,[18] Carl Schmitt,[19] Oswald Spengler,[20] Werner Sombart,[21] Othmar Spann,[22] Friedrich Hielscher,[23] Ernst Niekisch, and others.

The philosophical paradigm of the conservative revolutionary stems from the general conservative view of the world as an objective process of degrada-

---

18   Ernst Jünger (1895–1998) was one of the most prominent of the German Conservative Revolutionaries, but that was only one phase in a long and varied career. He volunteered for and fought in the German Army throughout the First World War, and was awarded the highest decoration, the Pour le Mérite, for his service. After the war, he wrote many books and novels, was active in German politics, experimented with psychedelic drugs, and travelled the world. He remained ambivalent about National Socialism at first, but never joined the Party, and he had turned against the Nazis by the late 1930s. He rejoined the Wehrmacht at the outbreak of war, however, and remained in Paris as a captain, where he spent more time with Picasso and Cocteau than enforcing the occupation. His objections to the Nazis were influential upon the members of the Stauffenberg plot to assassinate Hitler in July 1944, which led to his dismissal from the Wehrmacht. After the war, Jünger's political views gradually moved toward a sort of aristocratic anarchism. His brother, Friedrich Jünger (1898–1977) was also a veteran of the First World War and participated in the Conservative Revolution, and also became a writer and philosopher.

19   Carl Schmitt (1888–1985) was an important German jurist who wrote about political science, geopolitics and constitutional law. He was part of the Conservative Revolutionary movement of the Weimar era. He also briefly supported the National Socialists at the beginning of their regime, although they later turned against him. He remains highly influential in the fields of law and philosophy.

20   Oswald Spengler (1880–1936) was a German philosopher who is regarded as one of the principal Conservative Revolutionary figures of the Weimar period in Germany. His most important work was his two-volume 1922/23 book, *The Decline of the West*, in which he theorised that all civilisations go through an inevitable cycle of ages of rise and decline in power, with the present age of the West currently entering its declining period.

21   Werner Sombart (1863–1941) was a German economist and sociologist who was very much opposed to capitalism and democracy.

22   Othmar Spann (1878–1950) was an Austrian Catholic philosopher and economist who held neoconservative views based on the ideals of German Romanticism. He is credited with developing the idea of the corporate state, which was soon to become so integral to Fascism, and which Spann believed could be applied everywhere for the benefit of humanity. In spite of this, he did not support National Socialism, and he was imprisoned after the Anschluss in 1938 and forbidden to teach at the University of Vienna (where had had taught since 1919). He attempted to return to teaching after 1945, but was again rejected.

23   Friedrich Hielscher (1902–1990) was a German thinker who was involved in the Conservative Revolution and who was an active neo-pagan throughout his life. He participated in the anti-Nazi resistance during the Third Reich.

tion, which reaches its peak with modernism (a view shared by traditionalism). But, unlike the traditionalists, conservative revolutionaries think: why does God, who created this world, ultimately turn a blind eye to evil, and why do God's enemies win? One might suspect that the beautiful Golden Age, which fundamental conservatives defend, already contained a gene that brought about this degradation. Then the conservative revolutionaries say to the fundamental conservatives: 'You propose to go back to the state when man only suffered from the initial symptoms of the illness, a hacking cough, and talk about how well-off man was back then, when today this same man is on his deathbed. You merely contrast a coughing man with a dying man. Conservative revolutionaries want to find out how the infection itself originated and why the man started to cough...' 'We believe', the conservative revolutionaries say, 'in God and in Providence. But we think the original source, God Himself, the Divine Source, contains the intention to organise this eschatological drama.' With this vision, modernism acquires a paradoxical character. It is not just an illness of today's world, but a discovery in today's world of a phenomenon which began to take root in the very same past that is so dear to traditionalists. Modernism is not improved as a result of this realisation by the conservative revolutionaries, while tradition loses its decisive positivity.

The basic formula of the Conservative Revolutionary Arthur Moeller van den Bruck is, 'The conservatives used to try to stop the revolution, but now we must lead it.' It means that in joining, modernism's destructive tendencies, in part out of pragmatism, one must identify and recognise the germ that served as the initial cause of its destructive tendencies — namely, modernism itself. Then the conservative must carefully and permanently root it out of existence and, in doing so, bring about God's secret, parallel, additional, and subtle design. The conservative revolutionaries want not only to slow time down as do liberal conservatives or to go back to the past like traditionalists, but to tear out the root of all evil in the world's fundamental structure.

The Conservative Choice

Contemporary Russian conservatism must be simultaneously non-Communist (the Communist dogma has always denied the fact that the Soviet regime was a continuation of tsarism and treated recent democratic reforms in an extremely negative light), non-liberal (liberalism is too revolutionary and insists on a radical break from both the Soviet past and the tsarist legacy), and non-monarchic (monarchism wants to exclude both the Soviet and the recent liberal democratic periods from national history).

The peculiarity of Russian political life in the twenty-first century is that its main stages have been in direct and severe conceptual opposition to each other and succeeded each other not through natural continuity, but through revolutions and radical disruptions. This seriously challenges the formula of contemporary Russian conservatism: the continuity and identity of Russia and the Russian people are not plainly visible on society's surface; in order to establish consistent conservative views, one must make an effort that will raise us to the level of a new historical, political, civilisational and national consolidation. Contemporary Russian conservatism is not a given, but a task to be undertaken.

Consistent Russian conservatism must combine the historical and geographical layers of our national existence. I would like to remind you that, during the very first years of Soviet rule, the Eurasianists insisted on the civilisational continuity of the USSR in relation to the Russian Empire.

Contemplating contemporary Russian conservatism is basically contemplating Eurasianism, which is a synthesis of Russian political history on the basis of a unique geopolitical and civilisational methodology. Russia, viewed as Eurasia, reveals its permanent essence and its historical identity — from the mosaic of Slavic, Turkic and Ugrian tribes through Kievan Rus'[24] and Muscovy to the great continental empire, first 'white' and then 'red', to today's democratic Russia, which is a little indecisive but is now pulling herself together for a new historical leap.

I am convinced that political history will very soon force us clarify our positions and polish our rhetoric to make it more precise. We have no choice but conservatism: we will be pushed towards it *from the outside*, as well as from within. But what shall we do with the spirit of revolution, the

---

24 Kievan Rus' was a loose tribal confederation that had its capital in Kiev, and from which the modern-day states of Russia, Ukraine and Belarus are descended. It lasted from the tenth until the thirteenth centuries.

will, the blazing flame of rebellion which secretly languishes in the Russian heart and disturbs our sleep, inviting us to follow it to faraway lands? I think that we should invest our continental strength in a new conservative project. And let it be the new edition of our Revolution, the Conservative Revolution, the National Revolution in the name of a big dream...

Putin, Conservatism and the *Siloviki*

The basic paradigm of Putin and his supporters is, I think, a universal conservatism, which includes everything from the liberally enlightened to the social and fundamental forms of conservatism. The alternatives are liberalism and Atlanticism, which have been held over from earlier times in the form of some of the personnel among the presidential administration and its experts and advisors. Putin is personally a supporter of the idea of economic and social mobilisation for the sake of strengthening Russia's national sovereignty. It can be referred to as 'active conservatism', 'radical conservatism' and even a call for a conservative revolution. Putin would like to give conservatism some consistency and political resilience. This movement is noticeably slowing down due to the unwillingness and passive attitude of state officials, centrist parties, and possibly even the masses; the policy is dampened by an entourage that blunts its vector. There is no intellectually concentrated focus, no adequate institutions, and no political instruments capable of undertaking it. This is the reason many of Putin's speeches are passively conservative, hinting only at achieving satisfaction and preserving the status quo. This is the principal contradiction of Putin and his rule: subjectively Putin realises and recognises the need for active conservative measures to drag the country out of stagnation, but he cannot properly implement such measures. There is ongoing passive sabotage of Putin's initiatives by members of the President's closest entourage.

The second source of resistance is the oligarchs. They do not see the necessity of strengthening the national administration and are quite satisfied with the status quo. They are only interested either in subduing conservatism, stripping it of ideology and deconstructing it (Pyotr Aven and Alfa-Bank),[25] or in a gradual transition to liberalism.

The third source is the diehard liberals. They are few and their paladin is Anatoly Chubais, whose primary focus is the economy and administration rather than ideology. That said, Chubais does not, in fact, disagree with the official course; he merely ignores it in a friendly manner, remaining loyal to the authorities.

But one cannot rule out the possibility of a repeat privatisation of major holdings, such as that which was carried out in the 1990s. This re-privatisation phenomenon is practiced by many capitalist countries, where the role of the state and the administrative institutions in the acquisition of property is very significant. The bureaucracy rotates and new greedy civil servants appear, who were once corrupted and are now begging for more, and the owners think that they have already paid in full. The conditions for a re-privatisation in Russia are maturing. Legally it can be arranged in any way necessary and it can be accomplished politically as an intermediate stage of re-nationalisation stage or disguised as patriotism.

The first scenario would be the nationalisation of natural resources, with a subsequent re-privatisation disguised as a change in management structure. The second scenario would be a public demonstration of the oligarchs' unpatriotic stance (i.e., the purchase of an expensive yacht or a foreign football club) with subsequent legal and criminal persecution fuelled by the people's anger. Then the property will find a new, patriotic owner: the management will not be improved, the civil servants will be satisfied, the people will be subdued for a time; some will gain, some will lose, and somebody will go to jail.

The law enforcement agencies are now promoting Putin's initial strategy aimed at putting the country in order. These agencies play a very practical role in Russian society. The technology that is used for the management of the enforcement agencies is obsolete; they still use things like IBM 386

---

25   Pyotr Aven (b. 1955) is a businessman who served as Minister of Foreign Economic Relations and as Russia's representative to the G7 in 1992–92. Today he is the head of Alfa-Bank, which is Russia's largest commercial bank.

computers.²⁶ The enforcement agencies respond very weakly to Vladimir Putin, and the entire system constantly undergoes clearly visible glitches. The fact that there is a gap between a President's task and the quality and speed of its execution is not surprising. As far as the prosecutor's office is concerned, this is quite normal. Russia has never been and will hardly become a nomocratic society. The notion of '*the truth*' is much more important that the notion of the '*law*', and the truth we adhere to is the Tsar's truth. The President (the Tsar, or the General Secretary)²⁷ in a country like Russia is playing and will always play the central role for the enforcement agencies.

Vladimir Putin and the Empire

'Russian leaders, particularly Prime Minister Vladimir Putin, want to resurrect the Russian Empire,' said the American Secretary of Defence, Robert Gates. As Gates puts it, these 'imperialistic intentions obstruct US-Russian relations'. The Secretary of Defence also believes that these 'imperialistic intentions' are more characteristic of Putin than of Medvedev. It is Putin who is doing his best to make Russia the main player in the international arena — a fact that greatly worries the US. 'Are the Russians condemned to yet another attempt to build an empire?' asks Geoffrey Hosking, a Professor at University College London, in his book *Rulers and Victims: The Russians in the Soviet Union*.²⁸ This worries the British as well: Hosking asks, 'What exactly will the Russians choose: the present state of affairs, where it has lost parts of its territory lost, or a new empire?'

Again: Who are You, Mr Putin?

This question, posed at the beginning of Putin's career, was formulated during the transmutation of contemporary Russia's political language from modernism into postmodernism. The classical modernism of the Enlight-

---

26   The IBM 386 model was first developed in the mid-1980s.

27   The title of the leader of the Communist Party during the Soviet era.

28   Geoffrey Hosking, *Rulers and Victims: The Russians in the Soviet Union* (Cambridge, Massachusetts: Belknap Press, 2006).

enment views Putin more as a human being, a personality with particular features, and less as a politician. In postmodernism, a personality is an empty spot — fragments of a discourse in a linguistic context. Vladimir Putin's image stems not from knowledge of him or from an analysis of his actions, but from language games.

When people who know our President well hear what is said about Putin in the West, they fall out of their chairs. This happens because the Putin the West has imagined does not exist. There are reports and language games about Putin being created in both Russia and Europe, and the ugly picture that the West is given of him has nothing at all to do with our President. Westerners sees Putin as a 'political dwarf' without any ideology, a protégé of the most reactionary circles and of the most horrible secret services; a person neither with any political future nor any respect for democracy. We, on the other hand, deal with another Putin. He is a product of our ceremonial, mostly officious style.

Putin as the Symbol of Empire-building

The new, large Russia to be resurrected within the Eurasian space is an idea of a new sovereign empire. It is not Soviet, because that ideology is dead, but not Russian either, because we have no common religious vector here. At the new stage Eurasianism proposes the resurrection of the *Large Eurasian Space* in place of the former Russian Empire and the Soviet Union. This project is in strong opposition to Russian Westernists as well as Atlanticists. Putin came out of the Atlanticist regime of Yeltsin, but completely reversed Yeltsin's policy in less than 6 years. At the outset, the main idea was to integrate Russia into the Western world in order to become, as they said, '*a normal country*'. Today's norm for our political establishment, apart from ultra-marginal scum, is another idea: Russia is a great country, a country re-establishing its universal significance and leading an independent policy free from globalist pressure and the unipolar world. This is a geopolitical programme of empire-building. Eurasianism today opposes two things: liberal-democratic Westernism and narrow nationalism, the latter of which presents Russia as a mono-national state. Putin's presidential policy is directed by this Eurasian code.

Jean Parvulesco: 'This Simply Cannot Be...'

What is especially striking about the French visionary writer Jean Parvulesco, known for his extravagant fantasies, is that all of his writings tend to come true over time. I read the articles that he wrote between 1976–1979 in the Italian magazine *Orion*, where he described a situation that actually came about in Russia in 1991–1993. It described the 'Red-Browns', the union of Communists and nationalists, as well as the liberal institutions which would unite with the West and destroy the great Soviet Union. At the time, many people who read his articles said that Parvulesco was insane. Brezhnevism was rampant, and the Soviet bloc seemed impervious. Even we, his friends, were saying: 'This just cannot be, Jean! 'This is nonsense!' His answer was 'Just wait, Alexander...'

In his book *Putin and the Eurasian Empire*, now published in Russia, Parvulesco argued that there were people in the Russian military and secret service who based their work on a geopolitical perspective and who nurtured the idea of resurrecting the Empire on a continental scale. He predicted that, sooner or later, a man would emerge from the secret service and implement the idea of restoring the imperial geopolitical potential of Russia beyond Communist ideology. He would be guided by the values ingrained in the very core of Russian history. He would revive Orthodoxy, restore national identity and bring Russia back to its pre-Communist values. Parvulesco wrote this in the 1970s, when nobody could even imagine it, and 20 years later Putin emerged. Parvulesco singled him out immediately: 'He is a man of destiny, I've always written about him. I wrote about him long before I knew his name.'

In Parvulesco's writing, Putin does not exist merely as a person. There is the Eurasian Empire, the 'dogmatic course', and the building of the Eurasian Empire with Putin as an instrument of its creation.

Whether or not Putin was chosen in the secret corridors of the Russian secret service to implement this empire-building feat remains a mystery. This cannot be either refuted or confirmed. The 'Vladimir Putin and the Eurasian Empire' project is not just the past, the present and the future. A visionary acts in a space where the past and future coexist. Many biblical prophets describe the design of eternity, and the non-visionary, non-prophetic Parvulesco does the same thing.

The Eurasian Empire is Integrated into the Dogmatic Course of Events

Parvulesco paints a striking picture, very different from both official Russian perceptions and the Western ideas of Putin. He makes Putin part of global history on a par with figures like Alexander the Great, Napoleon, de Gaulle, Stalin, Hitler, Lenin, the secret services and great conquests. Parvulesco notices the smallest details: Putin's chance phrase or a gesture made during a foreign trip — all that is sufficient for a postmodern insight into the dialectics of the Empire.

What Putin and his entourage think about this surprising and attractive image of a historical person is less important than the way we understand the essence and contexts of the imperial project within which such transformations are possible. As the German Romantic Novalis[29] once said, we learn more about the essence of ancient times from fairy tales than from detailed historical chronicles. Only totally inept and mentally deficient people, like the early Ludwig Wittgenstein or the positivists, can argue that a researcher needs *atomic facts*.[30] There are no such facts: they have been searched for by people more dedicated than these contemporary Russian philistines, indeed by piercing and acute minds. Putin as an actual person simply does not exist, and the version proposed by Jean Parvulesco deserves serious contemplation because intellectually, stylistically and visually it revolves around the very metaphysics of our Large Space and our great people. This is why 'Putin as the builder of the great Eurasian empire' is the most correct and realistic understanding of his mission, while all the junk that is churned out both against him and in his support will soon rot away.

---

29 Novalis, the pen name of Georg Philipp Friedrich Freiherr von Hardenberg (1772–1801), was a poet and philosopher. Novalis says this in his poem 'When Geometric Diagrams...'.

30 In the philosophy of Logical Atomism, an atomic fact is the simplest type of fact, consisting of a quality in some specific, individual thing, such as a thing's color. Under the assumption that language mirrors reality, it can be proposed that the world is composed of facts that are utterly simple and comprehensible.

Putin as the empire-builder will survive, even if he himself rejects this image. He will still constitute the portrait of our epoch, not only of Putin himself but of Russia. The Eurasian Empire is inevitably integrated in the dogmatic course of things. This is understood by Robert Gates and Geoffrey Hosking, as well as by the entire Western elite that rules the contemporary world. The Eurasian Empire was, is and always will be, and Putin is obviously connected with it.

Eurasianism as the New President's Ideology

The Eurasian ideology is in perfect accord with the historical mission facing Vladimir Putin. The main problems of the current political situation are absence of a genuine consolidation of the political class around Putin, the uncertainty of the centrist parties' positions, the willingness of certain high-ranking officials to grab the opportunity to directly confront the President with the support of some important forces in the media and intelligentsia, and the preservation of an anti-Russian stance in the European Union and certain Republican circles in the US.

The 'inertial' (sluggish) scenario in the development of the political situation today, specifically the preservation of key tendencies (an apparent stability and the status quo) is unlikely. One should bear in mind some additional scenarios. Eurasianism is especially optimal as an ideology for the President to use in a critical situation. Eurasianism will add substance to the President's political position — a substance that was outlined at the beginning of his first term, but then postponed, effaced and replaced by tricks and superficial shows staged by political strategists.

Eurasianism will infuse a patriotic policy (a national idea) with active political content. Eurasianism mobilises not only the mostly passive forces that sympathise with the cause of strengthening the Russian statehood (the Russian majority, civil servants, and the masses), but also the active layers of society that have a neutral or even negative attitude towards this project (national and religious minorities, the intelligentsia, business magnates). Small people fighting for a great Russia!

Eurasianism proposes an unambiguous scenario for an international strategy: the middle path between globalisation and isolationism; it is 'partial globalisation' or the 'globalisation of Large Spaces.' This model implies a differentiating attitude towards other 'Large Spaces': European, American, Pacific, Arabic. This allows Russia to accumulate its internal potential and skilfully manoeuvre between the interests of other geopolitical poles for her own benefit.

Eurasianism involves infusing all the pro-presidential forces and, more broadly, all layers of society that realise their personal dependency on the cause of strengthening the Russian state with political content.

The potential size of the electorate that supports Putin as he is and which will be especially eager to support a Eurasian President is much broader than those ideologically lacklustre, artificial partisan entities with little potential for mobilisation and clumsy politics. Besides, proper handling of the Eurasian ideology will give the new President the possibility to choose a certain part of the national and socially-oriented electorate, which will give serious support to the political (Left-wing) opposition (the new President will not risk losing the support of the Right-wing sector due to the direct dependence on the Kremlin of some of these forces and the insignificant political share possessed by this sector as a whole).

Eurasianism foresees an ideological base to conduct a 'crusade' against extremism and various terrorist ideologies — radical Islamism, national separatism, superpower chauvinism and social (Left-wing) radicalism. Besides, Eurasianism not only fundamentally and substantively validates the necessity of strong ideological opposition to such things, but offers a positive alternative in the form of the values accepted and defended by Eurasianism itself: traditional Islam, the theory of the rights of the peoples and of ethnocultural autonomies (without prospective political segregation), geopolitical Eurasian patriotism, and a moderate, socially-oriented economic system. Eurasianism not only destroys the opponent ideologically, it also attracts the hesitant masses, which otherwise might stand in opposition to Russian statehood and the new President.

Eurasianism has its own formula for all the principal economic strata of Russian society. In the electoral sense, it appeals to the 'dispossessed majority' — to the working class that makes up the majority of voting Russians. Here social rhetoric comes to the forefront (social justice, nationalisation of natural resources rent, etc.). The cadres of Eurasianism are formed, in contrast, from representatives of medium-size and small businesses who have an adequate share of efficient and energetic civil servants (capable of mobilisation). For powerful Russian magnates, Eurasianism proposes to heighten their awareness of the direct connection between their business structures and the geopolitical destiny of Russian statehood itself (which is typical of all large national and transnational companies in the US, Europe, Japan, etc.). Thus, the Eurasian economy model satisfies the demand of the masses for social justice, encourages middle class initiatives, and inspires geopolitical responsibility in the magnates.

Eurasianism today is the ideological basis of the Eurasian political party, which will soon be restored. This party does not have opportunistic ambitions and does not aim to be in competition with other political-partisan projects. The Eurasia Party[31] should be viewed not as an alternative to the other pro-presidential parties but as a political and ideological laboratory for the development of a national strategy and ideology for the new President. Thus, Eurasianism can evolve quickly from a party ideology via a presidential ideology to an ideology of the state.

Putin and Eurasian Integration

The processes of integration in the territory of the former Soviet Union have always been a painful subject for Russian politicians. After the creation of an amorphous group with uncertain functions and the equally obscure name 'Commonwealth of Independent States' in the place of the USSR, no serious developments towards a large-scale integration took place in the former USSR. This was not due to the unwillingness of the leaders of the newly formed states: some of them, notably Kazakhstan's President Nursultan Nazarbayev, were actively engaged in the development of the economic and political integration of the CIS countries. In the 1990s, Belarus' leaders showed an acute interest in integration. The reason for the slowing down of

---

31   The Eurasia Party, established in 2002, is the political arm of the Eurasia Movement.

the integration projects in the post-Soviet space lies in the unwillingness of the Russian leaders themselves to deal with this problem.

Throughout the 1990s, Russian leaders, during those rare moments when they were capable of intellectual activity, thought that help would come from abroad, that Russia would fuse into the family of advanced democratic nations and would live its happy, fair bourgeois life. The awakening came in the late 1990s, when, following the bombing of Yugoslavia and the start of the second Chechnya campaign, a sense of understanding dawned on the existing elite: if the West is ever going to stomach Russia, it will do so only piece by piece. The threat of our country's disintegration not only forced them to strengthen the 'vertical power,' but to engage in foreign relations in earnest, primarily with the CIS. It turned out that while Russia was content to engage in bilateral negotiations with Belarus, the issues of multilateral CIS integration were already being tackled by Washington, which established organisations such as the GUAM Organisation for Democracy and Economic Development.[32]

Vladimir Putin was the first to realise that our previous course was headed towards a dead end. It was during Putin's presidency that Russia chose the path towards CIS integration (economic, military and political, from the creation of EurAsEC to the negotiations regarding the creation of a union with Belarus). Today it is hard to imagine Russia's foreign policy and global international relations in general without such organisations as the Collective Security Treaty Organisation (CSTO),[33] the Eurasian Economic Community (EurAsEC), the Shanghai Cooperation Organisation

---

32   GUAM stands for Georgia, Ukraine, Azerbaijan, and Moldova. It was established in 2001 as a means of accelerating democratic and economic reforms in these countries, and of creating the basis for eventual integration with Europe. In Russia it is seen as an American-backed plot to attempt to take these countries out of Russia's economic orbit, since the CIS also wishes to see these nations reintegrated with Russia.

33   The CSTO was formed in 1992 as a military alliance between the CIS states of Russia, Armenia, Kazakhstan, Kyrgyzstan, Tajikistan, and Uzbekistan. Azerbaijan, Georgia, and Uzbekistan subsequently withdrew.

(SCO)[34] and the Common Free Market Zone (CFMZ).[35] All of these organisations were established during Putin's presidency. Besides, the role of Russia, Kazakhstan and Belarus as the three staples of Eurasian integration in the CIS territory is due, in no small part, to the personal confidential relations between Vladimir Putin, Nursultan Nazarbayev and Alexander Lukashenko. The consequence of these confidential relations was the fact that the degree of cooperation regarding integration between the three countries is fairly high. As a result, Vladimir Putin resolved to create the Customs Union in 2006, which included all three countries within the EurAsEC.

Allow me to be straightforward: without Putin's participation, further integration would have been problematic. For example, integration suffered a blow with Gazprom's sanctions against Belarus, which were aimed at raising the gas prices for an allied nation, just as they were raised for the then hostile, 'orange' Ukraine. Kazakhstan would not want to experience such blows either: after the signing of the agreement on the construction of the Caspian Coastal Pipeline, Kazakhstan will deliver its gas to Europe via a Gazprom pipeline system and will be dependent on the prices set by this company. Nazarbayev would prefer to deal with a man who could, if necessary, clamp down on the gas behemoth in the interests of Russia and the common interests of the Customs Union and EurAsEC. The only way we could reach a mutual understanding on this issue with the majority of CIS countries, primarily Belarus and Kazakhstan, is by putting the integration into the hands of a person like Vladimir Putin.

Kazakhstan resolved to sign the Caspian Coastal Pipeline construction agreement, binding itself to Gazprom purchase prices solely based on the belief that unification processes of the post-Soviet space, which includes, *inter alia*, the fuel transportation issue, will be implemented by Putin. The actions of Putin, as well as of Russian leaders in general (in particular the Foreign Ministry), have recently confirmed that Putin will play a crucial role in the process of intensive Eurasian integration.

---

34   The SCO was formed in 2001 as a military and economic alliance between China, Russia, Kazakhstan, Kyrgyzstan, Tajikistan, and Uzbekistan.

35   The CFMZ is an economic cooperation treaty between Russia, Belarus, and Kazakhstan.

Vladimir Putin's landmark article about the creation of the Eurasian Union was published on 3 October 2011 in the newspaper *Izvestija*.[36] The theses proposed by Putin implied that the Eurasian Union, similar to the European Union, will be a single economic space in which immigration and border barriers will be removed between them. The steps taken by Putin after the publication of his article demonstrate that this was not merely words. The fact that he started to consistently implement the projects of the Customs Union, the creation of a free economic zone in the CIS and so on, show that we are dealing with a strategy and a programme.

The Project of Putin's Return: The Multipolar World

The Eurasian Union is not merely an economic initiative, although Putin stresses its economic aspect. If it were solely about the economy, why not stop at the creation of the EurAsEC, the Common Free Market Zone or the Customs Union? Putin talks about creating a Eurasian Union, which hints at something much more expansive. Since Kazakhstan's president Nazarbayev developed this model, and since our Eurasian Movement has been engaged in the issues of Eurasian integration and the creation of the Eurasian Union for many years, I can say with confidence that this is more than just an economic project: this is a political strategy, and Putin has set out to implement it. If Medvedev started his presidency with a project of modernisation, Putin marked his comeback with the creation of the Eurasian Union.

What is the Eurasian Union? It is, in effect, a political philosophy built around three main principles which form its cores. The first core is the necessity of the construction of a multipolar world as opposed to the unipolar world based on American hegemony that was criticised by Putin in his Munich speech. The project is not the construction of a global 'pole free' world with a non-existent centre, which would in effect disguise the domination of transnational corporations and the rule of the global elites.

---

36 An English translation of this article is available at www.russianmission.eu/en/news/article-prime-minister-vladimir-putin-new-integration-project-eurasia-future-making-izvestia-3-.

Neither a 'pole-free' nor a unipolar world is suitable for Putin. He speaks about a multipolar world with several regional poles of influence. Their balance creates a fair system of the distribution of powers and influence zones.

The multipolar world principle brings forth the second core of the Eurasian political philosophy: the integration of the post-Soviet space. This is the focus of Putin's programme right now. Russia alone cannot be an independent and complete pole in the multipolar world. In order to build this pole, Russia needs allies and integration processes in the post-Soviet space. It needs Kazakhstan, Belarus, Ukraine, Moldova, Armenia, and possibly Azerbaijan. It needs access to the depths of Central Asia represented by Kyrgyzstan, Tajikistan, and possibly Uzbekistan and even Turkmenistan. This is a long-term goal, but the creation of a pole of the multipolar world is necessary. Uniting our energy, economic, military and strategic potentials, as well as the territorial zones where natural resources are extracted and their delivery routes, we will transform ourselves into a genuine world power and into a real global player. We will return to the historical arena as a civilisation: the ultimate result of the creation of a multipolar world.

The third core of Eurasian political philosophy is the transformation of Russia from the liberal democratic model which was copied from the West during the 1990s into an altogether unique, Russian model of development. The peculiarity of our society is that we don't have a proper bourgeois nation, a single civil society based on individualistic, liberalist principles like America or Europe. The Russian system of values is radically different, and this system has both strategic unity around the Russian core and the polyphony of its ethnic groups — not nations but ethnic groups — that live in Russia's territories, in the post-Soviet space, and which constitute a civilisational unity. This is what Eurasianism in domestic policy is about: single strategic management, a single state and various ethnic groups, each of which does not represent a national or political entity but rather parts of the spiritual treasure of our common state. In the summer of 2011, Putin spoke about the necessity of differentiating between a nation and an *ethnos*. A nation is a single, unified state while ethnoses are multiple and different. It is very important here to avoid both separatist nationalism (small nationalism) and the nationalism of a 'big people'. These nationalistic models are incompatible with the Eurasian nature of our society. If we want to preserve, strengthen and expand our zone of influence, we must be Eurasians and base our politics on a Eurasian political philosophy. Putin declared all of this when he began to implement the Eurasian project.

I think that after a while, perhaps in a year or two, a serious refurbishing of our political system will be in order: a two-way shift in the balance of power between the centre and the regions. On the one hand, I think such notions as a 'national republic' within Russia will fall by the wayside. But, simultaneously, an expansion of the rights of ethnic groups will take place, along with policies aimed at strengthening and culturally reviving the linguistic, religious and cultural communities of the Russian territories. In other words, a two-way balance should be kept: at once centralised and decentralised under a Eurasian model, which is radically different from the idea of establishing a single individualistic civil society. This Eurasian political philosophy will be embodied by Putin after March 2012, and this is all very serious. As a Eurasianist, I surely know what actions will be taken next and what further actions will be taken after such significant strategic moves.

Eurasianism

The only strategy which lives up to the historical moment, to the new balance of power and the general mood of the masses, is Eurasianism. It is Eurasianism that can be an ultimate, genuine idea for Russia, as well as a strategy to stick to. Such a national idea has not previously existed in Russia: mostly, the country was torn between liberalism, which dominated the corrupt pro-Western elites, and the disparate, inconsistent and contradictory elements of nationalism which, in effect, aimed at the disintegration of Russia. This is why I am absolutely convinced that Putin must bet on the Eurasian model.

Putin's presidency over the next 12 years cannot follow the previous model. His potential for legitimacy has almost run dry and will not last long. The age of technology instead of the age of ideology, PR-campaigns instead of strategies, pop songs and gags instead of national ideas, is now over. The challenges of the new stage are incomparably more serious than those that Putin confronted and overcame before. If Putin tries to return to the same old models in his domestic and foreign policy, a collapse will become imminent. This is a new cycle and in order to assert himself in it and gain legitimacy, Putin needs a new strategy.

For a long time, Putin was kept from implementing this new strategy. All attempts to get Eurasian ideas across to him were blocked either by PR specialists who turned everything into a hotchpotch, or by ideological enemies — liberals and pro-Westerners. If Putin wants to be legitimate today, he will have to count on Eurasianism, because it also conforms to the multi-religious and polyethnic spirit of Russia, serves as the basis for the integration of the post-Soviet space and, in international politics, justifies the necessity of a multipolar world and the creation of a polycentric model. Polycentrism is often cited by Lavrov.[37] He recently mentioned the Eurasian Union during a UN session.

This is a new topic, and previously our leaders had never mentioned this Union. But it is Nazarbayev's long-cherished idea, as well as the idea of our own Eurasian Movement. The Eurasian Union has already become a political integration project. Previously, there had been no place for it; it had simply never been mentioned in official speeches. The people in the presidential administration, who were in charge of ideology in our country during the Yeltsin era, opposed the idea of the Eurasian Union at every turn. But this is over now, and the fact that Putin himself makes mention of the Eurasian Union is very telling.

Implementation of this project will require competent people, decisiveness and political will. This is a major problem. Putin can be dissuaded, and everything he has said may become merely empty rhetoric. The team in Putin's entourage responsible for ideological and political issues has extensive experience in doing away with ideological aspirations, and they can effectively turn an idea into a PR-campaign or a farce.

Again, the Western countries will do their best to prevent Eurasian integration, because it is an alternative world order to theirs. It is possible that Putin will be made to abandon the idea by force because they have too

---

37 Sergei Lavrov (b. 1950) has been the Foreign Minister of Russia since 2004.

much at stake. He will have to fight for his project. In my opinion, he could have introduced the idea back in 2001, but we can assume that he was pressured not to.

If Putin acts according to an 'inertial' model, drawing on semi-totalitarian, semi-postmodernist political consultants, he will likely fail. He will be declared an enemy of the West and simultaneously lose credibility within patriotic circles. Putin will be blown out of the water from both sides: he will be attacked by liberals and not supported by patriots. His only hope is Eurasianism. I think that if Putin does not become a Eurasianist in his next term, he will simply cease to be. He was right when he said, 'Russia will either be great or it will be nothing.'

Integration of Civilisations, Postmodernist Style

The EurAsEC and the Customs Union can be viewed as the economic entities of the Eurasian Union. The composition of the member countries within these integration structures is the core of the Eurasian Union. But the Eurasian Union is also a project of political integration. Nursultan Nazarbayev proposes to follow the European Union model. He even wrote a Constitution for the Eurasian Union, which replicates its European counterpart. So another question arises: what is the European Union, a confederacy, a national state or a new form of organisation for a political space, such as a 'postmodern state', as proposed by Robert Cooper?[38]

I assume that the Eurasian Union needs a special political theory — a theory of the multipolar world. Its subjects and actors should be not traditional modernist states (as in the Westphalian system),[39] but civilisations: a civilisation as a union. The entire international system should be reassessed

---

38   Robert Cooper (b. 1947) is a former British diplomat who subsequently worked for the European Union and currently is a member of the European Council on Foreign Relations. On 7 April 2002 he published an essay, 'The New Liberal Imperialism', in *The Guardian* in which he discusses the idea of the 'postmodern state'. The full text is available at www.theguardian.com/world/2002/apr/07/1.

39   The Thirty Years' War ended with the Peace of Westphalia in 1648, in which the nations of Europe recognised each others' territorial integrity. Some historians consider it to have been the first step in the development of the modern-day system of international relations.

for this purpose. This means that the Eurasian Union should become a new political entity with certain characteristics of a confederate state based on subsidiarity and broad regional autonomy, as well as certain traits of strategic centralism which is typical of classical empires.

The idea of the Eurasian Union is an idea of alternative postmodernism, different from both state-centric modernism and pre-modernist empires. Its main difference from pre-modernist empires is that the principle of political organisation of an international system on the grounds of a civilisation becomes a rational construct, and is reflected and described in technical terms. There is civilisation as inertia and as a *project*. Eurasianism proposes a project — that is, a forceful, constructed goal.

Today Putin speaks about the Eurasian Union as an intermediary project between Europe and the Asian-Pacific region, but this intermediary project is only the beginning. Europe was not built in a day and the fact that it bypassed a political aspect during its integration has yielded certain repercussions today. The economy alone is not a sufficient basis for building anything significant. The economy is a very unreliable entity and does not determine the course of history. *One should integrate on the basis of a project, an idea, and a common historical destiny — on the basis of the common civilisation and value system.* This is a strong combination capable of overcoming any obstacles. It could serve as the basis for the formation of a specific identity for Russia itself.

Putin will have to act decisively. The critical moment is approaching and he will have to act, whether he wants to or not.

In order to realise the idea of the Eurasian Union, it is necessary to reassess the entire existing international system. The Union is possible only if it is based on the theory of the multipolar world: this should be the starting point, and not the technical measures of economic integration. The establishment of a free market zone is a very important move towards the creation of the Customs Union at the CIS level, but the EU crisis has taught us that economics alone is not enough for a lasting integration. Absent a common political project and proper geopolitics, it is impossible to make anything stable. We should take that into account when building the Eurasian Union.

Eurasianism is a political philosophy which cannot be strictly classified as Right-wing and Orthodox-monarchic or as Left-wing, Communist, and socialist, let alone liberal. It is something original, painfully built throughout the course of the entire twentieth century. Eurasianism has a hundred-year-long history. Thus, this political philosophy has a history and a canon of texts, which is very important for any doctrine. as well as a Eurasian analysis of different historical periods. Starting with the First World War, it includes the works of Pyotr Savitsky and Nikolai Trubetzkoy, and in the 1960s and the 1970s came the works of Lev Gumilev.[40] We joined the movement in the 1980s and are continuing this line of thought. We analyse the events that have been unfolding for the last 25 years in terms of Eurasianism. Eurasianism is a hundred-year-old political philosophy. It was not simply formed and then discarded; it has perpetuated its existence. It exists in contemporary Russia as a compendium of political philosophy based on three principal aspects.

The Three Pillars of Putin

First. When it comes to foreign policy, the theory of the multipolar world should play a decisive role. I teach the sociology of international relations in the Sociology Department at Moscow State University, and I have found, to my surprise, that the theory of a multipolar world simply does not exist, although it has been fully developed in Eurasianism. Eurasianism is a multipolar world theory (MWT), not simply the desire for multipolarity. If we try and sum up the basic principles of the MWT, they are as follows:

1. A multipolar world is a radical alternative to the unipolar world (which exists now) in that it insists on several independent and sovereign centres of global strategic decision-making on a planetary scale.
2. These centres should be equipped and be materially independent to be able to defend their sovereignty in the face of a direct inva-

---

40 Lev Gumilev (1912–1992) was a Soviet anthropologist who attempted to explain ethnic differences through geological factors, especially in his book *Ethnogenesis and the Biosphere* (Moscow: Progress Publishers, 1990). He has been very influential on modern Eurasianism.

sion by a potential enemy, personified by today's most advanced power. This requirement basically implies the possibility to confront the material and military-strategic hegemony of the US and the NATO countries.
3. Many decision-making centres are not obliged to recognise the universality of Western norms and values as *sine qua non*[41] (democracy, liberalism, the free market, parliamentarism, human rights, individualism, cosmopolitanism, etc.) and can be fully independent of the spiritual hegemony of the West.
4. A multipolar world does not involve a return to the bipolar system, because there is not a single force today that can strategically or ideologically confront the material and spiritual hegemony of the contemporary West and its leader, the US. There should be more than two poles.
5. The multipolar world does not seriously consider the sovereignty of existing national states. Such sovereignty is confined to legal terminology and is not confirmed by sufficient enforcement, strategic, economic and political potential. In order to be a sovereign subject in the twenty-first century, a national state is no longer enough. Real sovereignty can only be possessed by an aggregate, a coalition of states. The Westphalian system, which still exists today, does not reflect the reality of the system of international relations and should be reconsidered.
6. Multipolarity is not an equivalent of either bipolarity or multilaterality because it does not place its decision-making centre (pole) either under the jurisdiction of a world government or under the club of the US or its democratic allies ('the global West'), nor at the sub-national level, under NGOs or other instances of civil society. This pole must be located elsewhere.

These six points set the pace for further developments and are a condensed expression of the main features of multipolarity. But this description, albeit significantly enhancing our understanding of multipolarity, is not yet a com-

---

[41] A condition without which something cannot exist.

plete theory. It is just a preliminary conclusion, a launch pad for further comprehensive theoretical thinking.

Secondly, there is the imperative of the integration of the post-Soviet space stemming from the above multipolarity. One can say that in a historical context, it is the restoration of the Russian Empire and the USSR on new terms. As the Russian Empire was different from the USSR, so the Eurasian Union is different from both the USSR and the Russian Empire. There is a different ideological base, different mechanisms, different actors and different integration models in play. In one case it is colonisation, in the other a socialist revolution, and in our case it is a voluntary specific integration model similar to the European Union, under the model outlined by Nursultan Nazarbayev in 1994.[42] But this theory of the integration of the post-Soviet space actually exists, and such is the second aspect of the Eurasian political philosophy.

Its third and final aspect is the socio-political structure of Russia. Eurasianism proposes a specific answer. We reject the creation of a national state, which leads to the levelling of all ethnic cultures existing within the territory of Russia. We reject the model of a civil society based on the principle of individualism which underlies the European Union, and we reject the model of ethnic separatism in which ethnic groups strive for political independence. These form the basis of the political Eurasian project for the Russian Federation: a single strategic management and a polyphony of ethnic cultures. We likewise reject any attributes of political independence within the Russian Federation (sovereignty or even the status of a national republic). Ramzan Kadyrov was absolutely right when he refused the presidential post and called himself 'the head of the Chechen republic'. This must become the norm.

The next necessary step is the abolition of the status of national republics. That said, Eurasianism does not want to diminish the ethnic, religious or cultural rights of any communities living within Russian territory. Both nation-

---

42   Nazarbayev outlined the idea for a Eurasian Union in a speech he delivered at Moscow University in May 1994.

alists and liberals accuse us of trying to do this, but we support Konstantin Leontiev's 'flourishing complexity'.[43]

The Constitution of the Russian Federation was copied from its European equivalents and not adapted to our cultural specifics. It contains a lot of mutually contradicting theses. For instance, it states that the subjects of the Federation are independent states and continues to say that the only sovereignty is possessed by the Russian Federation. This Constitution can be interpreted any way you like: in a Eurasian, nationalistic or liberal separatist way. This Constitution was largely the basis of the conflicts and bloody wars of the 1990s, and in itself it requires interpretation, not rewriting, which is something Putin is successfully accomplishing. He progressed from viewing the subjects of the Federation as possessing state status via the appointment of their leaders to the obvious reduction of their status as states.

Thus, we will create the possibility for both the preservation of territorial integrity and a possible integration of the post-Soviet space, without infringing on the rights of its indigenous peoples. In this regard, Russians don't even have their own federal subject, and they don't need it. We are a state-forming core. The Russians can speak their language wherever they want and all other Russian citizens, both Russians and non-Russians, must know the Russian language.

As for the protection of the rights of the indigenous peoples, this point is included in the Constitution. The ethnic processes are very complex. As a specialist in ethnic sociology, I can say that a definitive nomenclature of ethnic groups is unattainable. These groups vanish, emerge and split. Certain ethnic groups view themselves as something separate, such as the

---

43   Konstantin Leontiev (1831–1891) was a conservative philosopher who opposed democracy and liberalism. He believed that an alliance between Russia and Eastern nations such as India and China could help to ward off Western influences. He described 'flourishing complexity' as the second phase in the historical cycle of a civilisation in his book *The East, Russia, and Slavdom* (no English translation exists).

Mishari,[44] and the Kryashens.[45] They can be distinguished as separate ethnic groups based on religion or otherwise, and they can view themselves as a separate cultural or even ethnocultural phenomenon.

This is the reason why ethnic groups must not obtain legal status. Nevertheless, the authorities must constitutionally respect the rights of all ethnic groups and peoples which exist within the territory of the Russian Federation.

Eurasianism contains answers to all questions: from housing and utilities reforms to healthcare. In social politics, Eurasianism leans towards the Left, towards the socialist position. One can note Eurasianism's kinship with socialism, albeit not in a doctrinal, Marxist or atheistic sense but rather in an Orthodox or Islamic sense (in terms of the structure of Islamic communities).

Eurasianists are not dogmatists. Eurasianists have always called into question some elements of their programme. What matters is that economics must be organic, fair and holistic — that is, based on the principle of integrity. I personally like socialism, but I think that this issue is open to debate and discussion. On the other hand, with respect to the principle of multipolarity, we fully support Nazarbayev's idea of multipolar currencies, which states that every region of the world must have its own currency. We oppose dollar imperialism.

The Eurasian Union and the US

The US attitude towards the Eurasian Union will without a doubt be radically and expressly hostile. The creation of the Eurasian Union directly contradicts the adopted strategy of the US national security apparatus, which aims at unipolarity. The US seeks to prevent the emergence of a political, economic and military-strategic entity in Europe capable of limiting American control over the European zone. This was stated in Paul Wolfowitz'

---

44   The Mishar Tatars are a subgroup of the Volga Tatars.

45   The Kryashens are Tatars who are a subgroup of the Volga Tatars. Unlike most Tatars they are Orthodox Christians.

'Defense Planning Guidance' (1992)[46] and later fully reiterated in principal American strategy documents.

The creation of the Eurasian Union means the rejection of American hegemony and the transition towards building a multipolar world. In this world, the US may remain a great power, but only regionally, not internationally. Nobody in Washington seems to be prepared for this. It will result in a tangible conflict between Atlanticism and Eurasianism (which never really stopped anyway), a great war of the continents.

The Eurasian Union is a key pole in the multipolar world in a strategic, political and economic sense. Obviously, Eurasia's main strength is in its energy and natural resources. Nuclear weapons and huge territories are also of great importance. All of this leads to impressive geopolitical potential. At the same time, the Eurasian Union lacks access to advanced technologies, industrial potential, dynamic technical development and a sufficient consumer market. This makes Eurasia dependent on Europe and Asia, but not on the US.

This is why the successful establishment of the Eurasian Union requires a Eurasian-European and a Eurasian-Chinese partnership: 'Great Europe from Lisbon to Vladivostok' (as Vladimir Putin wrote) and the Moscow-Beijing axis.[47] Besides, the Eurasian Union would greatly benefit from a partnership with the Islamic world, as well as with Latin America, the Asian-Pacific countries and Africa. They are all potential poles of the multipolar world.

None of them is perfect and every pole lacks certain resources. Together, on the basis of a dialogue of civilisations, we can build a balanced and

---

46 The document was leaked to *The New York Times*, which led to an article, 'U.S. Strategy Plan Calls for Insuring No Rivals Develop' by Patrick E Tyler, published on 8 March 1992. The article is available at www.nytimes.com/1992/03/08/world/us-strategy-plan-calls-for-insuring-no-rivals-develop.html. The document came to be known as the 'Wolfowitz Doctrine', and came to be seen as an early statement of neoconservative thought on foreign policy and a forerunner of the policies that were later adopted by the George W. Bush administration.

47 Putin used this phrase in conjunction with a suggestion for a free trade agreement between Russia and Europe in an editorial published in the *Süddeutsche Zeitung* on 23 November 2010.

fair world order. Will all conflicts be immediately resolved? No. They can spring up at any time. Nevertheless, there are always ways to avoid them. Instead of wars and conflicts, we should start a peaceful dialogue. The clash of civilisations is not fatal in itself.

One must learn to build an international system on the basis of broad and thoughtful social and cultural anthropology and not on the basis of Western-style American-European cultural racism, colonialist liberalism, or totalitarian universalism based on purely Western values (which are individualistic, market-oriented, and capitalist). To achieve this, Putin will need a new kind of political elite: dedicated, tough and morally sound.

The Avant-Garde Nature of Neo-Eurasianism

Neo-Eurasianism, which appeared in Russia in the late 1980s and was developed by me and my colleagues from the Eurasia Party and the International Eurasia Movement, fully absorbed the elements of the previous Eurasian episteme, but complemented them with elements of traditionalism, geopolitics, structuralism, Heidegger's fundamental ontology, sociology and anthropology. We have done extensive work to accommodate the basic principles of Eurasianism to the reality of the second half of the twentieth and early twenty-first centuries, in light of the latest scientific developments and research.

If we are to take the Eurasian model of empire-building seriously, Putin will have to focus on the following aspects of it:

1. Eurasianism and neo-Eurasianism pertain to conservative ideologies and have the features of both fundamental conservatism (traditionalism) and the Conservative Revolution (including the social conservatism of the Left-wing Eurasians). The only movement that Eurasianists reject in conservatism is liberal conservatism, which continues to dominate Russia's domestic policy.
2. Eurasianism, aware of the universal aspirations of the Western *logos*,[48] refuses to accept this universality as inevitable. This is a key aspect of Eurasianism. It perceives Western culture as a local and

---

48 Classical Greek: 'idea', in the sense of an ordering principle.

transient phenomenon and asserts the multiplicity of cultures and civilisations which coexist at different points in a historical cycle. Modernism for Eurasians is a purely Western phenomenon and other cultures must expose these claims to Western universality for what they are in order to base their societies on their own, domestic values. There is no single historical process. Every nation has its own historical model that moves at different speeds and sometimes in different directions. Eurasianism is, in effect, epistemological pluralism. The unitary system of modernism, including science, politics, culture and anthropology, is contrasted with a multiplicity of epistemes built around the fundamentals of every existing civilisation: the Eurasian episteme for the Russian civilisation, the Chinese episteme for the Chinese civilisation, the Islamic for the Islamic civilisation, the Hindu for the Hindu civilisation, and so forth. It is only on the basis of these epistemes, stripped of Western features, that further socio-political, cultural and economic projects and constructions should be built.

In the twentieth century, modernity and Western civilisation were criticised not only by Eurasianist Russians but by Western thinkers as well: Spengler and Toynbee,[49] and especially by the structuralists, primarily by Lévi-Strauss,[50] the creator of structural anthropology. Structural anthropology is based upon the principal equality of different cultures, from the primitive to the most advanced. In this view, Western culture has no claim to superiority over even the most 'savage' and 'primitive' tribe. It should be noted that the Eurasianists Roman Jakobson[51] and Nikolai Trubetzkoy, the founders of phonology and the major representatives of structural linguistics in Russia, were Lévi-Strauss' teachers and taught him the basics

---

49 Arnold J. Toynbee (1889–1975) was a British historian who wrote a 12-volume study of the cycles of civilisations, A Study of History, between 1934 and 1961.

50 Claude Lévi-Strauss (1908–2009) was the most influential anthropologist of the twentieth century.

51 Roman Jakobson (1896–1982) was a Russian linguist who was one of the founders of what came to be called structuralism. He fled the Soviet Union just prior to the Second World War and lived for the remainder of his life in the United States.

of structural analysis that he readily acknowledged. Thus, an intellectual continuity can be traced: Eurasianism to structuralism to neo-Eurasianism. Neo-Eurasianism becomes in this sense a restoration of a broad range of ideas, insights and intuitions outlined by the first Eurasianists, which organically included the results of scientific activities carried out by various schools and authors (mostly conservative) that were developing simultaneously throughout the twentieth century.

Putin has declared his intention to build the Eurasian Union, but there are certain doubts.

Will the project of the Eurasian Union be confined to the economic integration of the post-Soviet space? Will Putin be able to insist on this Union as a strategic vector in Russia's development towards Eurasianism? Note that contemporary world globalism and the international liberal hegemony will resist this project and pressure the President by any means possible. Will Putin withstand this international pressure? Can the technical component of the Eurasian Union cancel out its strategic, attitudinal, historical and spiritual meaning? Will this vector of development help us draw important conclusions? Is the President capable of such a great construction? Can he see all the advantages and prospects of this project? Let's face it: in purely technical terms, the project will most likely fail because it has too many opponents and objections. The implementation of this project will require incredible will and determination. If it works, we will establish a theoretical and material base for the realisation of the multipolar world theory, and we will effectively implement the concept of Large Spaces united similarly to the European Union in place of national states. In this case, we will actualise the idea of multiple civilisations instead of a single global civilisation as promoted by the West. In this historical deed, we will enable the rejection of the individualism that is central to the liberal model and replace it with a pluralism of values, as well as the establishment of peoples, ethnic groups, religions and cultures as independent subjects. Their mentalities should not necessarily be moulded to accommodate Western requirements. And last, but not least is the revival of our common motherland — Great Russia at a new historical stage.

The West will be the first to object to this project, and they will be followed by the fifth column inside the country. Russian citizens will have questions about the advantages and benefits of such unification as well, namely, whether the construction of the great Eurasian project would have a negative impact on their standard of living for the sake of some sort of global achievement or special mission. But all the above-mentioned questions pale before this one: is Putin really standing on the threshold of Russian revival and thinking and acting in accordance with Russian history and the spirit of the people, moving towards the Eurasian Union, or is this yet another mirage which will dissipate as soon as we confront the first problems?

The Russian Order: The Relevance of the New *Oprichnina*

Eurasianism and the Elites

There is a concept called 'Eurasian selection'. This is a model developed by the first Eurasianists that is used to determine what sort of people should head the state. They analysed the experience of Genghis Khan, the steppe empires that emphasised military virtues (loyalty, honour, and 'long will'):[52] that is, specific ethical qualities which must serve as the basis of the selection of the Eurasian elites. Today's Russian elite does not meet these criteria.

Naturally, the best way to create an adequate political elite is through revolutions and wars. In such cases the strongest, the aristocracy, come to power. A time of peace is usually the time of mediocre leaders or sub-passionaries. According to Gumilev, there are a hundred sub-passionaries per

---

52 According to Lev Gumilev, in ancient Mongol civilisation, warriors who were dissatisfied with being subject to the authority of the elders of their tribes would sometimes leave the tribe and go off on their own, becoming known as 'people of long will'.

one true passionary.[53] They are different from the masses in that they want something but cannot achieve it, and they make up a class of the 'sub-elite'.

There is a popular Eurasian slogan: 'career or revolution'. If one can get a career, he will get on in life. If not, he will opt for a revolution. The only thing that will not be tolerated is obedience. A man of the elite, a man of a ruling type, is not ready to tolerate the rule of someone worse than him. And he will not tolerate it. He will either be integrated into this power and improve it or he will destroy it. No society can exist without an elite class. If a society does not have its own elite, its place will be taken by a foreign one. If we cannot rule by ourselves, somebody else will rule us. Eurasianists believe that a country should be ruled by the best representatives of the society. The basis of Eurasian method of selection is the aristocracy, the passionaries.

Is this scenario realistic today? In my opinion, given the current power structure, it is not. If the Kremlin doors remain closed and various scum, lackeys and buffoons squeeze their way in through a narrow hole, this door will have to be taken by storm, if not by my generation, then by the next. This is the Pareto principle[54] and not an urge towards revolution and chaos. This is why, I think, our leaders should reassess their attitude towards the elite and accept the Eurasian method of selection before it is too late.

The Russian *Oprichnina* as the Archetypal New Elite

The Russian *oprichnina* is both a historical and a supra-historical phenomenon. The word is derived from the Russian adverb *oprich* ('aside' or 'aloof'). In Old Russian, it was synonymous with *krome* ('besides'), that is, *na kromke* ('on the brim'), hence *kromeshniy* ('pitch dark'). For this reason, the *oprich-*

---

53 Gumilev termed those in an ethnic group who possess a drive to expand their group 'passionaries'. Sub-passionaries are those who lack this drive.

54 Vilfredo Pareto (1844–1923) was an Italian sociologist and economist whose theories were highly influential upon Italian Fascism. Dugin is referring to the ideas he discusses in *The Rise and Fall of the Elites: An Application of Theoretical Sociology* (Totowa, New Jersey: Bedminster Press, 1968). According to Pareto, elites are never overthrown by the peoples they govern, but rather are displaced by another elite.

niki were sometimes called *kromeshniky*. The *oprichnina* received the lands that were 'aside' from the main administrative territories — the *zemstva*.

Ivan the Terrible[55] created the *oprichnina*[56] for two main purposes: *the mobilisation of forces for the fierce struggle against the West and the restructuring of the administrative elite*, whose rigidity prevented the development of a solution to the new challenges facing Muscovy during centralisation. After 14 years of existence, the *oprichnina* was abolished. Whether it fulfilled its mission or not is still open to debate, but the point of its creation was to bring about a new and more effective system of state management capable of solving new tasks.

At the same time, the Italian sociologist Vilfredo Pareto proved that the establishment of entities similar to the *oprichnina* is a classic motif in political history. When the ruling elites 'freeze up' and are shut down, the important process of *elite rotation* comes to a halt. In order to bring new blood into the ruling class, it is sometimes essential to create *parallel hierarchies*. These hierarchies are based on personal qualities, energy, courage, passion, and ideological convictions — in short, on *energetic idealism*, as opposed to previous hierarchies where noble origin, wealth and clan connections guarantee a high position in the political-administrative system. Therefore, the Russian *oprichnina* is a textbook example of the law of elite rotation: a cadre revolution from above.

The parallel hierarchy is usually created on the basis of special ideologies or even cults. Hence the chivalric orders, mystical Islamic orders (*tariqas*), Indian Tantric sects, Taoist and Buddhist sects in China and Japan, and so on. Every parallel hierarchy has its sacrality, its symbols, and its charismatic pole located in the centre of the entire structure as the organising element. Many features of the *oprichnina* suggest that it employed certain elements of this sacrality: dog heads and brooms tied to one's saddle, aside from being an obvious metaphor ('bite the throats of the enemies of the state and sweep the evil out of Holy Russia'), hint at alternative meanings. A dog in

---

55   Ivan IV, or Ivan the Terrible (1530–1584), was Tsar from 1547 until his death. Conquering much territory and instituting many reforms, Ivan was the forger of the Russian Empire.

56   The *oprichnina* were a secret police created to repress the aristocracy between 1565 and 1572.

mystical symbolism is a 'guide for the dead', a sacred animal, which in various myths about journeys to the underworld leads a deceased person from death to an ultimate revival. The Dominican monks made a pun on their own name and spelled it as *Domini canes*, the dogs of the Lord, thinking of themselves as the dogs guarding the sheep (Christians) from the wolves (the heretics and non-Christians) and serving the Shepherd (the Christ). But, unlike sheep, dogs were at the forefront of battles against wolves. The *oprichniki* defended the sacrality of Rus and fought its enemies, both domestic and foreign. But, like all dogs, they retained something of the wolf.

The broom in ancient cults was a symbol of a *sacral marriage*. In Slavic tradition, before the arrival of the bridal procession, the house was swept with special 'wedding brooms'. The broom plays a central ritualistic role in the weddings and engagement ceremonies of many peoples. It has an express erotic symbolism. It is possible that the *oprichniki* had similar rituals too, and what is described as their 'excesses' and 'licentious behaviour' could, in fact, have a ritualistic sense in the same vine as the Shaivite Tantric[57] tradition.

The centre of *oprichnina* sacrality was the figure of Ivan Vasilievich the Terrible himself and the *symbolism of death* that constantly occupied his mind and his imagination. It is known that Ivan personally prepared three Orthodox canons, one of which was dedicated to the Angel of Death, the terrible Angel (and this canon is still widely used by Old Believers).

Therefore, the *oprichnina* was a parallel hierarchy with its own specific symbolism, rituals and purposes. But the *oprichnina* theorist Ivan Peresvetov (some authors dispute his existence and even claim that 'Peresvetov' was a pseudonym for Ivan the Terrible himself) was significantly influenced by *Turkish Janissaries*,[58] the militant Sufis[59] of the Sublime Porte,[60] another secret order with its own symbolism and rituals.

---

57 Tantra is a school of esotericism in Hinduism. Shaivites are worshippers of the god Shiva.

58 The Janissaries were the elite troops of the Ottoman Empire.

59 Sufism refers to the various schools of esotericism which are part of Islamic culture. The Bektashi Order of Sufis had close ties to the Janissaries. For centuries of Ottoman history, any Sultan that tried to disband the Janissaries would be overthrown by them, until they were finally defeated by Mahmud II in 1826.

60 Sublime Porte refers to the government of the Ottoman Empire.

Oprichnina has obviously matured in contemporary Russia. The situation is very similar to that of the seventeenth century: there are external threats (from Western pressure, NATO expansion, and the 'orange revolutions' in the CIS) and the internal disintegration of the vertical power (unprecedented levels of corruption, moral degradation, alienation, impotence, and degeneration of the comprador elites). There is a functional, psychological, social and ideological necessity for it. The Russia of Yeltsin, which has been somewhat solidified by Vladimir Putin, is gradually sinking, and is starting to melt and turn sour before our very eyes. The hopes for evolutionary patriotism are fading. The situation is quickly becoming critical. The parties are weak and illusory. The administrative vertical is incompetent and corrupt. The national ideology is gone. And even Putin himself, contrary to the wailings of his opponents, does not have anything in common with an authoritarian, charismatic dictator. So, *only an Order can save the day*, along with everything that it entails. What will serve as its centre? What symbols will it have? What kind of sacrality will it appeal to? These questions are open to debate.

One thing is clear: Putin is not Ivan, and the historical opportunity to resemble him is now lost. So, the new *oprichnina* must be organised under a different, non-authoritarian principle. The Order has only one Russia left: the parallel motherland, Holy Russia, covered by the rubble and sediment of history. There is an enemy, though: the Orange Atlanticist enemy, both external and internal. As the Pareto principle shows, parallel hierarchies are not always formed from above. They are created now and then by the counter-elites — the passionate types who did not find a slot in the closed, greedy and rapidly deteriorating ruling classes. These are all reasons for the new *oprichnina* to emerge in Russia, but its nature, character, structures and symbolism have not been defined yet. I am personally convinced that the ultimate ideology in this situation is Eurasianism, which was devised by its founding fathers as a Russian Order.

CHAPTER 6

Putin: What Next?

Putin's First Eight Years: A Conservative's Balance

How justified was the support of Putin provided by the conservative national patriotic forces and, primarily, by our Eurasian movement? *What did Putin achieve and where did he fail?* What did he *want* to achieve? Have our hopes been justified?

The Labours of Hercules: A Summary

Let me remind you that at the beginning of Putin's presidency I published an article, 'On the twelve labours of Hercules', comparing Vladimir Putin to Hercules. On his way to the top, Putin, in my opinion, almost immediately carried out six fundamental feats. First, he stopped the disintegration of Russia, suppressing Chechen (and, more broadly, North Caucasian) ethno-Islamic separatism. Second, he strengthened the vertical power and the territorial integrity of Russia, introducing the federal districts, taming the governors and subsequently abolishing their elections altogether.[1] Third, he stopped blindly following the Americans' lead and started to defend Russia's national interests in foreign policy to the point of worsening relations

---

1   In 2004, Putin changed the laws so that the regional governors were chosen by the President, subject to the approval of the regional legislatures, rather than through direct elections.

with Washington. Fourth, he stopped the wave of liberal Westernist Russophobia (stopping them from attacking the Soviet past and sparking interest in the Tsarist past) and cut down on ultra-liberal journalism, reducing it to the narrow peripheral platform of *Echo Moskvy* and Internet blogs. Fifth, he ousted the rebellious oligarchs, who aspired to control the political processes and the Russian economy, keeping those who accepted the new rules of the game at arm's length, in effect nationalising the principal mining and extraction monopolies. And finally, he set to strengthen Russian positions in the post-Soviet space, giving the green light to the agents of integration: the EurAsEC, the CSTO, and so on.

These accomplishments stood in sharp contrast to the programme of Yeltsin and his entourage and represented a direct antithesis to the policies of the 1990s. The six labours of Hercules which I have laid out without a shadow of irony and which I consciously admire provided Putin with the unconditional support of the majority of the population and the conservative patriotic circles, which identify their political interests with those of the Russian people and the logic of Russian history.

Has Putin deviated from those measures to the point where one could come to regret supporting him? The critical moment was the events of 9/11, when Putin seemed to betray the Eurasian geopolitical imperative by supporting Washington in the wake of the terrorist attacks and endorsing the invasion of Afghanistan, and allowing the Americans to establish their bases in Central Asia. Another unpleasant aspect of his policies at this time was the rejection of our military bases in Cam Rahn[2] and Cuba. Although though those were obviously erroneous and misguided decisions, they did not have serious repercussions, and Putin set out to make amends almost immediately afterwards. A new project in Cuba is already underway, under which Russia re-established cooperation by delivering arms after a protracted break. The business with Washington naturally failed to get off the ground and everything went back to normal. Washington's stated intention to construct anti-ballistic missile (ABM) sites in Poland and the Czech Republic, as well as NATO's consistent expansion eastwards, made any further progress along the pro-American course almost impossible.

---

2   A costal city in Vietnam.

The Labour That Putin Failed to Perform

The Second Entry in the Balance of Putin's Rule: Losses and Disadvantages

In my article about his twelve accomplishments, I described the remaining six labours that Putin faced. The most crucial was the seventh labour, which was *to follow the first six labours to their logical conclusion*. This meant tightly intertwining the Caucasus with Russia geopolitically and ideologically; creating an imperial system that combines strategic centralism and democratic self-governance at the grassroots level; following an independent and effective foreign policy course; developing a national ideology; finalising the cleansing of the oligarchy and stopping corruption; and embarking on the creation of supranational political entities in the territory of the CIS (the Union State of Russia and Belarus, the Customs Union, the Eurasian Union, etc.).

Putin *stumbled* throughout the course of this seventh labour. Putin either did not manage or did not want to bring the first six steps *to the point of no return*.

The crucial thing here is *irreversibility*: in 2008, Putin delegated everything to his successor, but everything that he had done could have been theoretically *cancelled and reversed* at any point. This is why this successor was potentially dangerous for us.

During Yeltsin's presidency, Russia was rapidly heading towards an abyss. *Putin suspended the collapse through a colossal effort*. Russia stopped at the last moment and found itself at the edge. *And Putin left her there.* She was not slipping anymore, but she also did not step back and embark on the path towards revival. Time stood still. Why is this situation so fragile? Let's discuss it in detail.

The Fragile Putin: Absence of a National Ideology and a Clear-cut Strategy

The Russian authorities remain unconsolidated, devoid of a common national strategy (besides pointless incantations), and are not united under a clear-cut state-building or national idea. All attempts to develop an ideology with Putin were either a flop or a bluff.

There is no strategy because there is no ideology and no common political philosophy. The political elite live in the moment according to the interests of their clan. Moreover, with Putin the authorities never realised the *necessity of stimulating the proper development of a national, historically responsible worldview*. Philosophical research and studies were replaced by arbitrary simulacra and political anecdotes. The authorities seem to believe that systematic and well-structured thinking is a merely a whim, a pointless or unattainable luxury not worth wasting one's time on. But this is an excuse used by all mediocre and indecent people (even those who are indecent to themselves): 'I have no time to think.' No time to think? Excuse me, but that means you are an animal. Animals are also always busy doing something: they wag their tails, look for food, and meander around without any particular direction.

Stealing as a National Idea and the Absence of Economy

With the absence of a distinct political philosophy, corruption becomes *the informal norm*. We might no longer be selling out the interests of the state to external forces (this was stopped by Putin), but the state is being divided internally, the 'patriotic' way — 'patriots' bargaining with 'patriots'. The absence of a national idea gave rise to the practice of corruption. Ultimately, the thief mentality became a national idea in itself.

That said, Russia still does not have an economy. There is economic growth, but no economy. Putin nationalised the monopolistic instruments used to sell resources, which had previously belonged to the oligarchs. This is a good thing, but the proceeds were not properly invested into the creation of an advanced, competitive economy. The industrial sector was destroyed in the 1990s and never recovered. The defence-industrial complex fares a little better, but patriotic PR tactics disguise the permanent shortage of financing for the development of breakthrough technologies. Generally speaking, economic development cannot be limited to a single sector (such as defence); without the development of the high technologies sector in the general structure, achieving success in the military sphere is impossible.

Putin repeatedly stressed the importance of 'tech cities' and new centres for technological development, but nothing specific, with the exception of Yudashkin's[3] posh nanotechnology military uniform that apparently caused entire military units to catch pneumonia,[4] has been accomplished. The Skolkovo Innovation Centre project,[5] which infatuated Medvedev for four years, has yet to properly kick off, in spite of the fact that the project's entire budget has already been spent.

Absence of Social Policy and the Schism of the Elites

From the patriotic standpoint, Putin's loyalty to liberal economic theory has always been his serious drawback. For eight years, the ultra-liberal Gräf, Kudrin and Nabiullina[6] have been in charge of the government's economic bloc. Liberalism is an antithesis of social orientation, and therefore 'national projects' were devised to satisfy social expectations. They were conceived as PR support for Putin's successor. The ideas behind these 'national projects' were solid, but the results of their implementation are controversial: there is no distinct social strategy, just populist slogans and certain helpful but unsystematic steps. Take, for instance, the monetisation of benefits or

---

3   Valentin Yudashkin (b. 1963) is a fashion designer.

4   Yudashkin was hired by the Russian military to design new uniforms for its forces. He designed 85 new uniforms in all, However, when Russian soldiers wore the new uniforms during the winter, hundreds of them fell sick, which was blamed on the uniforms being too thin. Yudashkin responded by claiming that the military had changed the designs without his approval and had altered the materials the uniforms were made from.

5   Medvedev announced the creation of the Centre in 2009 with the intention that it would serve as a means of encouraging and marketing new developments in Russian science and technology. As of this writing it is still under development.

6   Elvira Nabiullina (b. 1963) is an economist who was Minister of Economic Development and Trade from 2007 until 2012, and was then an economic advisor to Putin following his re-election from 2012 until 2013. After that she was appointed the Governor of the Central Bank of Russia, becoming the first woman in the G8.

the former healthcare minister Zurabov,[7] who, after resigning (something which the entire country had been begging for) was appointed 'advisor to the President' and sent to Ukraine.

The absence of a national ideology and rampant corruption automatically led to a split of the elites into rival clans. These clans wage oligarchic wars on one another for chunks of property. They have stopped using political and media resources in their squabbles (the Parliament and the media are strictly controlled by the Kremlin), but otherwise these conflicts have not been ended. The line-up of major players has changed a bit: some have been marginalised, others removed. New, 'patriotic' semi-oligarchs emerged out of the enforcement agencies, but many have remained in place since the Yeltsin era. They still fight to the death to preserve their interests.

They have recognised Putin's authority as a fact, but the future of this authority is uncertain: the oligarchs are too tough and greedy to be guided by purely moral principles. As soon as Putin loosens his hold on them, the cards will be reshuffled and their zones of influence immediately redistributed.

Russia's Weakness in Her Foreign Policy

An analysis of Putin's actions in the international arena demonstrates that, in spite of all his tough rhetoric, *Putin failed to resolve most important geopolitical issues in Russia's favour* (except for the Sochi Olympics and the 2018 FIFA World Cup). In the post-Soviet space, Russia, in spite of all her efforts, failed in every respect. The anti-Russian regime in Georgia has only grown stronger. The 'Orange Revolution' in Ukraine has won and prevailed over the 'Party of the West' (which had, in turn, betrayed Moscow) to the extent that the latter does not much differ from the 'orange.' The Union State of Russia and Belarus would remain on paper if it weren't for the new initiative to create the Eurasian Union, which exists only as a declaration.

Despite Moscow's protests and alternative proposals, American military facilities, including proposals for ABM bases, have appeared in Poland,

---

7   Mikhail Zurabov (b. 1953) was Minister of Health and Social Development between 2004 and 2007. In 2005 he suggested the monetisation of benefits for the elderly, which led to protests all over Russia. He currently serves as Russia's ambassador to Ukraine.

the Czech Republic, Bulgaria and Romania. The Atlanticists triumphed in Europe (Sarkozy, then Hollande and Merkel). The Americans and Europeans recognised the independence of Kosovo, ignoring our protests in the UN. They bombed Libya and are threatening Syria and Iran. In short, *Russia failed to effectively resist the practical steps being taken to establish a unipolar world.* Russia's energy potential is genuine, but in the contemporary world economy, the financial and technological sectors matter more than the natural resources provided mostly by Third World countries. And even the energy sector has run into some trouble: the inspections of Gazprom's European subsidiaries in September 2011 are hardly a friendly measure by the 'grateful consumers' of natural gas.[8]

The UN is becoming increasingly useless, and all Russian efforts to appeal to countries all over the world to consider moral issues in dealing with international problems have proven futile. Big-time policy relies on a key instrument — force and will, which Russia desperately lacked in the Putin era, let alone during the four years of Medvedev's presidency.

The above-mentioned points are the critical remarks *of a conservative patriot*. Obviously, the liberal Westernists will come up with reverse criticisms, although our assessments may coincide in some respects: they, too, criticise the absence of a stable economy and growing corruption. Western critics will also complain about the existence of 'authoritarian tendencies', 'mere simulation of democratic procedures', 'limited freedom of speech', 'discriminating purges of certain representatives of big business' and 'bureaucratic raids', 'the mysterious death of Litvinenko'[9] (and other figures) and the 'deterioration of relations with the West' — in short, the typical compendium of liberal critique, which we, on the contrary, consider to be the advantages and achievements of Putin's rule, with no irony intend-

---

8   In September 2011 the European Commission carried out unannounced inspections of Gazprom's facilities in Europe, alleging violations of the EU's antitrust laws by hindering competition in the Central and Eastern European markets. The European Commission later made formal accusations against Gazprom.

9   Alexander Litvinenko (1962–2006) was a former agent of the FSB who fled to England after making accusations against the FSB and Putin personally for their alleged role in many criminal acts, including the Russian apartment bombings of 1999. In November 2006 he was poisoned and died shortly thereafter.

ed. We view these trends as the positive results of the eradication of the 'damned 1990s'. But even if we dismiss the liberals' arguments, an unbiased analysis of the country's future prospects in 2012 reveals *a fairly gloomy picture*.

Defending the 'status quo' is futile as of today. It would mean consciously defending a social illness and a rush toward an imminent end. But the principal question today is: *does Putin himself realise the urgency of the situation and the seriousness of the maturing crisis?*

The Crisis of Representation

The inadequacy of the ruling elite, the absence of a guiding ideology, the uncertainty and controversial nature of Russia's political strategy: all of these points call the legitimacy of Russia's authorities into question, leaving Russia between a rock and a hard place. The main problem of contemporary Russia is the growing discrepancy between the actual state of society and the political elite's idea of this state. The masses are confused, while the elites exude 'stability'. The people are outraged by rampant corruption while the elites benefit from it, which further increases the huge gap between the rich and the poor.

Ethnic tensions and uncontrolled immigration have reached a boiling point, but the authorities continue to hope for a civil society, tolerance and multiculturalism (which are already being rejected in Europe). The people worship Stalin, and dream about a great Russia and social justice, but the authorities have launched a 'de-Stalinisation' campaign, professing liberalism and the principle of 'every man for himself', boasting about a closer resemblance to the US and NATO countries. The elite complain that they are 'not happy with the people', claiming that 'the human material is of very low quality'. The people respond in kind. A sense of alienation is growing.

The state has traditionally been the supreme value of the Russian people. Without a strong state, the rights and freedoms of Russian citizens will not make any political or social sense. This hypothesis has been the basis of the notion of a 'controlled', 'sovereign' democracy, which implied that Western democratic standards are secondary to the establishment of Russian sovereignty. The compensation for 'suspending democracy' must be a tangible and palpable success in a project aimed at creating a stronger state. But the project of strengthening of the state, which drove the political reforms of the early 2000s, has been curtailed. Today, the 'suspension of democracy' is not justified at all, and this leads to disappointment in the existing political course not only among the radical pro-Western liberals (who just can't get enough democracy), but among the pro-state patriots as well.

The Growing Deficit in Legitimacy

We are currently undergoing a crisis of legitimacy when it comes to Russian attitudes towards our political authorities. *Legitimacy is the informal approval by the majority of the policy that the authorities have chosen to follow.* Legitimacy is the indicator of the general state of society and the collective opinion of the majority. Legality is the compliance of the political regime with the existing legal norms. During the USSR's last years, the political regime was quite legal, but was losing its legitimacy. The Yeltsin regime, which had to attack Parliament in order to strengthen its positions,[10] never became fully legitimate. The oligarchs ruled the country and ethnic and religious tensions were rampant in the Caucasus. We almost lost Chechnya. Vladimir Putin saved Russia as a state and strengthened its sovereignty. These actions made his first two terms both legal and legitimate. In 2008, Putin used up his 'legitimacy capital' in the election of Dmitry Medvedev. At this point, the legitimacy of Russia's authorities changed.

In August 2008, President Medvedev acted decisively and boldly in the critical situation caused by the Georgian attack on Tskhinvali,[11] prevent-

---

10   In September 1993, the differences between Yeltsin and the Parliament became so severe, particularly over the issue of economic reforms, that Yeltsin attempted to dissolve it, despite the fact that he had no constitutional authority to do so. Many representatives barricaded themselves in the White House and other government buildings, and protestors surrounded the buildings to support them, Finally Yeltsin ordered tanks to fire on the White House, which was done, and shortly thereafter the Russian military occupied the building. Hundreds were killed or injured in the fighting.

11   In August 2008, the Georgian government attacked Tskhinvali in South Ossetia with the intention of securing their control over the region, This led to Russian intervention and the 2008 South Ossetia War.

ing genocide in Ossetia and defending Russian interests in spite of pressure from the West and by the internal network of its agents. But this event was only a minor episode, and Medvedev stuck to the liberal course when it came to most other issues. He surrounded himself with pro-Western advisors and experts, unpopular oligarchs, catered to the US and Obama and severely aggravated relations with Belarus. The modernisation project that he claimed to have embarked upon involved the destruction of Russia's identity and the replication of Western social standards. The national projects that he had handled prior to his presidency gradually dwindled. The 'de-Stalinisation' project proved to be totally irrelevant, because the memories of the Soviet period — social security, leaps in industry and its international achievements — became a nostalgic ideal for the masses, standing in sharp contrast with the injustices, the gap between the rich and the poor and the cultural deterioration that has marked the post-Soviet period. The opening of a giant monument to Yeltsin by Medvedev in Yekaterinburg and a smaller monument to Yegor Gaidar in Moscow symbolically recreated the atmosphere of the 1990s, a period of time that was perceived by the Russian public to be completely illegitimate.

The ultra-liberals, on the other hand, also lacked faith in Medvedev, because they considered him to be overly dependent on Putin. So, beginning in 2008, the gap between the elite and the masses, and between the authorities and the people, started to widen.

The Paradox of Modernisation

The modernisation project was President Medvedev's hobby horse. If we are to accept the axiom that Russia must develop in line with the West (a largely disputable thesis), then historically we are now faced with the necessity to create a bourgeois nation. The nations in Europe first appeared in the modern era, coming into existence alongside bourgeois reforms and the Third Estate's[12] rise to power. The idea of a nation is inextricably linked with capitalism, industrialisation and the rejection of the traditional collectivist men-

---

12 In pre-Revolutionary France, the general assembly of the French government was divided into three States-General: the clergy (First), the nobles (Second), and the commoners (Third).

tality. A nation is based on the principle of individual citizenship. That said, Ernest Gellner[13] and Benedict Anderson[14] have illustrated that nations are created artificially, and nationalism serves as the main instrument by which this is accomplished.

Russia, in spite of having the outward signs of an industrial society, is still a largely traditional society with an archaic and collectivist mentality. If we develop in accordance with the European model, then we must build Russia into a bourgeois nation along with all its essential attributes: individual identity and the formation of the egoistic *Homo oeconomicus*,[15] as well as the mandatory eradication and neutralisation of all original ethnic cultures. In this case, the bourgeois nation would be called a Russian nation and the instrument of its creation would have to be Russian nationalism. And since European nations had existed for several centuries before Europeans began switching to the model of a civil society, the Russian nation will supposedly face a long period of similar evolution (a century, at least). In addition, similar to European nations, its nationalism would have to be its principal guiding ideology. Therefore, modernisation in our historical context can mean only one thing: the creation of a bourgeois Russian nation backed by Russian nationalism.

But here we come across a contradiction. The Western countries are trying to overcome their national boundaries and create a civil society. This is the reason why their nationalism in all its various forms is subject to eradication and dismantling: it has already had its day. It appears that we are at different historical stages: we are facing the creation of a bourgeois nation while the West is moving towards the next social model, a civil society. We may fall victim to the 'Bolshevist' temptation to accelerate the historical

---

13   Ernest Gellner (1925–1995) was a British-Czech philosopher and anthropologist. Dugin is referring to Gellner's *Nations and Nationalism* (Ithaca: Cornell University Press, 1983) in which he argued that the nation-state is purely a product of modernity.

14   Benedict Anderson (b. 1936) likewise makes the argument that nationalism and modernity are linked in *Imagined Communities: Reflections on the Origin and Spread of Nationalism* (London: Verso, 1991), although he sees the nation-state in Europe as arising as an imitation of the rise of such states in North and South America.

15   Latin: 'economic man'.

process and skip a logically necessary stage of social development. Dmitry Medvedev (along with his advisors) fell for this trap with his version of modernisation: he tried to create a civil society in one leap, bypassing the necessary stage of creating a nation. This attempt resulted in a modernisation flop, a crisis in representation (the elites' idea of society does not reflect the actual state of things) and, consequently, the delegitimisation of the authorities and their political course.

Since the path towards modernisation has been established, nationalism is inevitable. But Medvedev and his circle rejected nationalism, along with the figure of Stalin who had made a decisive (albeit forceful) step towards Russia's industrialisation. And, finally, any modernisation in Russia was always forced from above, by breaking the resistance of the masses. Nationalism, Stalinism and authoritarianism are the three main reference points for Russian modernisation at its current historical stage, and if we don't employ all three, modernisation will remain an empty phrase.

End of a Political Cycle: Beyond the Grey Pole
The Dawn in Boots and Putin's Legitimacy

Yeltsin's power in the 1990s was politically illegitimate. What he and his entourage did was not supported by the majority of the population (liberal reforms, 'shock therapy', etc.). It was a dictatorship of the liberal pro-Western elite, the oligarchs, and a tiny number of top government officials. The people generally disapproved, but were not capable of protesting. The country, nevertheless, was on the brink of disintegration. Putin, who was initially pushed to the top through PR campaigns and powerful administrative resources, turned out to be the one who everyone had been waiting for. Compared to Yeltsin, he was a godsend. Putin initiated a number of reforms to the benefit of the people. He prevented the disintegration of Russia, conducted the victorious second Chechen campaign, strengthened the vertical power, exiled or imprisoned the most notorious oligarchs, started negotiating with the West in a harsher manner, re-established the national anthem, threw the ultra-liberals out of politics, introduced the federal districts, gave the green light to the integration of the post-Soviet space, took the non-conforming TV and radio channels away from the oligarchs, insisted on removing the notion of 'sovereignty' from the local legislations of the subjects of the Russian Federation subjects, enhanced the positions of the *siloviki* in power, and established appointment procedures for the governors. All this, and especially the sharp contrast with Yeltsin, made Putin fully legitimate in the early 2000s. He found the right balance between partial compliance with both the pro-Western oligarchic elites of the 1990s (in their moderate sector) and the masses, who were hoping for great power, a tough stance and order. Public support was evident: after Yeltsin's effectively anti-Russian and comprador course, Putin was perceived positively. Thus Putin's positive ratings were established. Putin satisfied the majority; he was a compromise who met the requirements of a particular political period.

In the first stage, Putin was opposed only by the representatives of the ultra-liberal and pro-Western forces ('the dissenters') financed by the US and the exiled oligarchs. This set the political paradigm of the 2000s. Putin made a 90-degree turn away from the Yeltsin course. Not a 180-degree turn, but a 90-degree turn. He did not turn in another direction, he stopped the process. He froze it.

The 2008 elections served as the final straw. Putin still had room to return to his previous course, and he could have enhanced his legitimacy with the masses (simultaneously weakening his legitimacy with the elites and the West) if he had remained President for another term. He would have been the Russian Lukashenko, loved by the masses, frightening to the elite and hated by the West. At the very least he could have appointed someone who stuck to similar policies as his successor, but he resolved to take the alternative route and delegate his powers to Dmitry Medvedev.

Medvedev's political image was designed to appease liberals, the West and the oligarchy. In order to highlight this point, he became the head of the board of trustees of the Institute of Contemporary Development

(ICD),[16] which was established on the basis of the 'oligarchs' trade union' and the RUIE, and was headed by Igor Yurgens[17] (the 'voice of the oligarchs') and a pro-Western ultra-liberal even prior to his election. It is obvious that Putin decided to use these four years (2008–2012) as a buffer period for improving relations with the West (either in a genuine sense or only allegedly) and as a 'return to the 1990s' (partial or in full). Overall, Medvedev's presidency meant a partial reversal of Putin's course. It was a transition from the preservation of the status quo and 'sovereign democracy' to 'modernisation' and 'democratisation'.

Almost three years, from 2008 to the end of 2010, were spent on the preparation and solution of merely technical issues, and it was clear that the Putin cycle was over by the end of 2010. For a period of time, Medvedev's steps to appease the West could have been reversed. They could have passed for a farce or a distraction, especially given the fact that, at the beginning of his presidency in 2008, Russia's decisive entry into Georgia easily passed for a continuation of Putin-style politics. But his refusal to supply S-300s[18] to Iran (Russia's principal strategic partner), his support for sanctions against Iran and especially the signing of the New START agreement[19] (which caused irreparable harm to Russia's defences) demonstrated that things took a turn for the worst, and the Gorbachev-Yeltsin line in Russian-American relations resurfaced.

Three Russias: The Grey, the Orange, the Black

In contemporary Russia there are three political zones which can conventionally be called Russia 1, Russia 2 and Russia 3.

---

16 The Institute was inaugurated by Medvedev in 2008 with the intention of introducing modernising reforms into Russia, such as in information technology and civil society.

17 Igor Yurgens (b. 1952) is Vice President of the RUIE and is Chairman of the ICD.

18 A surface-to-air missile.

19 New START (Strategic Arms Reduction Treaty) was signed by the US and Russia in 2010 with the intention of reducing the number of active nuclear warheads possessed by both. Some in the Duma objected to the fact that the treaty placed no limitations on the US' stated intention of building ABM sites.

Russia 1 is a model of the preservation of Putin's compromise: the continued balancing between the elites and the masses, between the West and national interests, and between conservatism and modernisation. Russia 1 is 'putinism' in a broad sense. It can be referred to symbolically as a grey pole, the Russia of Putin, of the vertical power, a specific crossbreed of the Family and the Peter Guys, 'Russian patriotism' and 'gaidaronomics', Orthodox bankers and unorthodox oligarchs. It includes both the Munich speech and Medvedev with his Institute of Contemporary Development, complicity in the murder of Gaddafi and the Skolkovo thefts.[20] Russia 1 has been, until recently, managed by the Kremlin's grey cardinal Vladislav Surkov, the chief architect of its political and ideological structure who was responsible for emasculating both the liberal and patriotic substance of Russian politics. He was a postmodernist in a Byzantine vein.

Until recently, Russia 1 has been the dominant force in the country's political system. It was the golden mean located between the orange pole and the black pole. Russia 1 includes United Russia, the pro-Kremlin youth organisations, the moderation of the informational sphere, and the community of experts — in other words, Russia's entire domestic policy that is controlled by the Kremlin. The emergence of the power tandem[21] in 2008 split the grey pole. Medvedev clearly settled between the grey and the orange, in spite of the fact that he had avoided crossing this line in the past: he did not release Khodorkovsky, he did not sanction the creation of a new political party, and he did not grant the 'dissenters' free access to the federal media. Medvedev's gradual strengthening as President meant a drift from the grey to the orange. Its horizon is easy to predict: the territorial disintegration of Russia, the escalation of civil conflicts, a return of the liberals, and a sharp decline in Russia's importance in the international arena — in short, a complete return to the 1990s.

The second pole, Russia 2, is unadulterated Westernism, liberalism and Yeltsin-style reforms. This pole attracts American political protégés in Rus-

---

20 In 2012 the Russian government filed charges against several of the directors at Skolkovo, alleging that they had embezzled millions of rubles.

21 The balance of power between Medvedev and Putin during Medvedev's term has been referred to as the 'tandem'.

sia, the exiled oligarchs, the 'implacable opposition' (the 'dissenters') and the liberal power sector. Figures like Yurgens, Voloshin, Pavlovsky,²² Gontmakher, Chubais, Budberg, Navalny,²³ Nemtsov, and so on fit the mould perfectly.

The focus of Russia 2 is on modernisation, democratisation, closer ties to the West, globalisation and the dismantling of Putin's vertical power. The majority of the Russian economic and political elite formed in the Yeltsin era sympathises with this approach or actively supports it. The radio station *Ekho Moskvy* shows Russia 2 in crystal-clear form. This is the orange pole. There is a distinct liberal segment in Russia 1 that consists of Medvedev, Voloshin, Chubais, the leaders of the mass media and the experts. This liberal segment is slowly transforming into 'orangism'. For example, Andrei Illarionov, after serving as Putin's advisor, found himself alongside Kasparov and Kasyanov (who himself was Putin's Prime Minister). This is a common front whose members share a similar outlook on the destiny of Russia. The liberals that remain in Putin's entourage can be designated as 'spies who keep an eye on Putin'. They prefer to work for the West from the inside and not from the ranks of the opposition, but as they get periodically ousted from Russia 1, they easily join Russia 2.

Russia 3 is the far less ideologically and organisationally consistent position of the Russian masses who work toward establishing order, a strong state, social guarantees (socialism), nationalism and patriotism. This political sector reacts very painfully to the westernisation of Russian society. Russia 3 is represented by a large social base, but there is virtually no political representation. This position manifests itself in the Rodina party,²⁴ the

---

22 Yevgeny Gontmakher (b. 1953) was the Vice President of the RUIE and is currently the Deputy Director of the Institute of World Economics and International Relations at the Russian Academy of Sciences.

23 Alexei Navalny (b. 1976) is a lawyer who is one of the most prominent critics of Putin, and the Russian government more generally, today, In 2012 he was charged with embezzlement.

24 Rodina (Motherland in Russian), or the Motherland-National Patriotic Union, was established in 2003 as a socialist and nationalist party.

Russian Marches,[25] the *Zavtra*[26] newspaper, or in the gatherings of football fans on Manège square.[27] This is the black pole. Nobody tries to appease Russia 3; the grey continues to put pressure on it, attempting to split it up, tame, or weaken it. The authorities have spawned multiple simulacra, operated from the Kremlin. But the importance of Russia 3 (as a source of political legitimisation) is constantly growing. It is difficult to predict what organisational forms it will transform into. The existing political parties, which could claim to play this part, are paralysed from the inside and do not play a significant role in this process. Their management is integrated into the grey zone and directly depends on it. The creation of new and efficient patriotic movements will not be permitted by the authorities. Today there is no organisational potential and no outspoken leaders in this area.

The black pole is confused, disjointed and far from any notion of consolidation. It is at best capable of spontaneous protests (like the gatherings on Manège square) instead of well-planned initiatives. It operates through flash mobs and the systematic sabotage of the political discourse, not only through direct opposition but also through indifference and passivity. When it comes to legitimate politics, the representatives from this sector cannot compete with the technologies of the grey (whose use bribery, deceit, media campaigns, psychological methods, understatement, defamation, and so on — along with direct force). Besides, there is no external support for Russia 3. If only for the purpose of aggravating the situation (in a limited scope), certain sectors of the grey zone can be included in the overall structure of the 'dissenters', but only under the supervision and strict control of the orange pole. Nevertheless, the amount of sentiment of this sort in society will constantly grow, which will become the most important, if not crucial, factor. The huge electoral success of Rodina in 2003 is an outstanding example. Some of the patriots sustained by the authorities,

---

25 The Russian Marches are an annual march by nationalists which takes place on or around 4 November, Russia's Day of National Unity.

26 'Tomorrow'.

27 Manège square is central Moscow. In recent years it has become a site of rioting by football fans and of demonstrations by nationalists. In December 2010 there was a riot involving thousands of protesters and a considerable amount of violence, and since then Manège has come to be associated with nationalism.

such as Nikita Mikhalkov,[28] cooperate with Russia 1, but the other sector, the street nationalists of all denominations, are getting closer to the orange pole (Potkin,[29] Demushkin,[30] etc.). There is continuity here too, which invisibly transforms the nationalist stool pigeons, supervised by the *siloviki*, into national democrats and racists patronised by the spin doctors of the exiled oligarchs and the CIA (an important function here is played by the manager Stanislav Belkovsky).[31]

And what about Putin? Putin is biding his time. It would be logical if he veered towards the black pole, where he is being pushed by both the American politologists and by the patriots who remain loyal to him. Everybody expects Putin to move towards Russia 3. But this is not happening. Putin is not moving in this direction and continues to occupy the same space, in the middle of the grey zone, so there is a discrepancy even in relation to the compromise model of Putin's first presidential cycle.

Time is Up: Reinforcement of the Flanks and Weakening of the Centre

The most important aspect is that, as of the beginning of 2012, Putin has virtually no time or political room for a new patriotic gesture, which he has been postponing for many years. He demonstrates his charisma and legitimacy by refusing to actively oppose the orange zone. The entire system is shifting towards the orange zone. And even in spite of the fact that Putin is the only candidate representing the authorities in 2012, many opportunities have been hopelessly lost. Putin's allegiance to the grey zone will not satisfy anyone in the new stage, neither the orange (naturally) nor the black. This means that, in trying to repeat what he managed to do in

---

28 Nikita Mikhalkov (b. 1945) is a filmmaker best known for his 1994 anti-Stalinist film, *Burnt by the Sun*. He is well-known as a Slavophile and nationalist and is an outspoken supporter of Putin.

29 Alexander Potkin (b. 1976) was the leader of the Movement against Illegal Immigration. Known for its street-level activism, it was banned in 2011.

30 Dmitry Dyomushkin is the leader of the Slavic Union, a neo-Nazi group which was banned in 2010.

31 Stanislav Belkovsky (b. 1971) is a Russian political analyst and a cousin to Boris Berezovsky. He is the head of the think tank, the National Strategy Institute, and is a critic of Putin.

the 2000s, Putin will confront a serious problem: the context has changed but the forms of his political thinking have remained the same. Putin has missed his window of opportunity.

A process of disintegration in the existing Russian political system began in 2011: the grey pole began to shrink, and the orange and the black (Russia 2 and Russia 3) were gaining momentum. Russia 2 started to play up to Medvedev in earnest, associating its own autonomous political course with him. As 2012 approached, support for this segment from the West grew rapidly. The creation of a centre of power which could synchronise this activity seemed to be underway.

End of a Cycle

The logic of events forces us to take our fascinated eyes off the top officials and the opportunistic riffraff serving them, and look the other way: at the people, history, society, the logic of the principal international tendencies in geopolitics, ethno-sociology,the transformation of identity, postmodernism and the global scale of the crisis of mankind (not only economic, but the crisis in values, culture, and anthropology as well), as well as at the problems of hegemony and counter-hegemony.

Russia is part of the world, and everything about this world is wrong. Unsurprisingly, things are not well in our country either. We need to broaden the horizons of our thought. Some problems don't have easy solutions because these problems are complicated by their very nature. A technical malfunction can be fixed by technical means, but historical problems cannot be solved in the same manner. You cannot avoid politics: if we decide not to deal with politics, it means we will be reduced to voluntary slavery. By refusing to lead a political existence, we delegate power to the first comer who doesn't turn away from politics as we do. But politics should now be sought in other areas.

The domination of the grey zone has run dry. We should look beyond its limits. The grey zone is coming apart, and this process is irreversible. Russia is nearing the end of Putin's cycle, and Putin's return will not automatically solve anything. Putin's return will bring about new questions instead of providing us with answers. We need to use our historical imagination, because our old tactics are no longer working.

Phantom Russia

Russia 1 is Putin's personal formula. It was founded at a time when Yeltsin's Russia was on the brink of a political and personal crisis in the political authorities. As Putin emerged, he removed the principal problems. He *removed them but did not solve* them, transferring all these processes to a different plane. The origin of the problems of the pre-Putin period lay in *the directly opposing interests and mentality of the* nouveau riche *comprador elites versus the patriotically- and socially-oriented masses.*

Putin was brought to power by the consensus of the Yeltsin elite: liberal democrats, oligarchs, media magnates; in short, by the 'Family'. But, at the same time, politically his emergence was presented as a step towards *the masses* and as an answer to their demands. The intuition of some genius spin doctor sensed in Putin a point for a *total compromise* within Yeltsin's society, a point where the elites and the masses perfectly balanced each other, a place of dead calm in the eye of a hurricane. Putin satisfied the elites (liberalism, democracy) and the masses (patriotism, a tough stance) simultaneously. This simultaneous satisfaction, when 'the *lion* and the *lamb* shall lie down together' gave birth to Russia 2. During all four years of his first term society, apart from the marginal lunatic fringe, enjoyed the effect of this conciliation. This effect transformed into high ratings. In doing so, society illustrated the following: 'We prefer the pause button to be pressed permanently. We cannot tolerate the contradictions of the Yeltsin period any longer.' From the substantive standpoint, Russia 1 is a freeze-frame, a screenshot of all the rhythms and energies that roared in the 1990s, shaking the country, tormenting the people and their souls. Strictly adhering to the rules, Putin himself acted as a cautious gardener, *carefully mixing test-tube, virtual patriotism with coyly disguised and inconsistent liberal reformism.* This style of rule was somehow 'regional', not 'imperial'; accurate, punctual, striving to avoid all things large-scale and radical, all things truly Russian — 'as far as the eye can see'.

First and foremost: *the compromise was not a synthesis.* The elite continued their evil deeds: they were siphoning off funds, conning the people and taking kickbacks. The masses degenerated, listening to Petrosyan[32] and cosy patriotic truisms, and drinking vodka. Nothing that was promised actually got done.

The first wave of problems with Russia 1 started in 2004, right in the middle of Putin's first presidency. Some sinister shadows lurked on the horizon and dark omens loomed — terrorist attacks, catastrophes, monetisation, Yushchenko's[33] face. This entire series of events coincided with the increasing external (American) pressure on Russia, which is definitely systemic rather that accidental: the Americans are building a world empire on our dime, strictly according to schedule. The freeze-frame period ended with the inauguration of Putin's second term and was marked by the murder of Akhmat Kadyrov in May 2004. Putin was supposed to offer our society an image of the future and to do it smartly and decisively. But it did not happen in 2004. Everything remained as it was.

An Unsuccessful Theatrical Interlude

Putin's entire second term was devoted to the problem of 2008. This was the year Putin's presidency came to an end, and under the Constitution no person could be elected President more than twice in a row. The idea was to preserve the power and control of the country without a direct confrontation with the West. Various options were considered, and the most disastrous one was then selected. Putin decided to replace himself with a loyal, blank and weak-willed administrator who had a 'liberal' image. His liberalism and lack of leadership qualities warranted unpopularity with the patriotic masses. Liberalism was supposed to pacify the West and suspend the radicalisation of Russia 2. In order to save himself and Russia 1, Putin decided to stage a situation in which Russia 1 was soon about to turn, consciously and without additional external and internal pressure, into Russia 2. According to the plan, Medvedev could maintain that he would remain

---

32 Yevgeny Petrosyan (b. 1945) is a comedian who has been well-known since Soviet times.

33 Viktor Yushchenko (b. 1954) was President of Ukraine from 2005 until 2010. In 2004, during his campaign, he was poisoned, which horribly scarred his face. When he lost the initial election, widespread allegations of voter fraud led to the Orange Revolution, which in turn led to a revote and Yushchenko becoming President.

for a second term and finalise the liberalisation of Russia until the very last moment, conceding to the West in every way. The liberals sensed a possibility of recoup. Everybody succumbed to it and everybody was cheated. After the announcement in the autumn of 2011 that Putin would return, all the masks came off.

Technically, the trick worked, but the time for serious and substantive transformations was gone forever. The disappointment of the elite and the masses reached a critical point. The four years of Medvedev's pseudo-liberal palaver infuriated all politically active people. In this situation, the return of Putin failed to please even his supporters. Russia 1 qualitatively lost its legitimacy. The scene was finally set for a confrontation with Russia 2. In March 2012, Putin returned for another 12 years and remained as inarticulate and elusive as ever. Historically, the Russia 1 strategy was a flop. It still exists and is still dominant, but its days are numbered.

The Orange Russia

Russia 2, 'the orange Russia', sprung up amidst the 2004 events in Ukraine. These events became a political turning point for Putin. Putin moved towards patriotism and superpower geopolitics, overstepping the mark on several issues. It was possibly a weak and uncertain attempt to propose a serious patriotic agenda. 'All for Russia! All in the name of Russia!' This could have been just the thing… But the blatantly inadequate methods, the poorly trained personnel who were dispatched to Kiev and total political inadequacy demonstrated at once that this course did not have any substantive base.

It later emerged that during Putin's first presidential term nothing had been done in the area of genuine geopolitics in the post-Soviet space, and the complex battle for Ukraine was hastily delegated to a team of cynical 'technicians' close to the Kremlin. These people were only capable of siphoning off funds, coming up scams and cranking film cameras. The liberally inclined Marat Gelman[34] and Gleb Pavlovsky played important roles.

That's how Russia 2, painted in orange, first appeared in the tents on Independence Square. The process started and the target year was 2008. If it worked in Kiev, the next time it would work in Moscow as well. Thus decided Washington, Langley and (correspondingly) the Russian liberal opposition itself.

What is Russia 2? Nothing new, really: it is Yeltsin's Russia, well-known from the 1990s, after plenty of sunbathing on Bermuda's beaches and skiing in Courchevel. Don't forget that, unlike Ukraine, Russia had already had one 'orange revolution' in 1991, and Yeltsin's rule was painted in this colour. Even the facial defects of Yeltsin and Yushchenko are vaguely similar: dead-pan, puffed-up, wicked and emotionless. 'The orange Russia' consists of the same old oligarchs, who are exiled, imprisoned, and scared but who are generally maintaining their resilience and high spirits; it is the urban cosmopolitan intelligentsia, totally irresponsible and only capable of destruction and ridicule; it is the journalists with permanently split personalities who are always outside observers of history without a chance of participating in it; it is human rights activists, liberal reformers, as well as greedy conformist officials who fulfil any orders from any authorities at the top. In short, it is the temporarily frozen and slowly melting, unbridled comprador elite and their writing-and-dancing clique of servants, which disgustingly calls itself 'the creative class': experts, PR specialists, spin doctors and the liberal bohemians exploited by them.

The elites started to leave Russia 1 for Russia 2, for the orange. After hiding under Putin's wing during a specific moment of political history and managing to calm down the masses, they are starting a new attack on statehood. The masses, in turn, started to turn away from Russia 1 for a different reason: they were no longer satisfied with the phantom nature of Russia 1, the ephemeral character of the state, nor the playful, irresponsible character

---

34 Marat Gelman (b. 1960) and Pavlovsky were the founders of the Foundation for Effective Politics, which is a think tank that disseminates media related to Russian politics, and was active in the Union of Right Forces in the late 1990s. He was also a director at Channel One. Today he is the director of an art gallery he opened in Moscow.

of the 'vertical'; 'orange' liberalism is alien to the masses, but gradually Russia 1 also started to lose their trust.

In 2008, Russia 2 was faced with a difficult scenario. Since the entire operation is supervised by Washington, the plan included the simultaneous intensification of terrorism in the Caucasus, escalating tension in the CIS, as well as social unrest in Russia herself. Putin only needed to mention a 'third term' and Russia 2 would be placed on alert for a full-scale all-round network war. Putin pretended that he voluntarily opened the Kremlin gates to Russia 2, represented by Medvedev, Dvorkovich,[35] Yurgens and Gontmakher. Note that the reformer Obama, who had just become President in November 2008, announced a 'reset' in relations with Russia. Even Brzezinski supported modernisation and believed in Medvedev. With Medvedev Russia would not have to be split, as Brzezinski had planned, because it would disintegrate on its own — what an economy of effort!

Russia 2 in its radical form subsided a little, waiting for Medvedev's second term.

In the autumn of 2011, when Putin announced his return as President, Russia 2 had no other alternative than to start a war with Russia 1. The Duma elections, badly staged by the authorities with endless violations and rigged ballots, the failure of Medvedev's fruitless presidency and, above all, a significant decline in Putin's credibility among the general public set the scene for a direct confrontation.

What does Russia 2 want? Unlike Ukraine, where the idea was to put a pro-Western politician in place of the pro-Russian one, in Russia herself this alternative is not viable. Russia is a country populated by patriotic masses. Therefore, the pro-Western elite who are in power cannot openly state their priorities: the masses would crush them for it. The overseas masterminds of the entire process clearly understand that. Liberalism and democracy have lost their credibility with the masses. 'The orange' pursue a strictly negative aim: destroying Russia 1. They are pushing for *total destruction*. Some of them are hoping to leave this country, some just want revenge, some want to cash in on the disintegration, some simply fail to understand the situa-

---

35 Arkady Dvorkovich (b. 1972) was an Assistant to the President during Medvedev's term. He is currently Deputy Prime Minister in Medvedev's cabinet.

tion clearly and are driven by emotion rather than prudence, and some genuinely hate 'this country'. Russia 2 is trying in vain to dissipate the ghostly Russia 1 to finish off Russia as such. Strange as it may seem, in a sense, it can serve as an inspiration to the masses: at some historical points the Russians were prone to nihilistic cults, love of death and a collective suicide impulse. The orange colour and the white ribbons[36] represent a playful death wish.

Russia 3 as a Project

One could draw a line here because, honestly, Russia 1 and Russia 2 are an exhaustive picture of what we have today. A pale spectre versus a happy death. But the voice of the Russian spirit opposes such harsh realism. Every nation at any point of its national history has a right to a spiritual uprising, to an awakening, to a vertical, persistent, unyielding stance. An uprising is always risky, but a Russian uprising against the forces of doom can happen as long as there are Russian people.

An uprising in favour of Russia 3, of its historical mission and its majestic destiny, of Russia as an Empire, of the great order, corresponding to the vast expanses of our lands, the height of our mountains, the depths of our rivers, has not yet been sold or taken away. Every Russian feels it in his heart, in spite of the fact that we allowed ourselves to become idiots and sank to an all-time low.

This is our eternal motherland, the absolute motherland, the Holy of Holies. This true Russia was bequeathed to us centuries ago. It is hidden from view but open to our spirit. We can hear her cry, we can sense her smoke, we can see her rays with our eyes closed.

We raise the banner of the universal gathering. We are signalling. Join Russia 3 when, like Marmeladov[37] said, 'There is nowhere else to *go*!'

---

36 In late 2011, after Putin announced his candidacy in the presidential election, protesters began to wear white ribbons in opposition to what they believed was Putin's intention of stealing the election.

37 Semyon Marmeladov is a character in Dostoevsky's *Crime and Punishment*. An alcoholic who has squandered all of his family's money, he says that one must go in seek of a loan even knowing that it will be refused, because 'there is nowhere else to go', and that sometimes a man must go somewhere since all men need someplace to go.

The Tactics for Today and Tomorrow

For the entire period since 2004, Russia 3 remained a project, a dream, a horizon. What we see today: Russia 1, United Russia, headed by Medvedev, who betrayed Libya, and, accordingly, by Yurgens and Gontmakher, with nasty elections and with an invitation to rejoice in the shameful state of this confused country which has lost its *raison d'etre*; without hope and without a strategy, without an Idea and purpose but constantly provided with entertainment and new gadgets; with Putin who basically ignored those who believed in him. And Russia 2, headed by radical pro-American stool pigeons, Russophobes, oligarchs who were removed from their plum positions and are now out for revenge, and psychotic liberals who view even this helpless and confused Russia of Putin's as a 'prison of nations' and as a 'cruel dictatorship'. Defending Russia 1 is not only repulsive, it is impossible. But one can't go to Russia 2 with a white funeral ribbon or to the ultra-nationalist stool pigeons who are rubbing their hands together in anticipation of another cycle of Russia's disintegration and relishing the idea of cashing in on it. We have finally come to the point where without the creation of Russia 3, a third force, a third political and ideological platform, one simply cannot go on living.

A Chain Reaction of the Authorities' Legitimacy

Russia was, is and always will be a major player in international politics — 'major' in terms of the laws that govern the geopolitical model of world domination. The creation of a unipolar world is only possible through the dismantling of the Eurasian system. Who rules Eurasia is not important: whether it is the Mongol Empire, the Russian Empire, the USSR or the Union State. 'Russia is the Heartland. He who controls the Heartland, controls the world,' Sir Halford Mackinder wrote.[38] It is extremely impor-

---

38 This is a paraphrase of Mackinder's original quotation, 'Who rules East Europe commands the Heartland: Who rules the Heartland commands the World-Island: Who rules the World-Island commands the world,' in *Democratic Ideals and Reality* (New York: Norton, 1962), p. 150.

tant for the West to break up Russia and turn it into a fragmented zone, an intention expressly stated by Brzezinski. The battle for Russia is in full force.

Everything now depends on the direction Russia will choose to move in. If globally she conducts a policy independent of the US, then together with other powerful countries and regions (China, India, Brazil and, possibly, even a united Europe) she may become the engine of a multipolar world, which will mean the end of the unipolar world and the end of American hegemony. If Russia has to drop out of this configuration, then the multipolar world will not be realised. The Americans have the means, resources and methods to restrain the other regions claiming to be poles of the multipolar world. Only Russia is capable of connecting them and of integrating them into a whole.

The ultra-liberals grouping together in the 'orange' Russia 2 are the exponents of the pro-American, treacherous course, aimed at surrendering our positions and helping the Americans maintain the unipolar world.

Back in the day, Putin's Munich speech was seen as Russia's return to her historical mission. We are not witnessing Russia falling back from these positions.

Putin is credited with stopping the disintegration of Russia through his policy. Unfortunately, this problem is not yet solved. Yes, the issue with Chechnya has been settled, but what is happening in Dagestan and other North Caucasus regions clearly indicates that the problem of separatism is ongoing and is on fertile ground. We can now see the downside of Putin's course and the possibility of backtracking. Putin started to do everything right but stopped halfway, without reaching the point of no return.

Take the conflict with Belarus, for example. Putin had adverse relations with Lukashenko, but he interpreted his differences with the Belarussian leader, first, not as a conflict of personalities, and second, not as a conflict of political personalities, but as a conflict over purely technical issues. Overall, Putin always adhered to the main idea of a strategic partnership between Russia and Belarus and was loyal to the idea of the Union State. Russian liberals and pro-American influence groups in the Kremlin tried to 'separate' Russia and Belarus even with Putin in power. But Moscow's policy towards Minsk ultimately hit the wrong track with Medvedev, who made ill-fated remarks addressed at Lukashenko. We are the older brothers of our Belarusian neighbour and we should forgive our younger brother whose actions we don't like.

Medvedev generally showed himself to be a man inexperienced in foreign policy, and he is not a quick learner, either. His video addresses and the innocent joy he displays at the cheap technological gadgets presented to him by the Americans, who quickly identified his weaknesses, deserve a special mention here. Sometimes his steps in international politics were implemented so clumsily that they were met with laughter and contempt. When Bush did similar things, it was not disgraceful for America because Bush was backed by a massive intellectual apparatus. Medvedev, however, was not 'backed' by anyone except the enemies of Russia. Medvedev's actions were the realisation of ultra-liberal and anti-national strategies. When Putin returned to power, he had to tackle the huge, newly-formed clump of unsolved and partially unsolvable problems, which had multiplied since he left to perform supporting roles in 2005.

A People's Front without the People

Early in May 2011, Prime Minister Vladimir Putin declared the creation of the All-Russian People's Front, a coalition of public organisations which allowed non-party candidates to be eligible for the 2011 Duma elections in accordance with the list of United Russia. But the very first meeting of the Coordination Council of the People's Front was held with the participation of Alexander Shokhin.[39] Excuse me for saying so, but Shokhin is the epitome of someone who is against the people. This means that the People's Front issue can be adjourned. It has no more sense than anything else that our authorities are doing. The Front will simply perform insignificant political and technical functions.

Still, the People's Front, the idea for which was proposed by me, must make one think: what is a people? When I say that Shokhin is the antithesis

---

39 Alexander Shokhin (b. 1951) has been the President of the RUIE since 2005 and is one of Russia's leading industrialists.

of the people, it opens up many meanings of the notion of 'people' because any notion is defined through its polar opposite.

One can single out several layers in the notion of a 'people'. We, the citizens of the Russian Federation, are a people inasmuch as we are not the citizens of Ukraine, France, Europe, or Turkey. The border between us and them is based on our citizenship, statehood, society, language, and culture. Thus, a people is contrasted with another people.

A people is also contrasted with an elite. A people is the majority, an elite is the minority. There are no societies where the majority lives in better conditions than the ruling minority. When we say 'a people' we mean the simple, miserable people who make up the lower and middle classes of social stratification.

A people is also an *ethnos* in some sense. A people is a composite element consisting of ethnic elements. It is somewhat different from an *ethnos*. There are ethnoses: the Chechens, the Avar,[40] the Great Russians, the Kalmyks,[41] and there is a Russian folk, or people, which integrates these ethnoses. At the ethnic level we stress differences and at the level of the people we stress unification. A people is an integral element which opposes disintegration.

A people is different from a 'population'. A people is a historical phenomenon, a people has a history. A population simply occupies a certain territory at a certain point in time. A people is a historically continuous succession, a process of existence that links generations. A people is always bigger than a population. A people worship their dead ancestors; a population lacks them (their dead souls are not classified anywhere). A people has descendants who are methodically conceived at night in order to multiply and populate future centuries and cycles to come. If history did not have this work done by the people, we would not have a historical memory and would not care about the future. A people is a historical notion, contrasted with a population as a purely statistical phenomenon.

---

40 A Caucasian people in the Dagestan region.

41 The Kalmyks, emigrated from Siberia to the Volga region in the seventeenth century. Today it is the autonomous Republic of Kalmykia, which is the only predominantly Buddhist country in Europe.

A people is a specific notion and simultaneously a historical, social, geopolitical, cultural, and sociological reality possessing a philosophical structure and all the attributes of existence. The People's Front should have responded to these deeply-rooted characteristics of the people. It should have been a front of the majority against the elite minority, a front requiring that the interests of the majority, miserable and inferior, be respected by the elite. The People's Front should have been an ultimatum to the authorities and the elite: 'Follow the people and you will become an elite, but if you go to Courchevel and acquire a face like Mikhail Prokhorov's,[42] you will be sent to the stables. This facial expression is insulting and is against the people.' Shokhin has exactly that kind of expression. The People's Front could be relevant if it followed the Russian trajectories of the national ethos; defended Russia before other countries; strived for the unification of the ethnoses in the face of separatism; stood for the nationalism of the miserable, simple people against the self-indulgent, anti-Russian Russophobic elite; and stood for history against the bluff of a consumer society. It would be a wonderful metaphysical, philosophical, political, ideological, and global program. Regretfully, Putin's People's Front does not have anything in common with such an understanding of 'people'.

Putin would be better off engaging in a genuine people's front and not in the People's Front that he is dealing with at the moment. The meaning of notions is the principal aspect of politics; semantics is what propels political processes. If we start with kōans: invite the self-indulgent bourgeois to a poor people's gathering, grant maternity leave to bachelors, or invite a thousand 'crowned thieves' and those who are notoriously corrupt to a people's front and claim that they are the best people, the entire point is lost.

---

42   Mikhail Prokhorov (b. 1965) is a Russian billionaire who ran for President as an independent in 2012. He owns the Brooklyn Nets basketball team.

Putin's Dead End
An Analysis of the Political Situation after 4 March 2012

In order to understand what is going on in contemporary Russian politics and what to expect, it is necessary to retrace the events that preceded our present situation. We will start in 2008.

Putin's two terms were over and he faced a dilemma: how to preserve power without violating the provisions of the Constitution. He could have had a third term in spite of the Constitution. He had credibility, and a people's referendum would have supported this idea without hesitation. But what about a fourth term? Another referendum? Some people urged Putin to do it, but he refused.

Another possible scenario: he could have chosen a successor from those who could stick to his course, like Sergei Ivanov or Vladimir Yakunin.[43] These superpower nationalists from the law enforcement agencies would soon be no less popular than Putin himself, but in four years they would probably not give the power back, so Putin brushed this option aside as well.

He could have chosen the pensioner Viktor Zubkov,[44] but that would have looked grotesque and Viktor Alexeevich would have sunk his teeth deep into the power structure (there are always people who can prompt him to do it and who will support him in the process). So this was not an option either.

The Manoeuvre

There was only one option left: to bet on an unpopular figure not capable of holding on to the position after March 2012, but capable of appeasing and alluring the West, as well as the domestic liberal opposition. In other

---

43   Vladimir Yakunin (b. 1948) has been head of the state-owned Russian Railways since 2005.

44   Viktor Alexeevich Zubkov (b. 1941) was Prime Minister of Russia from 2007 until 2008 and was Putin's First Deputy Prime Minister during Medvedev's term. Putin has named him as someone who could possibly be elected President. He is also the Chairman of the Board of Directors of Gazprom.

words, someone who could delay the imminent confrontation with Washington. This is what Putin opted to do, and this reshuffling was dubbed 'a tandem'.

And it worked! The West and the opposition seriously believed in Medvedev's second term and postponed their plan for Russia's disintegration. Expecting a rerun of Gorbachev, and believing that he would be able to personally continue with the disintegration of the country after 2012, they slowed down a little. Medvedev's entourage (I. Yurgens, E. Gontmakher, etc.) convincingly reported to the American and British secret intelligence services: 'Wait a little and we will do everything ourselves.' They waited until September 2011. In September, after the congress of United Russia, there was a showdown. Putin returned — more precisely, he showed us that, in fact, he had never left in the first place. The hopes for an 'evolutionary' disintegration of Russia were thwarted. Washington activated Plan B, that is, the more radical plan: their agents of influence received envelopes with the word 'revolution' inscribed on them. This is what upset the opposition so much: the feeling that they were duped by the Medvedev scheme. They started to hastily prepare for the 'Bolotnaya'[45] and 'Snezhnaya' revolutions, fastening white ribbons to their lapels.

Putin's own entourage played up to the liberals. While in power, Putin's corrupt officials did everything to increase the inefficiency and unpopularity of the authorities, but, after being fired, they pointed at the social and economic failures they had themselves created and shifted the blame to Putin. Good examples of this are Kudrin or Surkov, who called the people who gathered on Bolotnaya, 'the best people Russia has to offer'. Creating, almost singlehandedly, the utterly pointless entity of United Russia and making sure that not a single political idea sprung up from its ranks (thus delegitimising it), Surkov delegated responsibility and scurried to the government and then delegated it even lower, as usual, when the time came to pay the bills.

---

45 Bolotnaya is a square in central Moscow. In December 2011 a large protest against what the protesters believed would be unfair electoral practices in the upcoming elections happened there.

Thus, on 4 March 2012, Putin stood face to face with America and its network of agents, from then onward geared towards a revolution. This network has two segments: street level (Bolotnaya) and intra-governmental. They are directly related: Yurgens, Timakova,[46] and the like stand with one foot in the Kremlin and with the other foot in the ranks of the anti-Putin revolutionary crowd.

Besides, a gigantic layer of the corrupt Russian elite also plays into the anti-Putin revolution. Habitually selling and betraying everything, they don't mind selling their country out too, given half a chance.

Today, Putin finds himself in a difficult situation. He is back without having violated the law and there are no competitors left. The West fell for 'Perestroika 2' and the 'reset'. Mission accomplished. But at what price...

Why is the West against Putin?

Almost immediately after his first election, the West classified Putin as 'the bad guy'. He failed to become a 'friend' of the West. They sensed his persistency when it came to defending Russia's national interests. Putin embarked on a path of strengthening Russia and her sovereignty, daring to conduct, albeit partially and fragmentarily, an independent regional policy — a course that stood in sharp contrast with the policies of Gorbachev and Yeltsin. Initially softly and cautiously, then overtly, he challenged American hegemony and unipolar globalisation. In his Munich speech he called a spade a spade. After that, the West became disillusioned with the Russian president. 'This is a bad guy,' Washington resolved. 'Time to finish him off.'

Putin could be dealt with and on some issues he could even strike a compromise with the West (such as in his cooperation with the US on Afghanistan, relations with NATO, etc.). On economic issues he was liberal-minded and constantly avoided social policy, which made his domestic popularity genuinely justified. This was sufficient for the West. Putin did not exactly oppose global hegemony, but he did manage to slow it down. He disrupted the schedule of global 'democratisation' and 'de-sovereignisa-

---

46   Natalya Timakova (b. 1975) is a Russian journalist who was appointed Press Attaché to Medvedev in 2008. Since 2012 she has been Medvedev's Press Attaché in his role as Prime Minister.

tion'. That is why he was demonised and sentenced to deposition. Operation 'tandem' delayed the West's most radical scenario for four years, but did not remove it from the agenda. Today the process is underway.

Hegemony

We are talking about hegemony — a term that some might consider anachronistic. But Antonio Gramsci[47] gave a precise definition to 'hegemony' as 'a rule that is not perceived as such by those in power'. The difference between hegemony and direct power is that the existence of hegemony is not declared, not emphasised, and not fixed in documents, laws or agreements. Hegemony exists as a fact, and everybody is content with it, but it is rather implied than expressly declared.

Today we live in the conditions of expanding hegemony. It has two forms. The first is direct, express American hegemony (called 'unipolarity' or 'the American empire'), which is openly admitted by American neoconservatives. It was almost an official policy during the presidency of George W. Bush. The second is the disguised hegemony of globalism implemented through the global distribution of Western values, norms and procedures as a universal socio-political and economic organisation (the latter is sometimes called a 'pole-free world', in which the West dominates not in the name of a certain country but as an invisible centre, setting the global protocol and its system of codes and rules).

Both types of hegemony, in spite of the fact that their theoreticians are sometimes in discord, concur in that there should not be an independent and sovereign power that could act independently of the US and establish systems of norms, rules, interests and values significantly different from those of the liberal democratic, market-capitalist Western code. In the entire world, both in the West and in other regions of the planet, hegemony

---

47 Antonio Gramsci (1891–1937) was an Italian Communist who was imprisoned by the Fascists. He developed the theory of cultural hegemony, which (in brief) holds that a political group cannot maintain power without first persuading the members of a society that the ideas it propagates are the normal state of affairs, thus giving itself legitimacy. Therefore, control over the cultural apparatus of a society is a prerequisite for holding power, rather than being something which follows a revolution.

exists in the form of various institutions, networks, and groups of influence at various levels: from government entities to financial centres, transnational corporations, non-government organisations, centres supporting 'democracy and human rights', the international media, and various Internet communities. Where the government's official course complies with hegemony, these networks function publicly. When countries try to avoid hegemony, to defend their (even relative) independence, the agents of hegemony form the 'fifth column', acting in the name of 'democracy', 'human rights', 'civil society', and so forth.

Putin stood in the way of the expansion and strengthening of Western hegemony within the territory of the Russian state. In doing so, he engaged in a conflict with it. This is a key to understanding the political processes unfolding in contemporary Russia. Today the leaders of Bolotnaya act as operational centres of this same network of influence.

4 March

The elections of 4 March 2012 were utterly transparent, but their results still were, and had to be, contested by the radical opposition. In the virtual picture of the world created by the architects of hegemony, elections of 'bad guys' are automatically declared invalid because, in terms of hegemony, Putin is permanently 'illegitimate'. 'A good Putin is an absent Putin.' This is the axiom of global politics. In such a situation, what does the opinion of Russian voters amount to? Practically nothing. Hegemony habitually ignores the opinion of the majority in the cases where such opinion goes against its interests. For example, in the 1990s the liberal pro-Western team of Yeltsin and the young reformers unblinkingly ignored the referendum on the preservation of the USSR, and in 1993 it attacked the Parliament in cold blood. The West sympathetically accepted and approved that. Violence on the part of the supporters of hegemony is not violence, it is the 'side effects' of democracy. That is why the transparent and convincing victory of Putin in the first round did not impress the West at all.

Another question arises: how will Putin orchestrate his relations with the Russian masses? If he realises that the hegemony games are over and not one of his promises or statements in the liberal or pro-Western vein will be trusted by either Washington or the radical opposition, his last resort will be the Russian people and their backing. This will strengthen his position domestically, but none of his concessions will enhance his position in the outside world.

If Putin continues to manoeuver, he risks losing the domestic support of the masses as well. The opposition, working for hegemony, will cynically chalk it up and it will become their trump card, because there are not enough supporters of pure liberalism and Westernism to effect another revolution.

The Principal Trajectories of the Political Cycle Today

The plot of the first scenario is Putin preserving the old power model, based on a compromise between Western hegemony and support from the masses of the people. Putin's famous formula is a combination of 'liberalism' and 'patriotism'. Liberalism is intended for the West and the Russian economic and, to an extent, political elites, and patriotism is for the masses. Since these notions are mutually exclusive or, at least, mutually restraining, there has been no real shift towards either of these trends. Nevertheless, this model was successful in the early 2000s, although it started to malfunction in 2004–2005 and practically ran dry after 2008, when the successor, tandem and 'reset' issues came to the fore. It was a marked liberal shift, which logically led to the elimination of Putin along with the second half of his formula, patriotism. If Putin's declarations after the election continue to be ambiguous and elusive, stemming from this formula, where incompatible directives and trends sometimes pop up, like globalisation and sovereignty, democratisation and the strengthening of the vertical power, a path toward closer ties with Europe and focus on the independent development of Russia, next time this may arouse distrust, alienation and rejection among both basic sectors of society: the elite and the masses.

It is obvious that any attempts by Putin to attract the supporters of hegemony, liberals, Westernists, and 'democrats' will not be taken seriously by them. He will not be forgiven for the ruse with Medvedev and the associated failed hopes for the evolutionary disintegration of Russia.

At the same time, the masses, not seeing any serious steps by Putin towards a social policy and a national idea, will finally become disillusioned too.

In view of Washington's unanimous decision to remove Putin, the 'inertial' scenario will equal a gradual political suicide. The 'liberalism + patriotism' formula no longer works. But does Putin himself understand that?

If one foregoes emotions and wishful thinking, one has to admit that, unfortunately, it is this 'inertial' scenario that appears to be the most likely one. In this case we should expect serious perturbations, maybe even revolutions and wars.

The second scenario is capitulation, which means that Putin, realising the seriousness of his situation, decides to capitulate before the onslaught of hegemony and, rejecting patriotism, will move towards the West and clearcut liberalism. The possibility of taking this course, however, is in contradiction with Putin's psychological portrait. Theoretically, in this case Putin will have to make certain concessions to the West and start the process of 'democratisation', 'liberalisation' and the simultaneous de-sovereignisation of Russia. The moves to weaken the vertical power, to bring about the liberalisation of the electoral legislation and the revocation of the selection by Presidential appointment of the governors of the subjects of the Federation (the territorial subdivisions) can be interpreted as moves in this direction.

In this case the most problematic aspect is the following: sooner or later (rather sooner than later) liberals and their Western supervisors will propose that Putin delegate power to another political figure. This figure can be an opposition representative or a compromise variant like Dmitry Medvedev. According to the logic of global hegemony, Putin's offences are so grievous that he will have to pay a very high price. Putin surely understands this.

That said, Putin has already missed his chance to delegate his power to Medvedev peacefully. His decision to return to the Kremlin significantly reduced his chances, however small, to be forgiven by global hegemony. Choosing in favour of liberalism and the West will automatically cost Putin his power and subsequently cause fairly serious repercussions. This scenario appears to be unlikely.

The third scenario is the transfiguration of the empire.

The last possible scenario for Putin after 4 March is for him to, out of his own formula, select 'patriotism' as a priority. It will mean that he has finally and irreversibly resolved to bet on the masses, which are expecting order, justice, imperial power and a revival of the country from him. To achieve this one has to replace the slogans of 'stability' and 'comfort' with those of mobilisation, exerting effort and spiritual uplifting. Patriotism in this case will mean not only the preservation of the existing state of things but a leap upward. Not just conservatism but a conservative revolution.

This is an extremely difficult path. This scenario contradicts various tendencies and trends which started to take root in Russia in the 1990s. The main staples of this policy are the following (as I see them):

1. The formulation of a consistent and three-dimensional model for the strategic revival of Great Russia as an independent empire, capable of confronting hegemony in all its forms (both overt and implied). To do this it is necessary to rely on one's own resources and traditional values and look for supporters among the world powers that also refuse to recognise hegemony and which are interested in a multipolar, polycentric world order.
2. A radical rotation of the elites involving a mass replacement of the bureaucracy and financial oligarchy that was formed in the Yeltsin era, with new patriotic, ideologically motivated cadres (the new nobility).
3. A division of all spheres of corruption into two parts: corruption involving the betrayal of Russian national interests and corruption not involving such betrayal. Drastic, fast-paced elimination of the first part and gradual preparation for a struggle with the second. Today corruption is not just Russia's domestic problem, it is a transnational phenomenon with overseas connections. Only when corruption is confined within Russia can it be defeated.
4. A revival of spiritual and aesthetic culture, education and tradition. Russian society is overcome with moral degradation, cynicism and degeneration. The disintegration of the Soviet codes has been combined with the uncritical adoption of elements of Western post-

modern culture, which, in its turn, is deteriorating. This process must be decisively reversed. Culture has crucial importance for the existence of a society. A cultural revolution is necessary.
5. In economics a radical turn away from the ultra-liberal model is needed, aimed at the financial sector and natural resources trade, to the development of high technology, social policy and industry. From the virtual economy, which is increasing Russia's dependence on the flow of the global financial networks with their habitual crises and catastrophes, it is necessary to shift to real economy.

In order to realise this scenario Putin will have to make a serious effort. With the help of a course that focuses on meaningful, consistent and logically sound patriotism he will have a good chance to strengthen his position as the genuine leader of Russia and start the revival of the country in earnest. But to do this he will have to use extremely tough domestic measures, especially as regards the power elite, and he will have to confront significant pressure from the West and global hegemony.

The fact that Putin had not previously made any significant steps to prepare for such a turn in his policy impairs the prospects for the third scenario. Theoretically, however, this way exists and it is the only way that can help us to avoid revolutions and catastrophes.

A brief analysis of these three scenarios reveals an interesting perspective. Russia is definitely entering a zone of political turbulence. The country is starting to shake. The agents of influence for global hegemony and its network will take care of that, and the authorities will mechanically create suitable conditions for them (against their own will).

Previously we have analysed the situation in the political landscape on the basis of two poles: Putin on the one side and the radical opposition, embodied by Bolotnaya, on the other. If the Russian political geometry retains its bipolar structure, one can forecast the following process: the revolutionary 'Bolotnaya' pole, supported by the infrastructure and its potential for hegemony, will gradually increase this potential, using any failures on the part of the authorities to its advantage, and the authorities (especially if they use the first or the second scenario), on the contrary, will gradually lose momentum. In this situation the threat to the very existence of Russia as an independent state will grow drastically. The current bipolar system and the readiness of the West and its agents of influence in the radical opposition to start a revolutionary dismantling of the Russian regime is a very serious thing. And if only two positions remain (Putin against the Bolotnaya), the entire system will become extremely vulnerable.

This is why it is urgently necessary to form a third pole and to shift to a new political geometry. The third position has been ideologically formulated above as a third scenario for Putin, but the possibility that Putin may reject it and will not go in this direction should not be disregarded. In fact, such an outcome is highly probable. And if Putin does not go the patriotic way, it must be carried out by others.

Russia 3

Today we crucially need Russia 3, the third position, which is different both from Putin's Russia 1 and the Russia 2 of the Bolotnaya. The West strives for global domination anyway (either expressly or by implication) so in any country, especially in a key country like Russia, there is always 'the fifth column'. This is inevitable. Moreover, this 'fifth column' usually acts on both sides of the state: from the opposition and from inside the centre of power itself. The US and its NATO partners have extensive experience in this respect.

Russia 2 will be actively engaged in disrupting Russia's statehood, continuing the series of destructive processes that were begun in the late 1980s. This Russia 2, without counting on the half-hearted, compromise-prone and hesitant Russia 1, must be confronted by Russia 3. Its mission and meaning is to decisively combat the agents of global hegemony inside Russia, both among the radical opposition and in the segment which acts from inside the regime, betraying the country's national interests.

A determined 'anti-Bolotnaya' patriotic movement must be created today, with a clear goal: effective resistance against the 'colour revolution', directed not so much against Putin as a personality and politician, as against Russia herself; the realisation of the five points described in the third scenario.

Today Russia needs strong, supreme Russian power as urgently as it ever has. Whether it will be born through Putin's (Russia 1's) awakening or emerge as a separate phenomenon, independent of Putin, remains to be seen. In any case, preservation of the bipolar model — the Russia of Putin and the Russia of the opposition — is fatal in the current situation.

If the Bolotnaya opposition manages to present the situation as a confrontation between the regime and the dissatisfied, protesting masses who are crying for justice, this alone will become a significant victory for them. On the other hand, the people who care about their country cannot just relax, doing nothing and trying to figure out what decision will be made by Putin after 4 March. What if he makes the wrong decision?

Under bipolar politics the entire critical capital derived from Putin's various mistakes and hesitant moves from his unconvincing personnel appointments and failing anti-corruption campaigns will be automatically appropriated by Russia 2, for the benefit of global hegemony. Sooner or later this process will reach its critical point where the existence of a free, united and sovereign Russia will be problematic. The 'inertial' (and, sadly, most likely) scenario regarding Putin's behaviour will imminently lead to this situation. And if a third position emerges with a clear-cut programme using the five points above, as well as trustworthy leaders, at least the two poles will be strengthened simultaneously: the 'Bolotnaya' pole and the patriotic pole ('anti-orange' or Poklonnaya).[48]

Conservative Revolution as the Best Scenario for Russia

The formation of the third patriotic force is a national imperative. This force will drastically change the political map of Russia. Russia 2 blackmails Putin, demanding 'more democracy'. Russia 3, the patriotic Russia, must demand from Putin 'more patriotism'. If Putin effectively restrains

---

[48] Poklonnaya ('Adoration') Hill is the highest point in Moscow and is the location of Victory Park, which commemorates Russia's victory in the Second World War. On 4 February 2012, just before the presidential election, a mass rally of patriotic and nationalist groups was held there in opposition to the 'orange' protests occurring at the time. Dugin himself was one of the speakers.

the Bolotnaya and defends the country's interests, the patriots will support him, as they did at Poklonnaya Gora. Should he hesitate, Russia 3 must pressure the authorities. In a critical situation we should be ready to enter a tough confrontation with the internal and external enemies and even seize power, if necessary.

The only correct and helpful scenario for Russia after 4 March must be written by ourselves. We must pull ourselves together, summon our courage and raise the Russian flag of revival, struggle and victory high above our agonised society. It is wrong and irresponsible in such a critical situation to leave the country's future in the hands of any one man.

Conservatives are habitually loyal to the authorities. They can easily maintain the current state of things. But when this state of things is crumbling before our very eyes and the authorities are obviously incapable of stopping the forces that threaten to tear everything apart, it is the psychology that has to be changed. Today a conservative revolution is necessary, an awakening and a spiritual uprising of those who are devoted to Russia and are ready to fight for her against the global hegemony at any cost. Maybe it is the last battle. This thought has inspired numerous generations of Russians who have furiously defended their motherland, its freedom, its ideas, and its missions. The people, the masses should return to politics and become a vital political force. Not the clownish Duma opposition, acting as an appendix to either the regime or Western hegemony, but the force of genuine Russia, the Third Force.

Necessity of Awakening: The Search for an Idea

A political strategy can be built around a sound national idea. That said, none of Russia's four presidents took the trouble to formulate it. Basically, the country has been living in an ideological vacuum since Gorbachev. The absence of a national idea in Russia is sad and almost criminal. Paradoxically, this national idea is right there on the surface. The basis of the Russian ideology could be, for instance, integrity over atomisation, a unique historical development of the country, and a unique system of ethical values. A moral embodied in a slogan — this is what makes the national idea. But in

Russia such a delicate thing as ideology is delegated to spin doctors, puppet masters and managers.

The reason for this is that Vladimir Putin underestimates the importance of the notion of an 'idea'. He is an ingenious pragmatist, but ideas don't matter to him, especially compared to, say, American neoconservatives, who understand how potent ideas can be...

Today we are witnessing an almost exact rerun of the situation of the late 1980s, when the Soviet authorities were formally in control of the situation but did not know what to make of it. All resources were directed at solving purely technical tasks. Society was consumed with apathy and resentment. Besides, a small but closely-knit group of Western-oriented 'liberal intelligentsia' ('little people') was ideologically mobilised to topple the system and destroy the state. The entire process was supervised from abroad. The silent Russian people did not want this destruction, in fact they voted for the preservation of the USSR in March 1991,[49] but they were dissatisfied with the situation and did not intend to defend the status quo. The repressive apparatus was on the side of the authorities and the historical initiative on the side of the rebelling Westernists.

What did it all amount to in 1991? It amounted to the collapse of the USSR, the creation of an antisocial and unfair oligarchic capitalist system, the start of Russia's disintegration, the destruction of socialism and the coming of the roaring 1990s, which was the triumph of the comprador bourgeois and Russophobe elites. *Ekho Moskvy* and its ideology have secured their power.

In 1999, Putin 'froze' the situation, but he did not reverse it. At first it seemed that he was waiting for the right moment. Then it seemed that he was wasting his time. The Dmitry Medvedev scam was meant as a product for export: the US saw that Russia was headed by a 'liberal' and eased their pressure on Russia, expecting that during the second term this 'liberal' would ruin the country himself. The ultra-liberal opposition, hypnotised by the Institute of Contemporary Development, believed the same thing.

---

49   On 17 March 1991, a referendum on whether or not the Soviet Union should be preserved was held throughout the nation. 70% of voters elected to preserve the USSR, with a voter turnout rate of 80%.

All of this worked, and Putin organised his legal return, and the West had nothing to do but to accept it.

But these complex manipulations with the liberals and the West left the people and the Idea unattended. They were rendered a zero. Machiavelli warned that the worst thing a ruler can do is believe in his own lies...

So, what did Putin Fail to Do?

First, he did not propose an Idea for society, only techniques. This is why politics in Russia was given away to spin doctors and PR specialists. This was a fatal underestimation of the power of ideas.

Second, Putin failed to develop a strategy and responds only to current challenges. He does not have an idea for the future of Russia. He has only a limited understanding of the contemporary world. This world is very deceitful, complex, dynamic and aggressive. In order to correctly manoeuvre in it, one should analyse it closely and deeply.

Third, Putin failed to implement a practical rotation of the elites over the last thirteen years. The ruling elite was formed in the 1990s and maintains its destructive and privatising mission: hence the rampant corruption. Putin did not raise 'new people', he only gathered an additional group which is working under the same old conditions and rules.

Fourth, Putin did not create foreign policy instruments capable of an efficient confrontation with Western hegemony. He either played with the West or avoided it, or sharply criticised it. It was unclear whether Russia was saying 'yes' or 'no' to the existing world order. Maybe Putin thought that this uncertainty would give him free reign. It is possible but at the same time it blindfolds him.

Fifth, Putin did not give the people the principal things they needed: the satisfaction of their sense of right and wrong, and the feeling that social policy and solidarity were in place. Putin was afraid of a direct appeal to socialism. The people expected him to do that but they did not get what they wanted.

Sixth, Putin did not even start to seriously analyse ethnic problems and the issue of nationalities. In this sphere a hands-off approach was taken. After a decisive victory in Chechnya and stripping the Federation's subjects of their claims to sovereignty (which were the biggest and most genuine achievements of his presidency), Putin did not formulate a project of inter-ethnic balance nor a national model of political organisation. Multi-ethnic Russia, in the context of an objective worsening in terms of immigration, found herself in an explosive situation.

Seventh, Putin preferred to distance himself from society by way of adopting a mass media policy of the lowest order. The media has systematically lowered the cultural bar, corrupts the masses, and their control over political topics only aggravates the situation: the masses are subjected to entertaining programmes of forceful idiotisation, and political discourse is strictly controlled.

Eighth, Putin delegated the management of science and education to highly incompetent figures, who almost destroyed the existing system, clumsily copying the Western pattern. As a result of their experiments Russia's intellectual potential rapidly dwindled.

This is how Putin returned and continues to act, fully armed with these fatal mistakes. He remains without any idea or strategy, an adequate elite, a proper foreign policy, a socially oriented domestic policy, a model for the national organisation of society, nor a mass media with a culture-forming mission, amidst intellectual degradation.

Who is to blame? I think Putin himself. He coped with one historical challenge in the early 2000s, and failed to cope with the other. He was marked by indecisiveness, hesitation, the selection of the wrong strategies and good-for-nothing cadres. Yes, his entourage, who are responsible for the supervision of political processes, deceives him. But this just means that he wants to be deceived and does not want to face the truth. Putin must have a constructive plan. The situation could only be saved if the authorities wake up. Anything else will aggravate it and make it all the more catastrophic. Those who act against Putin are mortal enemies of Russia. Their successes are incompatible with our lives and with the country's existence, but the fact that these forces are looming again is Putin's fault.

Corrections of Mistakes: Is This Scenario Realistic?

There is one last thing: the immediate creation of a third force is crucial. It must stand against the rebelling ultra-liberals and the American networks of agents both inside the dissenting opposition and the Putin administration itself (where they are aplenty), as well as against those mistakes of Putin's which are impossible to accept and justify and which can easily become fatal for the country. Apart from Putin-Medvedev with their clique, Navalny-Nemtsov-Kasyanov with their clique should be opposed by a third clique, for the sake of the empire, social justice, culture, the Idea, national policy, strategy, a radical cleansing of the elite and an intellectual revival.

Putin's regime is not very inspiring today. But it is Russia, the people, the Idea, and the future horizon that are inspiring. They are worth fighting for with one's life. We lost our country twice: in 1991 and in 1993. We lost to the same forces: *Ekho Moskvy*, pro-Western liberals, the 'little people',[50] and the American agents of influence. These same forces are preparing for the third round: the collapse of Russia is ahead. They will overthrow Putin and the country (or what will be left of it) will perish under the rubble. This is just a revenge project by the forces that were staved off for a time in the 1990s. Putin did not finish them off. He did not break their necks. So now they are sticking them out again.

The Putin that we have Lost: Criticisms from Above

The emergence of Vladimir Putin in the Russian political arena thirteen years ago and his current 'semi-silence' is enigmatic. Nobody could understand who he was. Is he a Russian patriot and a loyal initiate into the secret service who skilfully uses a liberal's mask and only rarely shows his true colours (or more precisely, his iron face) or, on the contrary, is he a pro-

---

50 According to the mathematician Igor Shafarevich, who also writes in commentaries on Russia, Russian history has been marked by an opposition between the 'little people', who despise the morals and traditions of the majority, and the 'great people', which is the majority. He writes this in his untranslated book Russophobia.

Western liberal, subtly disguised as an enforcement agent and a supporter of empire, but at critical moments always relieving the tension in relations with the West and signalling: 'I am your man!' Putin is still elusive, contradictory, and mysterious.

After coming to power he made a drastic leap, which became a distinctive feature of his epoch as contrasted with the Gorbachev and Yeltsin era. He took a 90-degree turn in his course. He maintained capitalism, liberalism, and the Western orientation (as well as the other 'joys' of the 1990s: the oligarchy, corruption, the cynical comprador elite, the elimination of morals and the national spirit, the monstrous media, etc.), but at the same time he stopped the disintegration of Russia, the intra-oligarchical wars through the use of political parties and federal TV channels, the rebellious provinces and governors, the war in Chechnya (which he won), and the national republics' claims to sovereignty. After such a good start it seemed that the remaining 90 degrees were not far off and that Putin would just as quickly build an empire, integrate the post-Soviet space, arm himself with a Eurasian ideology, restore the status of religion and tradition, start reviving the culture, and restart the education of the spirit, values and customs of the people. But, alas, that was not to be.

Making a sharp 90-degree bank towards the 1990s, Putin suddenly stopped equally sharply. He deviated from the previous course by precisely 90 degrees, but no more and no less. The formula was discovered: 'liberalism + patriotism'. It was supposed to develop towards a consistent and consummate Eurasian patriotic position. Putin managed to balance on the edge of the contradictory 'liberalism + patriotism' position for as long as he wanted. He made society accept this particular Putin as an integral phenomenon. The ultra-liberal view him as a 'dictator'. This is not true. Putin prefers to act softly and uses force only in extreme cases. He does not like violence and resorts to it only in very rare circumstances which directly affect the interests of the state.

The ultra-patriots view him as a liberal, an 'agent of Western influence', and a 'protégé of the oligarchs and the global cabal'. This is not true either. The West hates Putin: he is a genuine threat to the global domination of the

American empire. The West would give (and gives) anything to eliminate him.

Putin is seen as a patriot and a nationalist. Seemingly that is not true either. An unexplained sphinx? In fact, Putin's mystery can be solved and we seem to be close to its solution.

Putin's New Formula?

The first year of Putin's third presidency made it absolutely clear for me personally why there was an aura of uncertainty around this figure. Is spite of Putin's repeated explanations of his course, both Russia and the West are still expecting surprises from him. The element of uncertainty was a specific trait in the style of Putin's presidency in recent years.

Today I can say who Putin is. This is no longer a mystery to me. In my opinion, if one sums up the principal aspects of his behaviour during the first two terms of his presidency, his ministerial term and the first year of his third term, one will come to the following conclusion: Putin constitutes a classical realist politician.

What is Realism?

I have recently written a new textbook on the theory of international relations — a scientific discipline/subject which was developed in England after the Second World War. Realism in international relations is not simply household realism or realism in painting, and not the so-called *Realpolitik*. The best interpretations of realism are given by the classical authors of this subdivision of international politics: Hans Morgenthau,[51] Edward Carr,[52] Henry Kissinger and their neo-realist followers: Kenneth Waltz,[53] Robert Gilpin,[54] John Mearsheimer,[55] and Stephen Krasner.[56]

The core of realism in international relations and, more broadly, in politics, is the principle of a contemporary national state as the major actor.

---

51 Hans Morgenthau (1904–1980) was a German-American political scientist who greatly influenced the understanding of international law and international relations. He is regarded as one of the most fundamental thinkers in the school of political realist thought. According to him, the most important aspect of international relations is how nation-states pursue their interests in terms of power. He believed that politics had immutable laws and that morality could not be applied to the actions of states.

52 E H Carr (1892–1982) was an English historian and international relations theorist. In his book The Twenty Years' Crisis, he divided ideas about international relations into two camps, utopians and realists. Although more sympathetic to realism, he was not uncritical of it, since he considered it without a goal or a basis for concrete action, and hoped for a synthesis of the two positions.

53 Kenneth Waltz (1924–2013) was an American political scientist who was one of the founders of the neo-realist school of political thought. He posited that international relations are in a perpetual state of anarchy since, unlike within a nation, there is no authority higher than the various nation-states that can impose order from above. Waltz believed that democracies seldom go to war against other democracies, and that therefore the spread of democracy throughout the world could help to bring about peace. Peace is also promoted when a single power has a monopoly on violence, as the United States currently has. Waltz believed that the US' present role as the pole of a unipolar world would be short-lived, however.

54 Robert Gilpin (b. 1930) is an American political scientist who, in recent years, has been attempting to apply political realism to America's policies in the Middle East. He has argued that when international relations reach a state of stability, they are defined by the rise of a new hegemon which then imposes its own systems on the rest of the world, bringing said stability. He sees the United States as the current hegemon.

55 John Mearsheimer (b. 1947) is an American political scientist. In the 1990s he postulated that, following the withdrawal of American and Soviet forces from Europe, Europe would eventually revert to a multipolar scenario, and believed that the proliferation of nuclear weapons throughout Europe could help to maintain peace. In 2006 he also published a study of the influence of the Israel lobby on American politics.

56 Stephen Krasner (b. 1942) is an American political scientist. He has argued that countries such as the US are threatened by weak states that lack stability, and that it is the responsibility of strong nations to stabilise weak states by inculcating in them the system of market-based liberal democracy.

For realists, the entire sphere of international relations is, absolutely and exclusively, an arena of the interaction of sovereign states. As regards international relations, liberals add to the list of actors of international politics the transnational corporations and Non-governmental organisations, and Marxists add international organisations that are created on the basis of class distinctions and which are beyond the borders of nation-states.

Three Principles of Realism: Sovereignty, the Prince, Leviathan

Realism is based on the three main political and philosophical principles: *Leviathan*, *The Prince* of Machiavelli and 'sovereignty' as defined by Jean Bodin), which underlie the theory of the contemporary state and became the basis of European international law (*Jus Publicum Europeum*) secured in the Westphalian system.

Realism in international relations is based on the premise that human nature is imperfect, that humans are prone to sin and weaknesses, and that there is permanent discord between people (Hobbes' thesis *Homo homini lupus est*: 'man is wolf to man'). The state and society exist precisely for the purpose of maintaining the individual in a neutral state, or at least to try to prevent him from total disintegration, if not improve him.

A pessimistic view of man, expressed in the idea that an individual who receives freedom will most likely engage in evil and unacceptable acts, underlies realism's treatment of politics. Realism declares the necessity of the state not only for the solution of foreign policy issues (where chaos and violence reign in the relations between states), but also as an instrument of domestic policy: restraining the individual from irreparably harming himself and his neighbours. The state must save man from the dark side of his own nature. People should voluntarily, through a social contract, delegate part of their powers and the option to be in charge of their own freedom to a strong state, Leviathan, and should laws be violated, the state ensures their observance. As Max Weber[57] noted, the state becomes the only insti-

---

57 Max Weber (1864–1920) was a German who is considered one of the founders of sociology. Weber writes about the 'monopoly of violence' by the state in his Politics as a Vocation.

tute of natural and legitimate violence, because it is a product of agreement and an embodiment of rationality in man, who thus overcomes his natural (beastly) state.

Unlike the traditional medieval state and, especially, an empire, Leviathan does not have any special mission, a spiritual or historical goal, or a divine purpose. Leviathan does not intend to improve human nature, it simply prevents anarchy and man's extermination of man. This is the beginning and the end of its function. Besides, Leviathan is created from below, is man-made, and is the product of a rational interpretation of his nature. This is how the state was interpreted in politics in the modern era.[58]

The next principle of realism in international politics is the sovereignty of Jean Bodin. It argued that a sovereign ruler is a ruler above whom there is no superior authority apart from God. Boden developed the idea of the state as an artificial organisation of life along rational lines whose supreme value is sovereignty as an absolute landmark in foreign policy. This means that there is no superior legitimate authority above the state which would oblige it to behave in a certain way in the international arena.

The figure of the prince or the 'new prince' created by Niccolò Machiavelli represented not a traditional monarch whose rule was guaranteed by social and political inertia, but a political figure facing the task of creating a state and a political system from scratch with the aid of his will and his mind. Here Machiavelli faced a problem of substantiating and validating political creativity based on rationality, will and efficiency.

The contemporary state is seen (or constructed) by him as a new political object, something that had not previously existed during the Middle Ages and in ancient times, and represents an apparatus for the efficient organisation of society in the interests of the ruler (new prince). The new prince, unlike the old prince, must not only preserve power in a given society with deeply rooted traditions and customs, which he has to observe, but he must create this society and these customs, secure his power and demonstrate his efficiency in practice.[59]

---

58   Thomas Hobbes, *Leviathan* (Cambridge: Cambridge University Press, 1996).—AD

59   Niccolò Machiavelli, *The Prince* (Cambridge: Cambridge University Press, 1988).—AD

Machiavelli's state does not have any purpose apart from being a power instrument of the 'new prince'; therefore all its institutions and principles should mandatorily have a rational end and constantly prove their efficiency. The volitional character of the new prince's rule is responsible for changing the political rules at a time when it is justified by certain purposes. The state is seen as a fully instrumental power mechanism, where everything comes down to the efficiency with which the ruling elite can seize and secure power. This leads to the optimal organisation of the political situation aimed at expanding and defending the national territories, as well as preventing civil revolts and the collapse of the state or a military defeat, which together constitute the principal responsibility of the rulers and is one of the main criteria of the efficiency and stability of their rule.

Realists view international relations as a field of anarchy (chaos) where every actor (the state) pursues his own self-interests. Therefore a war between sovereign states is a natural expression of the very nature of international relations as a battle between Leviathans. There is no higher instance than the state, and its relations with other states are driven only by its interests, wishes and possibilities, which are determined and realised by the political elite, that is the Prince, who is capable of proving the efficiency of his rule, maintaining power and securing his desired goals by any means.

Putin — an Absolute Realist

The description of realism in the Ministry of Defence's textbook and the model of Putin's rule show a striking convergence. Everything matches to the smallest detail. Putin's behaviour throughout all the preceding stages and at the present stage is fully integrated into the model of realism, with all its principles including those corresponding to Leviathan, sovereignty, and the new prince. In reality Putin, in spite of all societal expectations and the smoke and mirrors, ultimately has no long-term messianic ideology. In fact he considers the state as a manmade, rational, and pragmatic structure that is designed primarily for the protection of the sovereignty entrusted to it by Russian society. Putin relies on absolute state sovereignty and does not recognise the legitimacy of the demands made by the international community. Just like any realist, including American ones, he equates the decisions made by international institutions to nothing. Resolutions like the Kyoto

Protocol[60] and the Strasbourg court[61] are absolutely non-binding for him. The principle of a unipolar world as well as that of a world arbitrarily divided into several poles are equally unacceptable to him.

Putin is entirely convinced that the principles of sovereignty preclude the implementation of legal pressures against any state or its ruler by international institutions. He shares beliefs commonly attributed to modernism: that the relatively stable world order relies on balancing the principle of state sovereignty and the structure of international law. It is thanks to this that Russia did not surrender its nuclear weapons and maintains a strong potential to enforce its sovereignty. It is the fact that Russia is the only country aside from the US that has a nuclear triad — on land, in the sea, and in the air — that allows it to take an independent position in the international arena, and to have its own opinion and an independent foreign policy.' [62]

Putin sees a potential to keep the economy afloat and ensure Russia's energy sovereignty by utilising the country's abundant natural resources. The advantage for him lies in Russia's thousand-year tradition of independence (except for the period of the Tatar-Mongol yoke), as well as the deep historical, political, and ideological roots of independence and sovereignty that lies in the country's population itself.

Putin has the resources to carry out realistic policies. In areas where they lack their own forces, realist leaders usually resort to alliances and manoeuvring. In this sense, Putin plays a skilful game of chess in relations with China, the other modern realist government, as well as with Iran and other countries. He does not confront the West because he has no ideological grounds to do so.

---

60   The Kyoto Protocol is an international agreement signed in 1997 with the intention of reducing the amount of greenhouse gases emitted, including by the Russian Federation.

61   The European Court of Human Rights, which is based in Strasbourg, France, enforces the European Convention on Human Rights on the member states of the Council of Europe. The Russian Federation is a member.

62   From 'A Conversation with Vladimir Putin, Continuation,' dated 15 December 2011, available at www.rg.ru/2011/12/15/stenogramma.html.—AD

In a complete spirit of realism, Putin is inclined to consider international relations as ruled by chaos and anarchy: 'We are witnessing chaos everywhere, and we do not consider the position of our partners to be entirely correct. Why should we support what we think is wrong? Why should they demand that we implement their standards? Perhaps we will require them to implement our standards? Let's not demand anything from each other, let's treat each other with respect.'

It is quite obvious that all Putin has done in the past and all he is doing now fits completely into the classic understanding of realism in international relations. And just as two points are enough to draw a straight line, these facts allow us to make the following prediction: Putin will follow realist politics through to the very end. Most likely, his successor in eleven years will also be a proponent of the realist trend. This is a defined and pre-determined vector. Of course, realism as the future is not guaranteed in an absolute manner because the unpredictability of world events in recent years and months may interfere with this process.

Therefore it seems to me that the Putin enigma is solved. Putin is a realist. All the pros and cons, advantages and limitations of his rule are included in this thesis. This, in our opinion, is an axiom.

Thus, we live in a realist state and we have realist policies. All those who are discontented can leave! Anyone wishing to voice their opinions regarding alternative models of political policy — for example, it is liberalism that usually opposes realism but Marxism, postmodernism and positivism can also be that opposition — are welcome to the theoretical discussion.

Whether or not Putin will consider these alternatives depends on the correctness of their presentation and how respectful the dialogue turns out to be. Today, liberal squawking is not welcome and well-reasoned, rational counter-realist positions may well be considered....and set aside.

I think that Putin will no longer listen to anyone but realists. Earlier he pretended that he was listening to these and those and others, but now the subject is closed.

The second most important issue is whether or not the country has institutionalised Putin's realism. If we look carefully at the dynamics of Russia in recent decades, we can see that its liberal-democratic foreign policy era which propounded ideas of state de-sovereignisation, globalisation, integration into the world community, and supranational globalist values in domestic politics was very short, only lasting from 1986 to 1996 — between the end of the Gorbachev era and before the Yeltsin period. Beginning in 1996, after Primakov became the Minister of Foreign Affairs in the late Yeltsin years, Russian policy became realist. Under Putin, this same policy has practically been canonised.

During this time Russian society and its communities of experts, the mass media, journalism, and the entire educational structure beginning with the Moscow State Institute of International Relations (MGIMO) and ending with any institution studying and analysing international relations and international politics were all dominated by this totalitarian liberal discourse. In other words, realism became Russia's dominant foreign policy long ago but is still not reflected in its social institutions. It is fundamentally misunderstood and not analysed in scientific ways, and it is ignored in higher education. We are governed by realists and they define the course of our development, yet reflection concerning and the institutionalisation of this process has not occurred. The theory of realism in international relations and in the politics of the new post-Soviet Russia does not exist, and appropriate schools of thought and concepts have not been created. The *gap* between Putin's actual realism and the lack of understanding and institutionalisation thereof leads to falsification of the discourse. Putin's realism is often erroneously classified as patriotism or nationalism. Substitution occurs. Confusion occurs. Patriotism is emotion, feeling, a choice of values, the love of country, and not a theory. Realism is a specific paradigm of responsible, coherent behaviour in foreign policy and the proper theoretical conception of this behaviour. Realism involves the estimation of national interests in the classic scheme of calculation and not in some emotional need, looking for approval. In other words, realism is a scientific, rational, reasonable, sensible institutionalised position that can be analysed while patriotism and nationalism are controversial in terms of their coherence, are haphazard, and are emotionally coloured points of view.

It is wrong to characterise Putin as a nationalist or a patriot. Putin conducts himself precisely as a realist, but one who behaves as a realist in terms of the behaviourist model of international relations. Everything else is a black box. We do not know what is on his mind, and we do not want to know. As an actor, and as he operates, Putin is a realist. To say this is to reveal Putin's algorithm. I believe during the time when Putin revealed himself as a realist, he already had no need for the smokescreen of liberalism in international relations. (Incidentally in this sense, institutions such as the MGIMO in its present condition, with liberal faculties and educational systems offering no alternatives to liberalism or residual Marxism as norms for modern international relations, are completely unacceptable.)

A new model for understanding modern processes based on the paradigm of realism is necessary in global politics. We do not have a conceptualised Russian realism or a Russian answer to neo-realist models, such as those of Kenneth Waltz (the unipolar world), Richard Gilpin (the theory of hegemonic stability), or other Western developments. Russian realism should carefully consider a number of neo-realist schemes describing the modern world. I believe that one of the most important tasks of the modern era is the institutionalisation of a non-politically biased, scientific, cold, abstract, rigorous, balanced, and hyper-reactionary Russian realism.

I often participate in discussions with different experts and am amazed that the people representing our country at the international level have never even heard of Morgenthau and believe that the defence of state and national interests is equivalent to fascism. Such specialists are too incompetent to be tolerated in the classroom, let alone represent our country in the international arena. We need to eliminate these losers as a class. A society that does not ostracise these types is absolutely sick. We have lots of these anomalies, but as the nature of Russian's foreign policy discussion becomes something outrageous, the time has come to eliminate them. Our theories are dominated by an unchallenged, haphazard liberalism in international affairs that is poised to infect us like a virus. The impression is that our experts simply belch liberal jargon, spew it forth, and do so without even knowing or realising it.

By this token, the institutionalisation of Russian-style realism will benefit Russian liberalism in international relations because liberal discourse, as it appears on screens and in the press, is simply an affront to human dignity. The global discourse of liberalism in international relations, which incidentally is rather rational and well-reasoned, is nowhere to be found in Russia and will not be even in the long term. However, in order to begin the process of bringing Russian political science in line with the world's standards of rationality, it is necessary to *de-monopolise liberal discourse in international relations and institutionalise realism*.

One more thing which seems very important to me is a behavioural analysis of Putin's domestic policy. Until now, we have claimed that Putin is a realist in international relations. This claim can be taken differently, but there are things that need to be taken as evident, scientifically true and ostensive facts. 'Putin is a realist.' This is an ostensive fact. However, this is in regard to international relations.

Who is Putin with regard to domestic policy? They will say, 'a conservative'. This concept is vague, requiring additional commentary, especially since conservatives are susceptible to conservative strife. This is a paradox. Western political science does not know the domestic politics of realism. However, in Russia, such a phenomenon is possible. In Russia, everything is not as it is in the West. Here Communists go to church. Here the liberal democratic party is neither liberal nor democratic, and attempts to establish such a political party generally lead absolutely nowhere.

Perhaps Russia has its own political path, a *Sonderweg*, a 'special way'. Where this will lead and what will be the outcome, whether there are one, one hundred or no parties at all, or whether or not any of them will smarten up or continue to act like the sheep they are today is as absolutely unpredictable as chaos. Maybe the leader of the LDPR, Zhirinovsky, will remain in power another fifteen terms and will continue to make jokes as he edges closer to death. Maybe he will depart much earlier due to health issues seeing how twenty years ago he once required urgent hospitalisation.

True, many other Russian politicians also periodically require hospitalisation and are then released again. Everything in Russia is unpredictable. Maybe this is the way things should be, since any an attempt to hold people in Russia accountable for their words always fails. This has applied to all of our politicians beginning with the former Komsomols[63] and the Commu-

---

63   The Komsomol was the youth division of the Communist Party of the Soviet Union.

nists, then the former liberal democrats, and now today it is the Putin conservatives. Therefore, essentially, no one. The West never encountered such a situation. This complete disregard for any rational installations in party-political and ideological behaviour is a peculiarly Russian phenomenon.

I believe Putin operates precisely as a realist in domestic politics. Realising that the Russian ideology is generally difficult to understand, Putin has created his own political model. In foreign policy he began to act along the rational, Western model of realism in international relations and everything has turned out well. Then he also decided to act in the spirit of realism in domestic politics.

Once, about six years ago, one high-ranking official in the Kremlin surprised me by saying, 'We owe everything to Carl Schmitt.' I asked, 'And do you know who introduced Carl Schmitt into the Russian political context?' It was not important that the official did not know who introduced Schmitt's ideas to the Russian public, or who first published his works here. (incidentally, this was Carl Schmitt's essay, *The Concept of the Political*,[64] which was translated and published in the journal *Questions of Sociology* by Alexander Filippov.) But the momentum generated here by Schmitt's ideas was Eurasian and conservative revolutionary. The Eurasian international movement also took the trouble to translate and promote the works of other brilliant German thinkers. This, however, does not matter.

What matters is something else. Who is Carl Schmitt? He is a representative of realism in international relations and one of the most important, world-class political scientists. He is fashionable in the West today. There is a huge interest in him on both the Right and the Left.

Carl Schmitt is precisely the key to what Putin is doing in politics today and is going to do in the future. Schmitt is a realist in both foreign and domestic policy. Schmitt, together with Eric Voegelin (a political scientist from the same group of Catholic thinkers as Schmitt),[65] substantiated the neo-Hobbesian approach as a certain political approach within the frame-

---

64 Carl Schmitt, *The Concept of the Political: Expanded Edition* (Chicago: University of Chicago Press, 2007).

65 Eric Voegelin (1901–1985) was a German conservative political philosopher.

work of political theology.⁶⁶ These two political scientists never discussed parties, ideologies, parliamentarianism or authoritarianism, totalitarianism or liberal democracy, but they said that the most important function of the state is to maintain order and that the state should be completely free in a political sense of ideological convictions.

There, perhaps, is the key to the madness of our political system. The state is managed by some stringent and obvious principles. For example, people should not kill each other, commit acts of terrorism, destabilise the state, give away the state's oil for free, be guided solely by mercantilist economic models, and so on. Putin has projected realism in international relations onto domestic politics and thus reshaped the concept of our state and society. Yes, this means that Putin has forcibly applied realism to domestic politics. Putin is indifferent to debates in the Parliament. He is not interested in whether deputies are acting according to their beliefs. He is indifferent to everything that is related to political interests, and maybe to all politicians. The important thing for politicians is to not make a mess of things, not to sell children for their organs, not to give Russian oil companies to foreign owners, and for the people to not take to the streets and create mass disorder. You have every right to do as you will, as long as it does not interfere with the state's abilities to perform its basic functions. Once you start to interfere, you will be given a time-out. In a sense, this kind of realism is liberal, leaving the policy to our discretion. You can say whatever you want, but do not interfere with the roadway where people are going to work and driving the snowploughs. Snowploughs are more important than all parliamentary politics because they clear the snow. That is realism. A snowplough drives along and clears snow. Suddenly, it reaches Bolotnaya and it is bothered by the snow. Then it clears Bolotnaya. It is nothing personal. Sometimes representatives of all groups want to stop the clearing of snow. Those on the Right, Left, the liberals, and the Communists can sometimes actually gather together and do it. Putin looks at them and asks, 'What are these people doing here? In principle, I do not mind at all that

---

66 Political theology examines how theological ideas underlie modern-day social and political thought. Carl Schmitt argued in a book of the same name that modern politics merely presents theological concepts in secularised form.

they are, but why do they interfere with clearing the snow?' And then the President loses his patience and removes the people along with the snow. My hypothesis is that there is none of the authoritarianism or totalitarianism of which people usually accuse Putin. In fact, there is nothing even conservative.

Simple realism perceives the state and the institution of order, both politically and ideologically, to be free of convictions. The state remains indifferent to the content of political and ideological life, although this indifference exists within a certain framework, that is, within the framework of a safely and satisfactorily functioning government.

To the modern West, the idea of such a state framework is a novel one because it is accustomed to executing internal politics semantically. The West cannot live without semantics. They are used by parties on both the Left and the Right. The Right offers budget cuts while half of the Left stands behind tax cuts and the other half supports tax increases. In Russia, everything is the opposite. We have the Left fighting for tax cuts, as opposed to the Left around the world that supports tax increases, and we have the Right, contrary to all the rules, insisting on a progressive tax structure and demanding the expropriation of oligarchs... Today in Russia, the discussion contains anything but political connotations, and maybe this is good. Suppose that the connotations are separate, and policies have their own special functions so that the government can provide the necessary services to the disabled, as well as monitor public transport and the behaviour of people on the street. It does not matter what kinds of people are on the streets as long as they walk along the side of the road where there are no snowploughs or other vehicles passing by. It is only when the clear and precise rules are broken that the long arm of the law grabs them. It is nothing personal.

I think that in the last few years Putin has demonstrated that not only have we entered an era of realism, but we are deep inside the realist model of domestic politics. Dmitry Medvedev's term was a rather entertaining episode. Society began to ponder what would come next. Would it be a second Medvedev term bringing about the end of the country, realism, and everything else, including snow removal? But then Medvedev returned to his position and Putin to his. Now we are guaranteed another legitimate eleven years of Putin's realism and more, heading towards infinity. How long can this last? I think that everything in Russia is unpredictable until the last moment. Once we think that we understand something, it most likely means that we are mistaken, since we live in a world of historical dreams. This, perhaps, is the special charm of our national history.

I think that by fixating on Putin's realism in foreign and domestic policy, I am groping for some important reference points toward a rational explanation of what is happening in Russia. I think that any other way of looking at him would be less accurate and more absurd.

Putin's realism is frustrating and fascinating. It is frustrating because he no longer meets the needs of our time, and fails in addressing the critical and meaningful moments of our history and our existence. It is fascinating because conservatism, which is exposed in Putin's realism, is always fascinating and charming. But it is not enough. It always seems to us that it creates and conceptualises predominantly technical, short-term projects. Generally, in all fairness, it should be noted that a pragmatic approach in the spirit of Putin's realist theory of international relations has no systematic framework, or it simply remains unarticulated.

Putin's managerial elite have no rational models for calculating national interests and no concise and interconnected understanding of the functioning of geopolitical forces in the world in mind. Everyone in the field of upholding the public interest is guided by their individual views or by decrees from above in which logic is sometimes completely absent. Realism presupposes a calculation. Here Putin relies on his ingenuity and resourcefulness, his own and that of his inner circle. That is, there is not only no idea of a mission, there is also no systematic or systemic rationalisation in line with national interests. Here are the intuitionism and adaptive agility, entirely Russian traits, which help compensate for the lack of a systematic approach. But only for the time being, and this has nothing to do with the National Idea.

CHAPTER 7

Criticism of Putin from Above

A 'Reigning Idea' Is Insufficient

Today we are left with just one method: *criticism of Putin from above*. Criticism of his realism, his pragmatism, and the insignificance and formality of his actions. This criticism doesn't come from the right, or the left, or below. How can we comprehend this? Why from above? As both the formal and informal pinnacle of the power pyramid, how could anything exist above Putin? Inherent in the very notion of sovereignty is that above him stands no other institution of authority. That is the point. So what exists above Putin, if everything (in Russia) exists below or beside him?

The idea stands above. Putin himself, most likely, doesn't believe in the idea, but in the means and methods. That's his business. Sometimes even philosophers don't believe in the idea, let alone rulers. But ideas exist, and they stir the world, history, society, and humanity. If someone doesn't want to confront these ideas, if he avoids the intensive and trepidatious process of reasoning, then other people will think for him — others that don't distance themselves from reflection. Even American neoconservatives recognise that ideas have meaning. In this case, they're right. And so, there you have it: criticism of Putin from above means to offer criticism of his actions and strategies from the point of view of an idea.

We immediately need to determine: what idea? Ideas look different — there are liberal, globalist, Western, Marxist, and socialist ideas. We leave their adherents to their particular way of looking at things. For us, the reigning idea is the Russian Idea, the idea of Great Russia, emerging from centuries of history and careening towards full and bright fulfilment in the future. This idea has many different aspects — cultural, geopolitical, social, political, religious, psychological, ethical, anthropological, ethnological, in terms of values, and so on. But given this variety and inexhaustible abundance of meanings and aspects, the Russian Idea offers itself as something full, whole, and organic. And this whole idea — though approximate, intuitive, remote, and vague — is sensed and understood by every Russian person. To be Russian is to be a compatriot in the Russian Idea, in any manner — even in the most unexpected, paradoxical, dialectic, convoluted of ways.

How does Putin relate to the Russian Idea? He is somehow connected to it, in one way or another considers it, and associates with it. He is connected to it through his realism. Putin is uninterested in Russia as a government. Putin sees government as a value. Freedom, independence, and government sovereignty constitute its ideological foundation. Putin considers and pays attention to these questions. Putin's actions during his first presidential term explicitly prove this: he didn't waver for one minute about whether or not Russia needed the Caucasus, he won the Second Chechen War, he stopped regional opposition, he held on to South Ossetia, he abolished (in the end) elections for the regional heads of the Federation and, accordingly, in the national republics, removed from the constitutions of these regions any mention of sovereignty, and much else in the same spirit. Therefore he conducts tests of the Russian Idea and, in short, comes out *on its side*. In this sense, he is the only political figure in contemporary Russia endowed with a substantial amount of trust; in this sense, he is a Russian in the Kremlin (and, furthermore, certainly not German, as Alexander Rahr[1] called him).

Following the first test, we come to the next layer of the Russian Idea. As far as form is concerned — independence, freedom, integrity, and sov-

---

1   Alexander Rahr (b. 1959) is a German historian who has written a biography of Putin.

ereignty — Putin is doing fine. But let's move on to content. This is where we start to see problems. The liberal attitude towards government, inherent in today's world, generally prohibits itself from containing any level of substance. It's simply a 'night watchman', a 'lesser of evils, and a product of the 'social contract' put into effect so that 'people don't kill each other' (Hobbes and his Leviathan). Simply put, the modern era has restricted the formal aspects of and refuses to talk about the meaning and purpose of government or about its mission. Is it compatible with the Russian Idea? Absolutely not. Russians, for the entirety of their history, have understood government to be a sacrosanct value, as a repository for spiritual meaning. For centuries it was the realm of Russian Orthodox ideals, and in the twentieth century it was the global Communism idea. But in all circumstances, Russia has always conceived of itself as a government endowed with higher meaning and purpose. It has a specific Russian purpose, which sets it apart from other, neighbouring governments.

What do we see in Putin's case? Are there signs of resonance with this sacral aspect of Russian statehood? It doesn't seem so. Putin's conception of government is completely European, and wholly conforms to the principles of a nation-state. As far as we've seen, only the formal aspects of government hold meaning for Putin; he attributes no significance to the other aspects. For him, government is a technical construct. The primary, formal characteristic of a government is its sovereignty. Putin is ready to defend it, but the idea that Russia should have some sort of mission or purpose aside from its technical effectiveness, adequate management, and adept manoeuvring amidst the threatening elements of international relations and geopolitical challenges, has not yet taken root. His public appearances, efforts in the spheres of politics and ideology, and actions on the world stage testify to this. Throughout, we see just one aspect — technique, pragmatism, and practicality. That is absolutely not Russian, it is European.

Hegemony and Counter-Hegemony: A Battle of Minds
The Politics of Big Ideas

Today, Putin and his circle understand that Russia needs big ideas and big projects. The Eurasian Economic Union and Eurasian integration is a large and very serious project. The project is a bit of a paradox because we oppose 'Eurasianism' in Europe and Asia. We maintain that Eurasia is neither Europe or Asia, but simultaneously both Europe and Asia. A key component of this project is the desire to substantiate the uniqueness of Russian civilisation. When Putin talks about the Eurasian empire from Lisbon to Vladivostok, this is no accident. The discussion focuses on a particular reorganisation of the international landscape on the basis of a multi-polar world, which will not be oppressed by the West's universal values. Today even the West itself understands that it does not impel globalisation and is not capable of assimilating all of the world's cultures and civilisations, with its billions of people, and its populations that identify with different values.

Even Europe is collapsing, as we see with Greece and Cyprus. It's obvious that the West's universal global project has failed. From this situation arises a critical question: can we Russians use this window of opportunity, when the West's unipolar front has stalled? Putin, completely logically, offers a single solution: Eurasian integration, that is, the creation of a new civilisation, the purpose of which would be to strategically adapt the landscape to a new model, which includes a new pole in a multipolar world. Putin does this skilfully and pragmatically, using the available resources. Maybe everything will go smoothly. I am not certain of the idea's future success or failure as I — the author of the concept of the Eurasian Economic Union and Eurasian integration — as an author and as a political scientist, philosopher, and metaphysician, I see that Putin lacks historical temperament and scale in the execution of this project. A historical act is an anomaly with a plus sign. It is not the act of normal people, but of great, prominent, and serious historical figures. The unification of Eurasia, created here on our mainland, and that of a specific new civilisation's landscape, and the creation of a multi-polar world — all of this is an undertaking for great people. Putin is currently battling fundamental domestic problems and is occupied with pragmatic complications. He has normalised the situation in the country and has proven that he is capable of handling the situation, but thus arises an important question: is he really capable of standing toe-to-toe with the demands of history? He proposed the Eurasian Economic Union, but does he truly understand what it will require? Does he realise the difficulties he will soon face and the substantial efforts that are essential for the project's realisation? Does he recognise that the strength to do it that must come from Russia and our foreign and domestic policy?

Political Realism: The Politics of Body and the Politics of Soul

What is political realism in the twenty-first century? To what degree do desires, dreams, and ideals have a place in realistic policy? In any political arena, clear goals are always desirable.

Will is a fundamental component of human society, what with people as they are. Man is a being, endowed with a will that strives to make something that isn't there; to create something that doesn't yet exist. In philosophy, this is called the principle of 'impossibilia' — the achievement of that which is unbelievable, impossible, or utopian. This is what drives man to leave his mark on history. Will transforms a dream into a project, into a programme, into a plan of action — and, in the end, into reality. The creation of our international policy guidelines has required indisputable effort from the government, from the people, from politicians, and from scholars. But the battle between the enthusiasts and the sceptics will be decided by just one factor: the presence of will. What we hunger to do, we will do.

When we talk about the Eurasian Union, we exclude the furthest extent of our dream — the dream of the poet and diplomat Fyodor Tyutchev[2] — a universal Orthodox empire. Today, this seems unrealistic to us. But the realisation of the Eurasian Union, both short-term and long-term, is a practical and wholly feasible task. It is why we are willing to consider that

---

2   Fyodor Tyutchev (1803–1873) was a Romantic poet. He was a Pan-Slavist who detested the West.

the design of Russia's foreign policy in the twenty-first century should be political realism: it allows room for imagination, accomplishment, fulfilment, and passion, but is compatible with existing realities, sensibly assesses possibilities and resources, and does not create challenges it is incapable of overcoming.

Putin's actions regarding the Eurasian Union these days, during his third term, are absolutely correct. And difficult. I don't exclude the possibility that he is acting in spite of himself. He would have gladly focused only on Russia — which comes easily to him — and on not allowing the country to fall to pieces, exchanging one corrupt bureaucrat for another from time to time.

Putin does everything so slowly and incrementally that it is clear we will never make it to our critical point in history. But if we don't actively take part in history now, and instead simply follow the flow of inertia, at some point the situation will become critical. The world is entering a new chapter, with new challenges arising. Does Russia truly have a grand design — for itself, for Europe, for the East, for America, for its neighbours?

The EurAsEC is great, and every step in that direction, however small, is a historical success. But at the moment Putin is proposing the EurAsEC as an integration of elements on a purely material level. The first step of the project was the Union State of Russia, Belarus, and Kazakhstan. The Customs Union is a considerable proposal. For example, in nineteenth-century Germany between 1815 and 1848, a similar proposal by Friedrich von List led to the creation of a completely new economic and political situation in Europe.[3]

In my opinion, even Putin's approach to problems is purely corporeal, much like Epicurus.[4] He sees the population as an aggregate of material objects that one must feed, give the ability to move about, keep from falling off the roof, give the ability to buy a tram ticket so that they can travel

---

3   List suggested that an economic union could be beneficial for Europe. His ideas are credited with having been influential on the development of the European Economic Community. He established the first union for industry and trade in Germany in 1819.

4   Epicurus (341–270 BC) was a Greek philosopher who did not believe that the body and soul were separate entities, and that the soul did not continue to exist after death.

somewhere, put up signs so they don't need to cross the street without a walk signal, and ensure that they don't yell, don't do anything stupid, and are well-behaved. This is all materialism. Putin suggests uniting the post-Soviet landscape in the same way — on a materialistic basis. For example, if Ukraine doesn't want to do something, you can tighten or loosen the gas line. Without gas, it's cold — one starts to shiver and makes a concession. Furnace diplomacy.

Putin's current platform is about integrating concrete things: the Customs Union, the economy, the EurAsEC. Turn on, turn off, press, release, give, take. That is, all actions are on the level of concrete, material realities. I think that it's necessary to move on to the politics of spirit.

If a person is comprised not only of a body, but has a spirit, then there should also be a political spirit and a politics of a universal history, of historical ideas, and of fate. A notion of the identity of the post-Soviet landscape should exist, a Russian identity...

A spiritual Eurasia should appear. A Eurasian spirit. Right now Putin is concerned with the material Eurasia, the material Customs Union, the material integration, and the material rebirth of Russia. A physical Russia is being reborn. Or rather, Russia is not being 'reborn' so much as it is returning to its natural state of being.

Further, it is essential to have a political spirit. But to engage in the spiritual, it is essential to pay attention to how one cultivates a spirit. A spirit is a very delicate matter, more delicately constructed than a body. I surmise that to do that it is necessary to have a notion of the logic of world history and about why our country moves into certain territories, but not others; what drove Russian history; and who Russians, Ukrainians, Cossacks, Tajiks, Iranians, Europeans, Chinese, and Indians are. It is essential to have a fundamental understanding of the most significant pieces of history so as to unite some nations and confront others. You're not going to be nice to everyone. It is impossible to undertake that kind of historical project in such a manner that all nations of the world are satisfied.

At first glance, it seems that America is motivated only by material concerns, and is implementing the physical transformation of the world, but that's just an appearance. The basis of American unipolarity lies specifically in the idea of Manifest Destiny.[5] It is the result of a particular ideological and philosophical programme. A facet of Russian culture has always been its rejection of Western materialistic dominance. What is of principal importance for us is the discovery of an intellectual, spiritual, and philosophical agenda for Russia, the exploration of our own national fate, and the composition of our identity across centuries of history. The fact is that throughout history we didn't simply become materially stronger, conquer someone, colonise, develop, expand and entrench. We did those things as part of a definitive, historical mission of Russia. If we do not recognise and reconstruct that mission now, then it seems that any actions we take on the level of sheer materialism, even if they are successful, will amount to nothing more than pirate's plunder.

Globalisation and Hegemony

A great number of challenges stand before Russia, challenges unlike any she has seen in the last two decades. These challenges are not technical or technological, but ideological and philosophical. The theory of de-ideologisation, which was popular in the USSR during the '70s, turned out to be false. Ideologies don't simply vanish — they transform, camouflage their original appearance, and inculcate themselves through subtle techniques and by influencing the order of things. Today's process of globalisation is an aggressive imposition of Western liberal ideology and American values on a global scale. Under this ideology, the qualification has changed. Having conquered all other prevailing ideologies, liberalism as an ideology of the postmodern era moves from the subjective sphere to the objective sphere, becoming an existential fact and is transformed into the 'objective' order of things. Liberalism in the postmodern era virtualises reality, fuses with it, ceases to be a political theory and becomes a singular post-political practice. Spurred by the 'end of history', politics is replaced by economics (the market economy), and governments and nations take part in the melting

---

5   In 1845 Americans first began to speak of 'Manifest Destiny', which was the belief that America had a right and was destined to spread throughout North America. Some have claimed that this concept never really left the American psyche and that Americans still feel it is their right to spread their power and influence throughout the world.

pot of universal globalisation. The values of liberalism are said to be 'universal' and 'common to humanity', even though they are solely derived from the experiences of the European and American segments of humanity, people who live in a limited territory.

This kind of globalisation today is unipolar and puts the reins of world sovereignty into the hands of the US, which pretends not only to have control over global processes, but also over the establishment of the rules of the game (hegemony).

Along with the imposition of American values (the market, individualism, personal rights, liberal democracy, bourgeois parliamentarism, economic control concentrated in the hands of a few large-scale world monopolies, transnational corporations, etc.) comes the imposition of all other American interests. Those countries and governments that follow the US in their regional politics are labelled as 'democracies' (even if no such rule has ever existed in said country), and those that dare to proclaim their sovereignty are regarded as 'outlaws' or 'authoritarian regimes' or are accused of 'living in the past' (more often than not, without people like that there wouldn't be a foundation for anything). Globalisation transforms countries and people from sovereign subjects of international politics into instruments, over whom sovereignty is gradually passed from the hands of national governors to a supranational authority — to the embryo of a kind of 'world power'.

Gramsciism and Neo-Gramscianism in Politics

The modern world presents a variety of challenges to Russia, ones that are impossible to respond to using Putin's strategy of realism in politics and international relations. The thing is, Putin's realism relies on a strategy of material strength, technology, and power — what is referred to as 'hardware'. In the contemporary world, the primary battle is waged using the intellectual strategy of 'software'. The conversation focuses on concepts of hegemony and counter-hegemony.

The contemporary West has just barely won on this level, and only to the extent that its intellectual discourse and its global cognitive and cultural strategy, which has become predominant in the world, is actively influencing not just individuals but also the collective, the classes, the parties, and the economic and political structure throughout the world. The Western centres that manage global development understand very well that the contemporary hegemonic discourse is Western-centric and based on liberalism, being indefinitely replicated and ingrained in the depths of the social and intellectual landscape and thus penetrating the depths of everyday consciousness and the 'structure of things' throughout the world, works better than economic and social revolution. This approach softly brings about change in political and economic organisations and extends to a transformation in the lifestyles and thinking of all social strata and classes, countries, governments, and continents. Ideas are what rule the world, and today nowhere more effectively so than in economics and finance. Underestimating ideas, ideology, worldview, ideals, and ideal factors in history is one of Putin's mistakes that could prove fatal.

The understanding of hegemony in the broad discourse of political science was introduced by the Italian neo-Marxist Antonio Gramsci. The word 'hegemony' originally meant 'domination'. Marxism cultivated an understanding of economic domination, determined by the ownership of the means of production. According to Marx, this is economic dominion in the basic sense. Gramsci connects political domination with Leninism and sees it as a degree of autonomy of the superstructure in politics, in a situation where the political will of a certain (proletariat) force is able to change (activating a certain segment of superstructure) a political situation, even if the basis for that change is not completely ready.

In the contemporary world, domination holds special meaning in the sphere of superstructure that Gramsci correlates with 'civil society,' with a focus on intellectual figures. Gramsci believes that hegemony is the domination of forces of inequality and supremacy, not in the spheres of economics and politics but in the cultural sphere, in the communities of intellectuals and experts, art and science, philosophy and the everyday awareness of the masses. This third sector of superstructure, which exists independently of politics or political organisations (government, parties, etc.), enjoys the same level of relative autonomy as Leninism did in politics. Revolution, in this instance, from the point of view of Gramsci, has three aspects: in the economic sphere (by the classic Marxist laws), in the political sphere (Lenin's strategy), and in the sphere of civil society which presents itself as the sphere of freedom. In the last sphere, an intellectual can make his choice between conformism and non-conformism, between maintaining the status quo, namely that of the ruling bourgeois class and its ideology and practices, or he can choose revolution, that is, between hegemony and counter-hegemony. The choice that the intellectual makes does not depend on his economic means; that is, it is not determined by his relationship to the ownership of the means of production or to his political affiliation with a particular party.

Gramsci believed that the Western world was created through a hegemony in which the economy is dominated by a capitalistic system, politics is dominated by a bourgeois political force, and intellectuals put into practice the interests of the bourgeois political elite, and thus become capital. It would appear that everything is stable: the worldwide bourgeois elite is pursuing the triumph of the design of a unipolar world and the creation of a worldwide government.

But Gramsci believed that it is possible to mount a rebellion against this world, and invited non-conformists and revolutionary intellectuals to create a 'historical bloc' that is opposed to this hegemony.

Caesarism and *Trasformismo*

Why do the concepts of hegemony and counter-hegemony appear to be important for contemporary Russia, Putin's Russia? Is there agreement with the Neo-Gramscian analysis, that all countries can be divided into two categories: countries where hegemony obviously became stronger, that is, the development of those capitalistic countries that have industrial economies, and which are dominated by bourgeois parties in parliamentary democratic systems, and which possess market economies and liberal ruling systems; and countries where, due to different historical circumstances, that didn't happen? For the first group of countries, it is considered acceptable to refer to them as 'developed democracies', and to refer to the second as 'marginal cases', 'problem zones', or even to put them in the category of 'rogue states' or 'outlaws'. Gramsci referred to this second group as 'Caesaristic' (he obviously had the experience of Fascist Italy in mind). 'Caesarism' can be seen in a broader context, as any other political system, as taking place where the existing bourgeois relationships are fragmented and their full political formulation (as in a classic bourgeois-democratic government) takes too long. In 'Caesarism,' the main point is not the authoritarian principle of rule, but specifically a delay in the multidimensional installation of the full values of a capitalist system on the Western model. The reasons for this kind of delay can be varied: a dictatorial style of rule, clannishness among the elites, the presence of different religious or ethnic groups in power, the cultural specificities of a society, historical circumstances, the particular economic or geographical conditions of the country, and so on.

The main point is that these societies are not completely integrated into the core of hegemony. In these interim governments, the political ruling class is still not properly participating in the Western capitalist world, where capital, hegemony, and bourgeois political parties, which represent the interests of the middle class, control the agenda.

Charles Kupchan, in his book *No One's World*,[6] presents a model, which Gramsci calls 'Caesarism,' divided into three types:

1. the modern corrupt Russian autocracy and other, similar models in the post-Soviet landscape that appear to be dominated by corrupt groups on the top;
2. the Chinese system of totalitarianism, which concentrates all power in a totalitarian manner on the governmental level;
3. the petro-monarchies of the Middle East where religious or dynastic aspects of domination are included in the very political structure, in its own Caesarism, as with, for example, the Saudi sheikhs.

Let us stress one more time that Russia, according to this classification, belongs to the group of countries with Caesaristic rule.

Firstly, it is important that in these societies hegemony is simultaneously a force from outside (which stands on the side of a fully bourgeois government) and an internal opposition, which is otherwise tied to exter-

---

6   Charles Kupchan, *No One's World: The West, the Rising Rest, and the Coming Global Turn* (Oxford: Oxford University Press, 2012).

nal factors. Hegemony from both the outside and the inside compels Caesarism to partially de-sovereignise and to shift to a more globalist condition of hegemony.

Neo-Gramscianists in international relations maintain that 'Caesarism' can be considered 'sub-hegemony'; for that reason its strategy focuses on balancing the pressures of hegemony externally and internally, making certain concessions, but doing so selectively in an effort to preserve its power at all costs, and to prevent its abdication to bourgeois political forces who assert that the economic basis of society lies within the political superstructure. 'Caesarism' is therefore doomed to '*trasformismo*'[7] (we have taken the Italian term *trasformismo*) because of its continuous participation in hegemony, on the one hand, and its constant efforts to delay, deter, or falsify an end towards which it had been steadily progressing. Thus, *trasformismo* is a balancing process, one that China went through during the 1980s and that Putin's Russia is currently in, particularly during the Medvedev era, and also it has also been seen in some Islamic states recently. These governments, according to Gramscians, absorb some elements of the West — capitalism, democracy, the separation of powers in political institutions, help to form a middle class, support the desires of the national bourgeoisie, and maintain internal hegemony and international external hegemony, but do not do all of this thoroughly and not authentically, but as a façade in order to maintain a political monopoly that is not strictly hegemonic. Thus, representatives of critical theory in international relations regard Caesarism as something that will sooner or later be overcome by hegemony, as far as Caesarism is not more than a 'historical delay', and certainly does not represent an alternative, that is, it is not counter-hegemony in the real sense.

Specifically with this 'Caesarism', contemporary representatives of critical theory in international relations refer to the majority of countries as the

---

7   *Trasformismo* in political thought refers to the strengthening of the centre in a government with the aim of preventing extremes from either the Right or the Left from taking power. This was done in Italy in the decades before the rise of Fascism, and many believe that this caused political stagnation and corruption which ultimately made Mussolini's rise possible.

Third World, and even some of the major BRICS powers — Brazil, Russia, India, China, and South Africa.[8] Note that Russia is on this list.

Thus, in front of Russia lies at least one path — the most likely one, from the point of view of the Neo-Gramscianists, and connected to an incremental and slow transformation (*trasformismo*) of its economic and political structures, ideology, national lifestyle, culture, and traditions in a globalist liberal scenario, leading to the inclusion of the country in the global world of contemporary capitalism to be led by a single world government. Particularly, Russia's participation in this new world order will only come at the cost of losing Caesarism or its authoritarianism and sovereignty, which until this time were at the centre of Putin's polities, and to this day saves Russia from annihilation in the world melting pot of national governments.

The second, revolutionary variant of the dynamics of Russian society, which is an alternative to the last scenario, is the development of a Russian project of counter-hegemony connected with the concept of a multi-polar world and a multitude of civilisations, cultures, and strategic poles on the Earth, who help to preserve the integrity of Russian civilisation. This demands the development of a unique Russian-Eurasian answer to the call of the contemporary West, as well as the project for a multi-polar world, a plurality and a dialogue of world civilisations.

The Historical Pact

According to the theory of Neo-Gramscianism, there is a concept of a 'historic pact' possessing two multi-directional vectors: the side of hegemony and the side of revolution. Hegemony, from Gramsci's point of view, is not fate but a choice. It is the same as choosing political parties. Eventually each person is free to choose between capitalism and Communism, liberalism and socialism, and along the same logic, between modernity and tradition. In the same way, class, party, nationality, and gender of the individual are secondary. In order to make a choice on the intellectual level it is absolutely

---

8   BRICS was established in 2006 with the intention of bringing together a series of countries with developing economies.

not necessary to be disadvantaged. Any intellectual may stand up on the side of counter-hegemony and engage in a revolutionary historical pact. It is not necessary to be thrown out of a social system (this is a main principle of Gramscianism).

One representative of Neo-Gramscianism, Stephen Gill, describes a historic pact as a meeting of intellectual conformists who favour hegemony within the framework of the Trilateral Commission or the Bilderberg Club.

Chronicles of Global Hegemony: Bilderberg and Its Russian Subsidiaries

Today the Western world multiplies the structures of hegemonic orientation, turning them into effective conveyors for the replication of bourgeois-liberal discourse. Texts, concepts, programmes and recommendations, planned coups, colour revolutions, and the unconscious behaviour of crowds, all show the giant reservoir of strategies used by liberal hegemony. The Bilderberg Club plays an important role in Putin's Russia.

The first meeting of the Bilderberg Club took place in 1954. The Club was finally made official in 1960 thanks to Jozéf Retinger,[9] a dignitary of the European Freemasons whose theories suggested that the world should be unified under the auspices of liberal-democratic regimes. Conceived as a restricted area for the coordination of the hegemonic political, economic, intellectual and media projects of the Western world transnationally, hey initially avoided publicity because it included most of the leaders of the world's media.

Between 1960 and 1970, the Club's activities were opened to the public and Bilderberg was seen as the prototype for a world government and a supranational organ for capitalism. Shortly thereafter, two powerful American ideologues entered the club — the liberal democrat Zbigniew Brzezinski and the Republican realist Henry Kissinger, both of whom would serve for decades as permanent members of the Bilderberg Club and the Trilateral Commission, which was established in 1974. One can also add the Council on Foreign Relations (CFR) to this list.

---

9   Jozéf Retinger (1888–1960) was a Polish political thinker who was one of the founders of the European Movement and the Council of Europe.

These three highly efficient and supranational structures serve as the vanguard of international affairs and can be considered as the model for a world government, or more precisely, its shadow cabinet.

After the collapse of the USSR, the Bilderberg Club began to invite political figures from Russia. According to Russian researchers, the principal institution of Russia's integration into the world government was the Council on Foreign and Defence Policy (CFDP) headed by Sergei Karaganov.[10] The Council and its members were practically a subsidiary of the Bilderberg Club. Karaganov also served as an observing member of the CFR, an organisation which is usually limited to American politicians. In addition, Karaganov attended almost all the meetings of the Trilateral Commission as an outside observer.

Russian specialists with connections to the CFDP were essentially 'agents of influence' or 'lobbyists' of the shadow world government. In America, lobbyists that advocate for the rights of their governments in the US Senate or Congress (for example, the Armenian or Israeli lobby) are legally registered. In Russia there is no such practice. Almost all the specialists entering the CFDP in the various stages of its activity acted as lobbyists for world government. Of course, lobbyists and agents are not entirely spies. They are citizens who are simply working in the interest of world government. CFDP documents and journals contain the names of several prominent Russian politicians over the years. They contain not only Anatoly Chubais, Gozman[11] and Sergei Karaganov, Grigory Yavlinsky, and Lilia Shevtsova,[12] but also almost all leading experts of the time including Vyacheslav Nikonov, Vitaly Tretyakov,[13] and Natalya Narochnitskaya,[14] and among others.

---

10   Sergei Karaganov (b. 1952) is a political scientist who has been an advisor to both Putin and Yeltsin. He has been a member of the Trilateral Commission since 1998 and served on the advisory board of the Council of Foreign Relations from 1995 until 2005.

11   Leonid Gozman (b. 1950) has been the leader of the Union of Right Forces since 2011.

12   Lilia Shevtsova (b. 1949) is a political scientist who is recognised internationally as an expert on Russia and the Kremlin.

13   Vitaly Tretyakov (b. 1953) is a well-known journalist and political scientist in Russia.

14   Natalya Narochnitskaya (b. 1948) is a Russian politician who has served in the Duma as a member of Rodina.

Some of these figures, who today have become national heroes, were actively lobbying for American interests in Russia in the 1990s. For example, the literature includes information that indicates that at the beginning of the 1990s, Vyacheslav Nikonov used Russian agents to pass ciphers to the American leadership by order of Vadim Bakatin,[15] then the chairman of the KGB under Yeltsin.

As sad as it is, it is our history and we have to talk about it because Vladimir Putin has made serious efforts to free Russia from foreign influence. In order to do this, it is necessary to immediately revise the entire structure of the CFDP, because every other member is a lobbyist for world government consciously engaged in activities on their behalf.

All hegemonic organisations including the Bilderberg Club, the Trilateral Commission, and the Council on Foreign Relations generally have the same function. There are specialists who are continuously involved in all three organisations. These include Henry Kissinger and Zbigniew Brzezinski as well as Russian experts associated with the CFDP and its periodical, *Russia in Global Affairs*. Virtually all Russian experts from the CFDP have worked with Western institutions associated with Bilderberg or participated in the activities of one or more of the structures in its network, in one way or another. When asked what role Russia is given in the process of creating a globalised world, we can say that it was, at least until recently, an active participant in the process. 2013 is the first year in a long time that no Russians were invited to any of the meetings.

I have been following these globalist clubs for several years. Even before the collapse of the Soviet Union, I wrote articles and books which, predicted, to take an example, that if the representatives of the Trilateral Commission, in particular Brzezinski or Kissinger, visited Moscow, then the Soviet Union would be destroyed within two or three years. All this happened. For a long time I have been following these clubs' activities and can definitely say that the current absence of Russians in these structures is telling. It means that Putin's modern Russia stands strictly behind sover-

---

15   Vadim Bakatin (b. 1937) was Minister of Internal Affairs under Gorbachev, and was then appointed as chairman of the KGB in August 1991. He was the last such chairman, serving until January 1992, when the KGB was abolished.

eignty. Together with other countries which seek a multipolar world, Russia is gradually liberating itself from the control of these global networks. It is escaping, but is still not out entirely because such individuals as the Bilderberg veteran Anatoly Chubais and newcomers such as Igor Yurgens or Arkady Dvorkovich still continue to pursue this line.

So these globalist social clubs — Bilderberg, the Trilateral Commission, and the CFR — not only discuss political issues and exchange views between those who are influential upon Western society including politicians, experts, representatives of the financial circles and the media, but also on many occasions develop strategies for world politics. It is precisely these clubs that are the real foundation of world hegemony by the modern liberal West and in the spirit of unipolar global hegemony (today the US performs this function).

In 2013 Turkey is on the Bilderberg agenda. What decisions will be made at the meeting? We cannot know anything about this process except that at the Club's meetings, it will develop a consensus on behalf of 'global humanity' as represented by the political elite. Behind the scenes the Club is making important decisions that affect every society. Do members of the parliaments in any country draft their own laws or make their own decisions? As a rule, decisions are not made by parties or committees. Rather, they are developed in the 'think tanks' within these committees, which are made up of just a few people.

Today in America and Russia, there are hundreds of centres servicing the global liberal model. In Russia these include the liberal institutes, funds, organisations, the Higher School of Economics, the Institute of Contemporary Development, and a huge number of liberal experts like I. Yurgens and Gontmakher, and of course modernisation projects like Skolkovo.

Today it is globalist clubs like this that decide how multinational capitalists and the West deal with Syria, Turkey, Iran, North Korea, and finally Russia. This type of discussion is officially impossible in any country, state, parliament, or government. In this case, decisions are not made either in America or in Russia, but rather in independent organisations which are more versatile than any one state can be, and which act on behalf of the world's globalist organisations. These globalist clubs do not have any legal status and thus they are not required to disclose their decisions.

The Bilderberg Club's decisions are non-binding. Nominally, it is an abstract intellectual project. Nevertheless, at some point the Club's projects become binding and uncontested.

Most recently, Vladislav Surkov conducted an advisory council meeting at the Kremlin similar to those conducted in the Bilderberg Club. As a rule, the President's administration always invites creative people to its meetings. Participants in these strange meetings can be hippies, analysts, bankers, artists, filmmakers, Internet pornographers, bloggers, and even schizophrenics. This motley crowd discussed a number of seemingly irrelevant topics that later became parts of Putin's agenda.

Today, ideas rule the world. Intellectual decisions in the non-political superstructure can (in Gramsci's understanding) upset the world order, begin and end revolutions, remove dictators and autocrats, and bring down economies. The mechanisms that develop a global liberal strategy, a hegemonic strategy, are finely tuned.

Although in America, Europe, and Russia there are completely different forms of decision-making, the results are the same. The work of these globalist clubs is leading a number of organisations and states in different parts of the world to begin implementing synchronous and coordinated political steps, to harmonise their actions and to speak with one voice in world affairs. This is how world's politicians, economists, the media, the intellectual elite, and the world's aristocracy determine the fate of the world, its worldview, and its mindset. All of this together makes up the body of global liberal hegemony.

Is it possible for Russia to counter a strategy like this? Is Russia itself falling into the web of this mechanism, willingly or unwillingly, explicitly or implicitly? Has Putin thought about this network of intellectual centres, clubs, and other forms of organisations that once could have been called counter-hegemonic? Indeed the Izborsk Club[16] is but a drop in the ocean.

---

16 The Izborsk Club is a patriotic group of experts founded by Putin which advises him on matters of policy.

Worldwide clubs of global hegemony also had a hand in the collapse of the USSR. In 1954 a group of specialists gathered at the Bilderberg Club to combat the Soviet Union and turn capitalism into a global system besides which there would be no alternative. In 1991, less than forty years later, this goal was achieved. This inevitably leads to the conclusion that powerful intellectual groups and organisations work behind the scenes and represent the major segments of global politics, global intellectualism, and global strategic thinking. Forty years of intensive work brought about excellent results.

Here is one example: one day during a private meeting with Brzezinski, I asked him how the West managed to persuade Gorbachev to withdraw Russia's troops from East Germany. He smiled and said, 'We tricked him.'

The structures of the Western intellectual clubs operate using extremely delicate strategies. They rely on strategies of deception, geopolitical lies, techniques of psychological warfare used against the subconscious of the masses, and on new memes of mass liberal culture. They work as the vanguard of modern trends in religion, philosophy, and psychology. They also use the images of global revolutionary practices against models of counter-hegemony. With these ideas, they permeate the deepest levels of the subconscious minds not only of every man and woman on the street, but also of the minds of the world's most rational intellectuals. They do this ultimately, whether through soft or hard power, to condition humanity towards the Global Liberal Empire.

Many experts who have participated in the meetings of the Trilateral Commission and the Bilderberg Club have expressed their anger many times against the complete illegitimacy of these organisations that operate according to a model of global dictatorship. Some of these experts indignantly left these organisations and exposed the illegality of their decisions, but then soon dropped from the public eye. They seem to still be alive and working but their positions in society seem to have been reduced to nothing. These clubs operate through strategies of obstruction and ostracism.

Roger Garaudy[17] needed to speak out in support of the Palestinian movement only once before he disappeared from the list of respected intellectuals in France and was forgotten. That Abbé Pierre,[18] one of the most respected politicians in France who fought for the rights of homeless people for forty years, supported Garaudy dissuaded no one. We know how the mechanisms of demonisation work. Accordingly, no sane person invited to the Bilderberg Club would ever discuss what goes on there because he knows what would be in store for him in the future.

Thus operates the giant hegemonic machine of the Atlantic West. But at the same time, it is not worth it to demonise the situation too much and overestimate the power of and the lack of alternatives to these global hegemonic structures. Their secrecy should also not be overestimated.

Secrets are often revealed. If we look at what Western international relations theorists write regarding the need for the legal establishment of a world government, we see that it is the official programme of any liberal in international relations, authorised by the leaders of Bilderberg who sit back comfortably and relax in Europe or America, knowing their agenda will be pursued. Any liberal in international relations prescribes the establishment of a world government as the best and most necessary prospect and hope for world order. The idea in itself is absolutely legal.

Therefore we should not overestimate the importance of Bilderberg and similar organisations. These are just parts of the liberal hegemonic idea. These ideas also include open and formal talks of a theoretical nature and based on the scientific theory of liberalism in international relations, which asserts the need to create a unipolar world, the establishment of a world government, and the reduction of the sovereignty of nation-states. Each liberal, whether or not he or she is a participant in the CFDP, Surkov's 2020 Forum, or some other organisation, serves as an agent of this global

---

17   Roger Garaudy (1913–2012) was a prominent French philosopher who had fought in the French Resistance, later became a Communist, and converted to Islam in 1982, becoming a staunch supporter of the Palestinian cause. He also claimed that the Holocaust is a myth.

18   Abbé Pierre (1912–2007) was a French Catholic priest and a member of the French Resistance. He served in the French Assembly and was a crusader for the plight of refugees around the world.

project. It is nothing personal. The establishment of a world government is as important to liberal hegemony as the proletarian revolution, expropriation of the expropriators, and the abolition of private property was to the Communists. If you are for Communism, do not be surprised by the extermination of the bourgeoisie, the disappearance of private property, revolution, and revolutionary terror. You actively want and encourage this. If you are a liberal, then do not be surprised by the destruction of nation-states, the reduction of your country's sovereignty, and the abolition of all forms of identity other than that of the individual. You fight and strive for this, and because of this, you will be responsible if things go wrong and situations arise that are unintended, and that are not liberal or hegemonic.

The Counter-Hegemony and Counter-Society

The counter-hegemonic conception is brought forward by a specialist in the field of international relations, Robert W. Cox, as a generalisation of Gramsci's theory and its application to the current global situation. He states that all systems of international relations today are built to provide service to the existing hegemony. Everything that is told to us about the relations between states, the meaning of history, and of wars and invasions is pure propaganda from the oligarchic elite of world hegemony. To a large extent, this construct rests on the intelligentsia or intellectuals, who are opting for and serving hegemony.

But intellectuals are free not to choose hegemony. As Ernst Niekisch wrote, 'There is no fatalism inherent in the nature of human society. Fatalism applies to the changing of the seasons and to natural disasters. The dignity of man is such that he can always say "no". Man can always rise up. He can always stand up and fight, even against what seems inevitable, absolute, and invincible. And even if he loses, he sets an example to others. Others take his place and also say "no". Therefore, the most fateful and fatal of events can be overcome with strength of spirit.' This means that in any country, under any economic or political system, or in any intellectual space, including the fields of philosophy, science, art, analytics, and journalism, it is possible to find or develop an alternative set of values to the liberal system by choosing a personal or collective position that is anti-bourgeois, anti-liberal, anti-hegemonic, and responsible. This particular historical idealism allows us to consider Western liberal hegemony as a phenomenon that is principally defensive, transformable, rotten from within, and subject to deconstruction and elimination. It is a sort of colossus with feet of clay against which joint efforts can prevail.

An Intellectual Revolutionary Alternative

Robert Cox poses a question about the establishment of an intellectual revolutionary alternative which he calls 'counter-hegemony'. He talks about the need for a global historical bloc of intellectuals from around the world who opt for a revolution to critique the liberal status quo. The most important thing about this is that it does not have to be done on a Marxist basis. Cox thinks that the historical process is open, and in this respect the domination of capital is a construct. In this respect he is pointedly different from the neo-Marxists, including Wallerstein.[19]

The post-positivist, constructivist, and postmodernist ideas of Cox conclude that the conditions of globalisation necessitate posing the question of counter-hegemony as globally as you would pose the question of bourgeois liberal hegemony. Passive resistance to global hegemony by states exercising *trasformismo* is absolutely insufficient and leads to the fall of Caesarism.

Cox introduces the concept of counter-society in contrast to today's global society dominated by bourgeois-liberal principles. How is counter-society established? It is established through contrary principles. All that is good in a global society must be destroyed, and in its place should be built a society with the opposite characteristics. Instead of principles of universal domination, develop principles of local community. Instead of the liberal monologue, create a dialogue of organic culture.

---

19   Immanuel Wallerstein (b. 1930) is an American sociologist who is known for his work in post-colonialist theory and anti-globalisation. He is a critic of capitalism, claiming that capitalism is not centred in any specific country but rather is synonymous with the global economy itself.

To Conceive of Counter-Hegemony

John M Hobson is a specialist in international affairs and the author of *The Eurocentric Conception of World Politics*,[20] a book in which he criticises American racism. Hobson writes that it is a brilliant idea to build a model of counter-hegemony when there is a popular desire and demand for one. The description of the principles of counter-hegemony takes up only 2 to 3 pages in his book. That is why it is necessary to start from the beginning, and figure out how to conceive of a counter-hegemony.

In order to conceive of counter-hegemony, first hegemony, as a universalism of liberalism, must be soundly conceived of and understood as a unified monolithic context. Gramcianism proposes itself as a strategy of counter-hegemony — a spiritual alternative to liberalism in the context of contemporary society. In the beginning, it is necessary to think of counter-hegemony as a society of non-liberalism. That is why it is necessary to construct the non-liberalism of tomorrow, and not the non-liberalism of yesterday. In other words: the non-liberalism of the future, and not the non-liberalism of the past. The avant-garde elements of contemporary counter-hegemony are the 'theory of the multipolar world' and the 'Fourth Political Theory' (4PT) which are being developed in Russia in the context of the International Eurasia Movement.[21]

What is the non-liberalism of the past? It is the anti-liberal ideologies of the twentieth century, those that were historically vanquished by liberalism (Communism, conservatism, and fascism). All of these ideologies were defeated by liberalism, and were consequently thrown on the trash heap of history. The bearers of archaic, Marxist, fascist and conservative-monarchical discourses have already demonstrated that they could not endure the

---

20   John M Hobson, *The Eurocentric Conception of World Politics: Western International Theory, 1760–2010* (Cambridge: Cambridge University Press, 2012).

21   The following works are devoted to the problems of developing a 'Fourth Political Theory': Alexander Dugin, *The Fourth Political Theory* (London: Arktos, 2012); and Alain de Benoist, *Against Liberalism: The Fourth Political Theory* (St. Petersburg: Amphora, 2009). (The latter book is a collection of Benoist's essays; there is no corresponding title in French or English.—Ed.) There are also Websites dedicated to the development of the 'Fourth Political Theory': 4pt.su and konservatizm.org/konservatizm/theory/list.xhtml.—AD

historical battle with hegemony. That is why these ideologies, as far as the establishing of a counter-hegemonic project is concerned, can be seen as peripheral.

In order to win against its ideological enemies, liberalism in the twentieth century used opposition to totalitarianism (in which the conservative and Communist projects participated against their will). To fight its ideological enemies, liberalism in the twentieth century also used freedom and liberty, or 'freedom from' — negative freedom.

Today, liberalism has won out against all others. 'Freedom from' is now an irrefutable right. We live in a liberal world, where an individual does not have to free himself from anything, in principle, except from the ground and from his own humanity. We have now discovered the purest essence of liberalism: freedom from everything, which is nothing more than pure nothingness and absolute nihilism.

Today, against the hegemonic triumph of liberalism, stands a sluggish Caesarism in its last days. *The End of History and the Last Man* by Francis Fukuyama could not have anticipated this. However, in the meantime...

Non-Liberalism of the Future

What does it mean to think of the non-liberalism of the future? It means to think of a non-liberalism which is born from the dehumanisation of man and the loss of gender identity, a non-liberalism born out of a type of man who has nothing. It means to see the horizon of liberalism as an absolute victory over Nothingness. It means to offer an alternative not from without, but from within. It means that ultimately, liberalism will move beyond the boundaries of sociology and will become a thoroughly anthropological issue. Society disintegrates, and then there is post-society. There is only an isolated liberal citizen of the world, a cosmopolitan, who, in fact, does not belong to any society.

The Italian philosopher, Massimo Cacciari, calls this 'a society made up entirely of idiots', a society which loses the ability to communicate amongst themselves, and losing everything that they have common. As such, they have their own unique languages, and carry out a rhizomatic existence.

Here, we come to the last frontier of humanity. This is where counter-hegemony will take off.

The principal course of counter-hegemony, in its anthropological iteration, is the idea of a radical rethinking of freedom. Liberalism must not oppose totalitarianism, because by doing so it only fuels its destructive power against the principle of freedom in the sense of 'freedom for', freedom as defined by John Stuart Mill. Approaching the problem in which the individual is placed above the whole of society from the standpoint of anthropology, it is not conservative values that work against liberalism, but something radically different. This radically different thing is an understanding of the person, that is, freedom against liberty, and a person against individualism. In Christianity, such a person is seen as the fusion of the divine with the individual. The personality is born at the moment of baptism. In religion, the idea of personality is described in various ways, and it is especially beautifully represented in the works of Marcel Mauss.[22] In any society, it is an archaic concept of the person when the person is at the centre of attention. This is not an individual; it is the intersection of some spiritual or generalised species,- an eidetic subject.

An individual must rise against 'freedom from' and should act in favour of the 'freedom to' and not in favour of a lack of freedom, or in favour of some form of collective community. We must accept the challenge of nihilism, in the sense of Martin Heidegger's strict nihilism. Furthermore, Martin Heidegger proposed building a philosophy upon the inner individual according to the principle of *Dasein*.[23]

To conceive of counter-hegemony, one must think creatively. Personal freedom is at the heart of counter-hegemony.

---

22   Marcel Mauss (1872–1950) was a sociologist whose work also had a significant impact on anthropology, particularly Claude Lévi-Strauss.

23   In German, *Dasein* literally means 'being there'. It is one of the principal concepts in Heidegger's thought.

A Model for Counter-Society: A Pact among Intellectuals

The counter-society model must be open at the top; such is the principle of freedom. At the head of this society, there must stand those who are the most open to the heights of temperance, and who are not fixated on themselves. For Plato, this was philosophers who were contemplative. Plato's Republic can be seen as the political expression of Platonism, and the philosopher stands at its head. The philosopher does not so much rule as thinks, contemplates, and creates opportunities for individuals and societies to become sacred. The principle of the unsacred makes up the backbone of the theory of counter-society. Modern power should not only be intellectual, but should also be opposed to profanity. It must restore the elements of the sacred, the holy, and the vertical dimension - everything that was cast aside by modernity, leading humanity to the emptiness and meaninglessness of its modern liberal iteration.

The political philosophy of verticalism must be a platform for the new, historic pact of intellectuals. If we create this pact on the basis of pragmatic alliances alone, we will not succeed, because liberalism will take over these formations sooner or later.

A historic pact of intellectuals must necessarily be global; it cannot be limited to any one nationality, country, or culture. For example, even the totality of the Islamic world or the Chinese cannot do this. It requires counter-hegemony and a counter-hegemonic global association of intellectuals on the basis of an open philosophy and on a global scale. Around this pact of intellectuals, there should be a constellation of multi-scale systems, symmetric with those envisaged by Joseph Nye in his description of the transactional system of liberalism (where actors are states, parties, movements, industrial groups, religious groups, and even individuals all in one).

The Will and Resources of the New Elite Civilisation

Massimo Cacciari's Archipelago

The axis of counter-hegemonic strategy should be the construction of the will, and not material resources. The will comes first, and then resources. This shall proceed from the global counter-hegemonic intellectual elite, which will be responsible for dialogue between civilisations.

A civilised elite is a new concept. It currently does not exist. We are talking about a combination of two elite qualities: a deep assimilation of civilised culture (on the philosophical, religious, and moral levels) and of a high degree of passion, the kind that will push a man to the heights of power, prestige, and influence. Modern liberalism channels passion exclusively into the fields of economics and business, creating a privileged society that advances a very specific type of individual (which the American sociologist Yuri Slezkine calls the 'mercurial type').[24]

The mercurial elite globalism of mondialist nomadism, expounded by Jacques Attali,[25] must be overthrown in favour of a radically different type of elite. In every civilisation different 'planets' can dominate, and not only furtively. The mercenary Mercury reflects its installation through the managers of cosmopolitanism. The Islamic elite is clearly different; we see an example of this in modern Iran, where politics (Mars) and economics (Mercury) are subordinated to spirituality in the hands of its spiritual leaders, the Ayatollahs (Saturn).

However, 'the world' is only a metaphor. Different civilisations are based on different codes. The primary thing is that the elite is obliged to reflect

---

24   Yuri Slezkine (b. 1957) characterises the Jews as 'mercurial', since they provide services to other peoples who produce food (which he terms 'Apollonian').

25   Jacques Attali (b. 1943) is a French economist who served as an advisor to Mitterrand. In his book *A Brief History of the Future*, he speculates that the next phase of capitalism will bring about a polycentric world defined by nomadism, which he believes will result from the development of social media and demographic pressures. The ultimate result of this would be a world in which nations cease to have meaning, dominated by an ultra-liberal economic system.

the codes in itself, whatever they may be. This is an essential condition. The will to be in power is inherent in any elite and must be intertwined with the will to have knowledge. In other words, intellectualism and activism should be united. Technical efficiency and values (often religious) should be combined in such an elite. Only such an elite will be able to participate fully and responsibly in the dialogue of civilisation; they will embody the principles of their traditions and engage with the representatives of other civilisations.

What resources can this constitutive intellectual elite depend on? First of all, it is the Second World, which Parag Khanna writes about,[26] the BRICS countries, and those states that have not received anything or are not in the first caste under the existing status quo. This makes up most nations in the current state of hegemony. Note that these countries will not take up the intellectual projects of counter-hegemony of their own accord.

The ruling regimes in these countries, if they do not step up, will continue to engage in *trasformismo*. Counter-hegemonic intellectuals must counterattack them, including in their own projects, instead of waiting until they are summoned to work within the administration of a state. It is important to understand that the states engaged in *trasformismo* will be engaged regardless of the place. China, Iran, Azerbaijan, India, Russia, and all the BRICS countries are undergoing continuous *trasformismo*.

Counter-hegemonic intellectuals should seize the narrative and dictate the agenda of these states to enable them to implement Caesarism as far as possible. Although the goal of counter-hegemony is something different, these countries hold great potential. They are a good resource and a tool to achieve that goal. This is an acceptable strategy. For example, Russia is a country with nuclear weapons that it can use as an argument against hegemony. This looks really impressive.

Also, as a counter-hegemonic resource, groups that are relevant to the historic pact are: the anti-liberal orientation of various parties throughout the world (regardless of whether they are Right or Left), socialists or conservatives; various movements of the vertical-open type : cultural, artistic,

---

26   Parag Khanna (b. 1977) is an Indian-American expert on international relations, and he is the author of the 2008 book, *The Second World: Empires and Influence in the New Global Order*.

aesthetic, and environmental; whole social classes and industry, as for example the peasantry and global industry, which sooner or later will become victims of the banking and financial system, as well as the tertiary sector of the economy, which is already collapsing in the face of the growth of speculative globalist financial capital; and traditional religion, which, in essence, is non-liberal except for those religions of a liberal orientation, which are basically secular and relativistic.

The task of the historical counter-hegemonic bloc is to combine all of these resources into a global network. For this, the 'archipelago' concept of Massimo Cacciari is especially useful, and which he applies to Europe, though this idea can be spread wider. Massimo Cacciari argues that between the universalist *logos* and the anarchy of atomist idiots, there exists a personal *logos*, the *logoi* of particular civilisations: cultures that use a complex model in which dialogue and the integration of Right and Left into a single historic pact can make significant progress.

Russia and the Hegemony

From the point of view of the authors of the theory of counter-hegemony, Russia is currently a field of a typical *trasformismo*, and what is called Putinism is nothing short of Caesarism. Putinism opposes hegemony in the face of internal opposition and the 'white ribbon carrying' *Echo of Moscow*, as well as foreign hegemony, which puts pressure on Russia from the outside. It attempts to maintain a balance between Caesarism, which is trying to steer towards modernisation on the one hand, and on the other towards conservatism, in an attempt to hold onto power by any means. This description looks extremely crude, but rationally and realistically there are no ideas, no ideology, no goals, and no understanding of the historical process. There is no *telos*[27] here; it is simply the Caesarism of a Gramscian. This is how we have arrived at all the inconsistencies and reticence, hesitation and indecision, and balancing and unpredictability of Putin's policies.

However, the opposition put up by the internal and external forces of hegemony against this Caesarism need for Putin to move in the right direc-

---

27 Classical Greek: 'purpose' or 'goal'.

tion; this is necessary for intellectuals of the counter-hegemony. However, *trasformismo* is an adaptive-passive strategy; this means that sooner or later, the purpose of this *trasformismo* will destroy Caesarism. In this sense, it is a negative initiative that looks like modernisation and which objectively leads to the strengthening of the middle class, the classic enemy of the state, as well as the bourgeoisie; capitalism and individualism are the enemies of a concrete society, and humanity as a whole.

How soon will Caesarism fall? History shows that it can carry on for a very long time. Theoretically, it should fall, but it continues to exist, sometimes becoming quite successful. It all depends on how successfully or unsuccessfully *trasformismo* is implemented. In this doomed passive strategy, sometimes the most paradoxical way can be the most efficient.

It is quite obvious that if we accept that over the past 13 years Russia practiced precisely this strategy, it should be recognised that general ideological pragmatism is omnivorous, and it will continue to exist, despite an outcry. Nevertheless, it is worth noting that it was successful *trasformismo* that saved the state from the fact that its representatives have not yet destroyed the global hegemony.

Today, it seems to us that we should not identify the national interests of the Russian Federation with that line of strategic planning seen in Putin's rule, which can be perfectly described by the term *trasformismo*.

However, this is not enough. The right strategy requires a completely different sort of type; it requires something thoroughly counter-hegemonic in its very essence. The right strategy must promote the theory of a multipolar world, rooted in the activities of the historic pact of anti-globalisation.

Another important initiative is the International Eurasia Movement's Global Revolutionary Alliance.[28] This is a quite active strategy that can be developed in parallel with Russia, being both Russian and international. Even if there are conflicts of interest between the Global Revolutionary Alliance and Europe or America (and there are a lot of them), this point should not embarrass, let alone stop anyone. People choose the same coun-

---

28 The Global Revolutionary Alliance is the international wing of the Eurasia Movement. They maintain a Website at www.granews.info.

ter-hegemonic ethics even when they run contrary to those societies in which they live.

In rejecting hegemony, we need not rely on power. Now, we have the ability to say 'yes' because we are on the same side as the current political power in our country: we oppose hegemony and those in power are against hegemony. However, even if hegemony triumphed in Russia, this situation should not influence the decision-making of the counter-hegemonic intellectual elite, as it should work in the name of fundamental objectives. Only by focusing solely on the concept of eschatology, on *telos*, and the target, rather than on short-term benefits, can victory and success be realised.

This historic pact of intellectuals, with their open philosophy of verticalism, can be in solidarity with the Russian Federation in its present state as one of the most important elements of the counter-hegemonic archipelago.

Putin's nuclear Russia is a great island in the archipelago; it is perfectly suitable for waging external revolutionary struggle. It is a wonderful base for training people who need to promote eschatological revolutionary activities on a global scale. This is a valuable tool, but without it things would continue all the same. We must look for contacts with China, Iran, India, Latin America, with counter-hegemonic forces in African countries, Asian countries, Europe, Canada, Australia, and so on. Everyone who is dissatisfied is a potential member of the counter-hegemonic archipelago, from states to individuals.

These are different things: Russia's national interests, as far as they pertain to counter-society, go beyond its territory and the archipelago. Counter-hegemony must think outside the ideological constraints of sectarianism if we want to create a counter-hegemonic bloc. The composition of the bloc must include all the representatives of the anti-bourgeois, anti-capitalist forces: Left, Right or even those who defy classification (Alain de Benoist[29] has consistently stressed that the divide between 'Left' and 'Right' is outdated. Today it is far more important whether someone

---

29 Alain de Benoist (b. 1943) is a French political philosopher who was the founder of the French 'New Right' school of thought, who has been very influential on Dugin and the Eurasia Movement.

stands for hegemony or against it.) Thus, modern Gramscianism calls for a counter-hegemonic bloc, a Global Revolutionary Alliance, that brings together all the enemies of capitalism and those who oppose the hegemony of Eurocentrism and racism (which are implicit in the ideas that underpin the universality of Western cultural values, the superiority of Western civilisation and modernisation). When placed in the context of the theory of the multipolar world, the theory of counter-hegemony occupies specific cultural and civilisational areas in the non-Eurocentric universal plurality. Modern counter-hegemony should be inclusive, that is, it should encompass all critiques of hegemony, from both the Right and the Left, and it should be inclusive of the positions and theories beyond the political ideologies of modernity. This is the Fourth Political Theory, about which I wrote a book of the same name, and which has been published in many European and Asian languages.

4PT
What is the Fourth Political Theory?

The model of globalisation functioning today forces all countries, nations and civilisations to make a fundamental choice: to accept the hegemonic liberal model or to look for their own, individual modes of development; to choose the path of resisting globalisation and thus find their own answers to its challenges. To maintain the status quo today without responding to globalisation in some way is impossible, because the passive observation of its unfolding 'of its own accord' inevitably leads to de-sovereiginisation and the introduction of governing structures from the outside; in other words, to countries losing their independence and freedom. The *trasformismo* trend in Russian politics is currently leading to just that.

History challenges Russia not just with liberalism and post-liberalism, but also with postmodernity, globalism and hegemony. Today, it is easy to see that the 'brave new world' of globalism, postmodernity and post-liberalism has no place for Russia in it. The issue is not just that the world government and the world state will eventually abolish all national governments altogether. The issue is that the entire span of Russian history is a dialectic struggle with the West and Western culture, the struggle to maintain its own (often only intuited) Russian truth, its own messianic idea, and its own version of the 'end of history', be it expressed through the Muscovite Orthodox tradition, the secular empire of Peter I,[30] or the global Communist revolution. The best minds of Russia saw the West headed towards the abyss, and today, looking at where the neoliberal economy and postmodern culture has taken the world, we can see clearly that this intuition that drove generations of Russians in search of an alternative was more than justified. The current economic crisis is just the start. The worst is yet to come. The inertia of post-liberal movement is such that there is no possible way to change its course. 'Liberated technics' (Oswald Spengler)[31] will seek more and more efficient, but purely technical and technological means to save the West. This is the new stage of technological and technical advancement, this worldwide spread of the nihilistic stain of the global market. It is clear that Russia must seek a separate way. Its own way. But therein lies the issue. Dodging the logic of postmodernism in a single country is not that simple.

What can be used to oppose global liberal hegemony in this day and age? The twentieth century was the century of ideologies (liberalism, Communism, and fascism). All of them were products of the new age (modernity), and each of them offered a worldview and sociopolitical project. Two of these have already proven fruitless, and liberalism is in crisis today — meaning the collapse of the world's financial system, economic crisis, and the degradation of capitalistic social strategies.

We need an alternative. This alternative to liberalism should be utterly new: invented, discovered, or even hard-won, if you will. Perhaps it will be an insight, but we must think and *live* in this direction — towards the expectation of some counter-liberal ideology.

The liberals are agonising. What is to replace the collapsing ideologeme and take its place?

---

30   Peter I (1672–1725), or Peter the Great, attempted to overcome traditional Russia, which he regarded as backwards, in favor of importing Enlightenment ideas from Europe.

31   Spengler discusses this idea in his book *Man and Technics* (London: Arktos, 2015).

This open question is what is called the Fourth Political Theory. It requires close attention. It cannot be solved with technology. Today we are living not in a simple glitch of the system, but in a full-blown collapse of the liberal order. This systemic and structural crisis will not leave anything as it has been. If Putin ignores the severity of this challenge to his worldview, we risk being simply buried under the debris of the inevitable collapse of the liberal system.

For Russia to persevere, even now we must be directing intellectual effort primarily towards the coming alternative, towards what is to come to replace collapsing liberalism.

There is no ready answer. Both will and imagination must strive to grasp the realities of the globalist world, to decipher the challenges of postmodernity and create something new; something different from the defeated ideologies of the past centuries (Communism, fascism) and the victorious one (liberalism), which was found to be wanting by the majority of humankind.

Russia needs a new political theory: the Fourth Political Theory. It's the fourth because the first two political theories, Communism and fascism, lost the historical battle in the twentieth century, and the third, liberalism, proved unsatisfactory to the majority of humanity. We are talking about a theory specifically, because any projects that merely touch up the surface and that are aimed at repairing the situation, and to correct the status quo will only be an utter waste of time. It is a political theory specifically because politics must not fade from human history, which would turn politics into 'government as an act', a merely technical manipulation of the world's managers. For Russia, it is the question of life or death, Hamlet's question. If Russia chooses 'to be', this automatically means creating the Fourth Political Theory. Otherwise, the choice is 'not to be', and Russia will quietly fade from the arena of history, merge with the globalised world, and become reimagined and governed by others.

4PT as a Universal Ideology

The Fourth Political Theory is a model for the political organisation of a multipolar world, and which should arise to replace contemporary unipolarity. The basis of this theory lies in a critical re-evaluation of the traditional political ideologies formed in the nineteenth and twentieth centuries. In the broadest terms, the Fourth Political Theory as a basis for a new worldview and the architecture of a multipolar world can be described through the dialectic rejection of the three primary ideologies that existed in human history: liberalism, Communism and fascism.

The Fourth Political Theory opposes liberalism as an ideology that puts the individual at the centre, but adopts the values of freedom. This value should, however, fit a different idea, and take for its social subject something other than the individual.

A review of the second political theory, Marxism, is informed by the inadequacy of the historical prognoses of Marx himself, who predicted the inevitability of the socialist revolutions in the developed bourgeois societies of Europe (where they never happened) and rejected the possibility of such revolutions occurring in the societies of Asia and Russia (where they happened only partially).

Historical materialism, uncritical faith in progress and dogmatic atheism are unacceptable aspects of Marxism; but alongside those, Marxism also gives a precise analysis of the alienation rampant in a bourgeois society, justly criticises capitalism and the mechanics of allocating surplus value, and predicts its inevitable crises and describes their mechanics. The critique of capitalism can be transferred to current circumstances as well, while singling out class as the subject of history can be dismissed as inadequate. The Fourth Political Theory accepts the Marxist analysis of alienation in bourgeois society.

When it comes to the ideologies of the 'Third Way' (fascism, National Socialism, etc.), it's imperative to reject racism as the idea of an inherent superiority of the people of one race over another. At the same time, the Fourth Political Theory expands the critique of racism to not only biological racism and nationalism, but into all forms of the acceptance of inequality in human societies, whether based on cultural, religious, technological or economic grounds. The Fourth Political Theory rejects all forms of racism and refuses to consider 'race' or the 'state' as the subject of history. In the context of international relations it translates into the acceptance of the equality of all societies and civilisations, and all nations and cultures across the globe regardless of skin colour or their level of development. Likewise it refuses to single out any one specific set of values, Eastern or Western, as universal. Certain aspects of the 'Third Way' can be seen as positive — primarily the interest that some of its atypical and dissenting thinkers took in the values of 'peoples' and 'ethnicities' in world history, and these concepts should always be used in the plural. Other important aspects are its legal theory of 'Large Spaces' and the theory of the 'rights of peoples' and 'political theology', as developed by the thinkers of the German Conservative Revolution (the Right-wing anti-Hitler opposition).

The Fourth Political Theory and Heidegger's *Dasein*

The Fourth Political Theory rejects the capitalism, individualism and 'religion of money' within liberalism; in Communism, materialism, atheism, progressivism and the theory of class struggle; in fascism, all forms of racism, totalitarianism and the idea of the dominance of one culture over another. On the other hand, the Fourth Political Theory borrows the idea of the value of freedom from liberalism; the ethical ideal of justice, equality and the harmonious development of coexistence based on the overcoming of alienation from Marxism; and from the 'Third Way' it takes the values of *ethnos*, nation, religion, spirituality, family, and the sacred.

These principles are entirely sufficient to construct a pluralistic and open system of intercultural and inter-civilisational dialogue.

The subject of the Fourth Political Theory ought not to be the individual, class, race or the state, but *Dasein* — human existence, present and well-grounded in its organic, cultural, linguistic and spiritual history. The term *Dasein* is the basis of Martin Heidegger's philosophy and is borrowed by the Fourth Political Theory as essential to understanding the subject of the contemporary political process.

From the philosophical standpoint, the Fourth Political Theory can be attributed to the fields of phenomenology, structuralism, existentialism, ethno-sociology and cultural anthropology. All these philosophical and humanitarian fields of study focus on the variety of human cultures and see this variety as the highest value and the treasure of the human spirit, something that must not be eradicated and levelled out but carefully preserved, supported and protected in every way. All conflicts and disagreements should not be solved via violence, universalism and colonisation (whichever apologist phraseology it may hide behind), but through harmony and a dialogue between civilisations.

The Fourth Political Theory is an answer to the challenge of postmodernity, which stems from the logic of forgetting the essence of being and in removing humanity from its ontological and theological (spiritual) roots. It is impossible to respond to that with 'one-day solution' innovations or PR surrogates. It appears that in order to solve the most pressing issues of the global economic crisis, in order to resist the unipolar world, maintain and preserve sovereignty, and so on, it is essential to turn to the philosophical basis of history and to make a metaphysical effort. The Fourth Political Theory cannot emerge on its own. An exertion of will is required here, conceptual work: a disagreement with postmodernity and with the status quo; with the inertia-propelled development of history; with the disappearance of politics from life; and with the utter alienation of the individual from the sphere of politics, spirit, culture, civilisation, and from humanity in general. The Fourth Political Theory is a crusade against postmodernity, and against the post-industrial society, liberalism and globalism. This is the strategy of riding postmodernity; much like how the Eastern practices offer to 'ride the tiger'.[32] This is a search and a discovery of weak points in the global systems and the hacking of those points. It is not possible to just walk past postmodernity, globalism and hegemony and merely ignore them. Hence why the Fourth Political Theory must turn to the precursors to modernity and to what modernity actively fought, but what became almost entirely irrelevant to postmodernity. We must turn to tradition, to pre-modernity, archaism, theology, the sacred sciences, and ancient philosophy. In Russia's case that means turning to the full Orthodox tradition,

---

32   To ride the tiger means to cling to his back rather than have to deal with his fangs and claws. The Italian traditionalist Julius Evola used the term as an analogy with the best way of dealing with the modern world for those who are dissenters: try to ride along with it without getting caught up in it, rather than attack it directly.

to its sources, to the mystical Orthodoxy of Byzantium, to even more ancient Platonic and Neo-Platonic doctrines, to the archaic layers of tradition, and to the highest super-rational creeds. Within the framework of the Fourth Political Theory we are also talking about a profound philosophical comprehension of being, about opening up the deep ontological source of human existence, and a careful understanding of the philosophical depth of experience that was made by Martin Heidegger — a thinker who made the unique effort of trying to construct a fundamental ontology — a deep, paradoxical, piercing teaching about being.

The Fourth Political Theory cannot be a task undertaken by an individual or even a limited group of people — it is for everyone to partake in. This effort must be a collective one. Representatives of other cultures from both Asia and Europe can help us here, as they feel the eschatological tension of the moment just as sharply, and they are just as desperately seeking an escape from the worldwide dead end.

The Fourth Political Theory must be developed by various peoples and cultures, and everyone can contribute. However, Russia, located in Eurasia, at the intersection of the cultural and civilisational tendencies of East and West, is destined to stand at the focal point of this conceptual process by the merit of its location alone. It comes as no surprise that the first systematic thoughts concerning this theory emerged in Russia.

Gramscian counter-hegemony calls for the formation of a counter-hegemonic block, a Global Revolutionary Alliance which joins all those opposing capitalism and hegemony, Eurocentrism and racism, all of which are implicit in the idea of the universality of Western cultural values, the superiority of Western civilisation and modernisation. In the context of the theory of the multipolar world and the Fourth Political Theory, the theory of counter-hegemony gains a concrete cultural and civilisational space of a non-Eurocentric pluralistic universe. Contemporary counter-hegemony must be inclusive, which means engaging with all types of resistance to hegemony; this involves the Left and the Right, and positions and theories that are outside the boundaries of the political ideologies of modernity within the framework of the Fourth Political Theory.

Conclusion
'He is Simply the Best'

This book contains reflections on Russia, its government, and its policies and problems during the past 13 years. It is an uninterrupted, if emotionally charged, flow of reflections, philosophical evaluations, and disjointed notes, held together by an unwavering and painful concern about the fate of the Motherland, Great Russia, and about our incredible and mysterious people, for whom I feel a boundless love and worry about infinitely with all my heart. Naturally, these reflections are bound to turn to power and its embodiment: Vladimir Vladimirovitch Putin. Hope and disappointment do not simply swap places here, but follow one another, coexist even. It is clear that we cannot calmly stand by as many painful processes emerge. We want to question those in power: 'Why are you dawdling? Why are you standing there instead of doing something?' There is a desire to force something, to somehow encourage, perhaps even exclaim: 'Vladimir Vladimirovitch, please, please fire this (or other) PR-monster who is letting you down, and making you seem like a buffoon or an idiot!', even if maybe those things should be ignored. My analysis constantly moves to the sphere of ideas, to structures and concepts that move and construct themselves following a different logic — in the cold, introspective skies of connotations. This comparison of earthly strife and the clear shining light of abstract ideas is what is truly important.

Nietzsche said once, after being rejected by Lou Andreas-Salomé:[33] 'If I were God, I would have created Lou Salomé differently.' If I were the President of Russia, I would have done everything differently, not like Putin has. I accept some of it as correct, but see some other things as mistakes. Sadly, the final balance is the same: he's exactly half right and half wrong. Putin is so steady in his self-defence and even imposing of his half-rightness — he takes no side steps. I am confident that it will cost him. 13 years in power is a very long time. He will not change, and this is very nearly a sentence — ot

---

33 Lou Andreas-Salomé (1861–1937) was a Russian-born intellectual who lived most of her life in Europe. Although she spurned Nietzsche, with whom she had a close relationship, she had affairs with Rainer Maria Rilke and Sigmund Freud, among others.

my sentence, but the sentence of the Russian Idea. I say that with the most sincere regret and sorrow. So far, Putin embodies the empty, technological present, which is getting harder and harder to bear. However, the moment you compare Putin to the leaders of other countries (Western ones, of course), you end up at the other extreme. There are no equals, he is simply the best. And that is the truth.

Vladimir Putin's Last Chance

What is the essence of Putin's position today, the Putin of the third term? I have always aligned myself with the 'third term party'... and it arrived. What can we expect?

Today we know several of Putin's formulas that I have been reflecting on for many years. The first one is simple and contradictory at once: 'patriotism plus liberalism'. Now it's being joined by two more, possibly clarifying the first: 'Putin the realist' and 'Putin as the embodiment of the idea of Caesarism and *trasformismo*'.

Each of these formulas and all of them together form Putin's own brand of a 'Putin kōan', his own personal ideological antimony, reflecting the structure of his personal and power-related compromise. The essence of the formulas reflects that our President is equally close to sovereignty, superpower statehood, vertical power, nationality, and religion; as well as to Westernisation, modernisation, effective management, and liberal reformism in the economy. We have lived in the structure of these formulas, combining the incongruous, in these *coincidentia oppositorum*[34] for the last 12 years. It seemed like an eternity, and yet flew by in the blink of an eye. Russians supported Putin for his patriotism — the people and the masses; the ordinary people and many an extraordinary person. Because of his liberalism and because he maintained the economic domination of the big bourgeoisie, or, essentially, the oligarchy that was established in the turbulent '90s, he was put up with by the economic elites. At the same time, all the active political forces were eager for Putin to step outside this compromise, in which patriotism was balanced by liberalism and the pro-Western liberal

---

34   Latin: 'unity of opposites'.

reforms were cancelled by leaning on sovereignty and the consolidation of vertical power. And yet Putin kept delaying year after year, hesitating, insisting on his vision. He forced the masses to obediently endure the economic injustices of uncontrolled capitalism and the unrestrained orgy of corruption, while he forced the elites to falsely don the robes of patriotism. The theory of international relations calls this *trasformismo*, a doublethink policy in which the autocratic ruler defends the sovereignty of the country against the world's hegemony, while eventually being forced to make concessions. Gradually this doublethink becomes unbearable for both the patriots and the liberals. The 'Putin kōans', which society has more or less accepted, are today utterly unbearable. They just stopped working.

What will Happen Next?

The first possibility is that Putin will habitually turn to his tried and tested formula. The *'trasformismo'* strategy can last a very long time. But we have seen that the liberals will actively undermine it, and the patriots who are not required to believe in it, might just believe that it's a simulacrum and a fake, and the political authorities will not do anything decisive. That means that Putin is seriously risking the loss of his real electorate in the folk, his strategic reserve — the trust of the patriotically-minded masses. In other words, the 'patriotism plus liberalism' formula will not work at all under the new circumstances.

There is one option left: patriotism without any impurities, such as Eurasianism and conservatism without any simulacra or postmodernism. This is the only logical and responsible choice for the third term.

The programme for such a conservative turn is exceedingly clear and in many ways natural for Putin himself. Most likely this is how he organically understands the world, the country, and history. In the past there were limiting factors; let us not discuss right now whether they were baseless or grounded in reality, but there were. Now, there aren't any. That is why all that remains is pure patriotism. And the gesture is already prepared: the liberals, partially getting ahead of themselves, have already irreversibly identified Putin with patriotism and have sentenced him as a patriot, conservative and populist. All that remains is for Putin to become the thing that his sworn enemies already see him as — which is also the thing that his friends of today, the patriots and Eurasianists, want to see him as. There is just one small thing left: to firmly take ownership of the image that had formed in the oppositional minority's mind a long time ago and that would be accepted by the popular majority, and which would be organic and natural for Putin himself. If it does, finally, happen (and Putin's pre-election articles, the meeting of patriots on Poklonnaya Hill, the founding of the Izborsk Club, and some symbolic cabinet reshuffling all give us reason to see it as a distinct possibility), what can we expect?

The answer is simple: at the age of 60 a new Putin will be revealed to us. Putin the patriot, minus the liberalism. Putin, the supporter of a multipolar world, and the opponent of American hegemony. Putin, Eurasian, the supporter of a great continental empire and of Russian civilisation.

A lot for a 60-year-old.

Just enough for a political leader. And yet...there is no room for error. In the next 12 years — the last years this can happen — it's paramount to win the battle for Russia or... (I don't even want to say it out loud).

Then we wait for the following: real steps towards integrating the post-Soviet space and the creation of the Eurasian Union; a huge leap forward in the field of defence; the development of a consolidating idea, aimed at strengthening the cultural code of our Eurasian civilisation; a turn towards conservative values and even traditionalism, morality, spirituality, and morality in the fields of education, culture, and in the mass media; a transition from a liberal economic policy to a social and mobilising one; a defeat of Western networks of influence over the elite, the culture, the community of experts, and the government; a reorganisation of the structure of inter-ethnic relationships based on the principles of respect for the Russian nation while taking into account the interests of all ethnic and confessional groups; emphasis on the renewal of the political and governing elite with new, passionary personnel; leaning on advanced technologies and the real economic sector while overcoming resource dependency; stricter measures against corruption tied to transnational institutions and which are part of the systems of external governance; the authorities siding with the people (the wide Russian, Eurasian masses) and selecting new active and passionate personnel from the bottom into the governing elite; and accepting a singular orientation towards multipolarity, polycentrism and effective resistance to American hegemony in foreign policy.

Can this be accomplished while maintaining the inertial order of things in today's Russia? Can it be done with the current personnel and the rather relaxed psychological state of society, which is mostly preoccupied with simple survival?

I will respond paradoxically and unexpectedly that yes, it can. The thing is, Russia is politically structured on the principle of vertical symmetry. The one at the top is everything. Furthermore, the higher up and more authoritarian the ruler, the closer he is to the masses and the more stable his rule. The elites, who break up the society from the top and the bottom, always oppose the ruler and the people alike. If the ruler makes a single move specifically looking to lean on the wide popular masses, he gains unlimited possibilities, and doesn't have to account to anyone after that. Call it what you will. It's Russian; it was and most likely will be. Due to this feature of Russian society an autocratic ruler can carry out any reforms, or none at all.

So, if Putin makes a decision at the age of 60, it alone will be enough. Personnel will appear, the psychological state will change, energy will appear along with resources, and the inertia will disappear. This doesn't mean that everything will go smoothly: one must not underestimate the pro-Western elites and especially their American patrons. But there are very real chances for success. So, it appears that whether or not the 60-year-old President wants to or not, he has to choose one thing: patriotism. And that's it.

This is not an ultimatum or a self-fulfilling prophecy. It's nothing personal. Such is the logic of cycles in politics, ideology and the electoral process, as well as in the personal biography of a major politician. It is cold math that is this time giving all of us hope and giving us a chance.

When Putin was 48 and he had just emerged on the horizon of Russian politics, I expressed genuine enthusiasm for his authentic actions (the second Chechen campaign, hitting the oligarchy, stopping the flow of radical Russophobia in the media; in other words, the liquidation of Yeltsinism) and his clear declarations (accepting sovereignty as the highest value, multipolarity, and orientation towards the Eurasian Union). This was reflected in my text 'Dawn in Boots'. Time has shown that I was clearly getting ahead of myself. Ahead were 12 years of delay, wasted time, and empty political tricks. It was a simulacrum of dawn. In other words, 12 years were stolen from the country, from history, politics, Eurasianism, and from me personally. It's impossible to just forget that. The former trust has been compromised. The emotions are gone. To some extent or other, the patriotic majority feels the same. It may not say so, and may not be able to express it, but it feels it.

That's why it is possible today to say without irritation or hopefulness: 'Vladimir Vladimirovitch, this is your last chance.'

And also our last chance, because if they topple Putin, the country will go down with him.

The final gesture is on the agenda: a radical transformation of the formula, minus liberalism. There is no more time to warm up. None. Now or never. One's sixtieth birthday doesn't allow for words like 'later' or 'gradually'.

APPENDIX I

The War on Russia in Its Ideological Dimension:

An Analysis from the Perspective of the Fourth Political Theory

(April 2014)

The Coming War as Concept

The war against Russia is currently the most discussed issue in the West. At this point it is only a suggestion and a possibility, but it can become a reality depending on the decisions taken by all parties involved in the Ukrainian conflict — Moscow, Washington, Kiev, and Brussels.

I don't want to discuss all the aspects and history of this conflict here. Instead I propose to analyze its deep ideological roots. My conception of the most relevant events is based on the Fourth Political Theory, whose principles I have described in my book under the same name that was published in English by Arktos Media in 2012.

Therefore I will not examine the war of the West on Russia in terms of its risks, dangers, issues, costs or consequences, but rather in an ideological sense as seen from the global perspective. I will instead meditate on the sense of such a war, and not on the war itself (which may be either real or virtual).

Essence of Liberalism

In the modern West, there is one ruling, dominant ideology: liberalism. It may appear in many shades, versions and forms, but the essence is always the same. Liberalism contains an inner, fundamental structure which follows axiomatic principles:

- anthropological individualism (the individual is the measure of all things);
- belief in progress (the world is heading toward a better future, and the past is always worse than the present);
- technocracy (technical development and its execution are taken as the most important criteria by which to judge the nature of a society);
- Eurocentrism (Euro-American societies are accepted as the standard of measure for the rest of humanity);
- economy as destiny (the free market economy is the only normative economic system — all the other types are to either be reformed or destroyed);
- democracy is the rule of minorities (defending themselves from the majority, which is always prone to degenerate into totalitarianism or 'populism');
- the middle class is the only really existing social actor and universal norm (independent from the fact of whether or not an individual has already reached this status or is on the way to becoming actually middle class, representing for the moment only a would-be middle class);
- one-world globalism (human beings are all essentially the same with only one distinction, namely that of their individual nature — the world should be integrated on the basis of the individual and cosmopolitism; in other words, world citizenship).

These are the core values of liberalism, and they are a manifestation of one of the three tendencies that originated in the Enlightenment alongside Communism and fascism, which collectively proposed varying interpretations of the spirit of modernity. During the twentieth century, liberalism defeated its rivals, and since 1991 has become the sole, dominant ideology of the world.

The only freedom of choice in the kingdom of global liberalism is that between Right liberalism, Left liberalism or radical liberalism, including far-Right liberalism, far-Left liberalism and extremely radical liberalism. As a consequence, liberalism has been installed as the operational system of Western civilisation and of all other societies that find themselves in the zone of Western influence. It has become the common denominator for any politically correct discourse, and the distinguishing mark which determines who is accepted by mainstream politics and who is marginalised and rejected. Conventional wisdom itself became liberal.

Geopolitically, liberalism was inscribed in the America-centred model in which Anglo-Saxons formed the ethnical core, based upon the Atlanticist Euro-American partnership, NATO, which represents the strategic core of the system of global security. Global security has come to be seen as being synonymous with the security of the West, and in the last instance with American security. So liberalism is not only an ideological power but also a political, military and strategic power. NATO is liberal in its roots. It defends liberal societies, and it fights to extend liberalism to new areas.

Liberalism as Nihilism

There is one point in liberal ideology that has brought about a crisis within it: liberalism is profoundly nihilistic at its core. The set of values defended by liberalism is essentially linked to its main thesis: the primacy of liberty. But liberty in the liberal vision is an essentially *negative* category: it claims to be free *from* (as per John Stuart Mill), not to be free *for* something. It is not secondary; it is the essence of the problem.

Liberalism fights against all forms of collective identity, and against all types of values, projects, strategies, goals, methods and so on that are collectivist, or at least non-individualist. That is the reason why one of the most important theorists of liberalism, Karl Popper[1] (following Friedrich Hayek), held in his important book, *The Open Society and Its Enemies*,[2] that liberals should fight against any ideology or political philosophy (ranging from Plato and Aristotle to Marx and Hegel) that suggests that human society should have some common goal, common value, or common meaning. (It should be noted that George Soros regards this book as his personal bible.) Any goal, any value, and any meaning in liberal society, or the open society, should be strictly based upon the individual. So the enemies of the open society, which is synonymous with Western society post-1991, and which has become the norm for the rest of the world, are concrete. Its primary enemies are Communism and fascism, both ideologies which emerged from the same Enlightenment philosophy, and which contained central, non-individualistic concepts — class in Marxism, race in National Socialism, and the national state in fascism).

The source of liberalism's conflict with the existing alternatives of modernity, fascism or Communism is quite obvious. Liberals claim to liberate society from fascism and Communism, or from the two major permutations of explicitly non-individualistic modern totalitarianism. Liberalism's struggle, when viewed as a part of the process of the liquidation of non-liberal societies, is quite meaningful: it acquires its meaning from the fact of the very existence of ideologies that explicitly deny the individual as society's highest value. It is quite clear what the struggle is attempting to achieve: liberation from its opposite. But the fact that liberty, as it is conceived by liberals, is an essentially *negative* category is not clearly perceived here. The enemy is present and is concrete. That very fact gives liberalism its solid content. Something other than the open society exists, and the fact of its existence is enough to justify the process of liberation.

---

[1] Sir Karl Popper (1902–1994) was an Austrian-British philosopher who was well-known for his defence of the principles of liberal democracy.

[2] Karl Popper, *The Open Society and Its Enemies*, 2 vols. (London: Routledge & Kegan Paul, 1945).

Unipolar Period: Threat of Implosion

In 1991, when the Soviet Union as the last opponent of Western liberalism fell, some Westerners, such as Francis Fukuyama, proclaimed the end of history. This was quite logical: as there was no longer an explicit enemy of the open society, therefore there was no more history as had occurred during the modern period, which was defined by the struggle between three political ideologies (liberalism, Communism and fascism) for the heritage of the Enlightenment. That was, strategically speaking, the moment when the 'unipolar moment' was realized (Charles Krauthammer). The period between 1991 and 2014, at the midpoint of which Bin Laden's attack against the World Trade Center occurred, was the period of the global domination of liberalism. The axioms of liberalism were accepted by all the main geopolitical actors, including China (in economic terms) and Russia (in its ideology, economy, and political system). There were liberals and would-be liberals, not-yet liberals, not-liberal-enough liberals and so on. The real and explicit exceptions were few (such as Iran and North Korea), so the world became axiomatically liberal according to its ideology.

This has been the most important moment in the history of liberalism. It has defeated its enemies, but at the same time it has *lost* them. Liberalism is essentially the liberation from and the fight against *all that is not liberal* (at present or in what has the potential to become such). Liberalism acquired its real meaning and its content from its enemies. When the choice is presented as being between not-freedom (as represented by concrete totalitarian societies) or freedom, many choose freedom, not understanding it in terms of freedom *for* what, or freedom *to do* what... When there is an illiberal society, liberalism is positive. It only begins to show its negative essence *after victory*.

After the victory of 1991, liberalism stepped into its *implosive* phase. After having defeated Communism and fascism, it stood alone, with no enemy to fight. And that was the moment when inner conflicts emerged, when liberal societies began to attempt to purge themselves of their last remaining non-liberal elements: sexism, political incorrectness, inequality between the sexes, any remnants of the non-individualistic dimensions of institutions such as the state and the Church, and so on. *Liberalism always needs an enemy to liberate from.* Otherwise it loses its purpose, and its implicit nihilism becomes too salient. The absolute triumph of liberalism is its death.

That is the ideological meaning of the financial crises of 2000 and 2008. The successes and not the failures of the new, entirely profit-based economy (of turbo-capitalism, according to Edward Luttwak)[3] are responsible for its collapse.

The liberty to do anything you want, but restricted to the individual scale, provokes an implosion of the personality. The human passes to the infra-human realm, and to sub-individual domains. And here he encounters virtuality, as a dream of sub-individuality, the freedom from anything. This is the evaporation of the human, and brings about the Empire of nothingness as the last word in the total victory of liberalism. Postmodernism prepares the terrain for that post-historic, self-referential recycling of nonsense.

The West is in Need of an Enemy

You may ask now, what the Hell does all of this have to do with the (presumable) coming war with Russia? I am ready to answer that now.

Liberalism has continued to gain momentum on a global scale. Since 1991, it has been an inescapable fact. And it has now *begun to implode*. It has arrived at its terminal point and started to liquidate itself. Mass immigration, the clash of cultures and civilisations, the financial crisis, terrorism, and the growth of ethnic nationalism are indicators of approaching chaos. This chaos endangers the established order: any kind of order, including the liberal order itself. The more liberalism succeeds, the faster it approaches its end and the end of the present world. Here we are dealing with the nihilistic essence of liberal philosophy, with nothingness as the inner (me)ontological principle of freedom-from. The German anthropologist Arnold Gehlen[4] justly defined the human as a 'deprived being', or

---

3   Edward Luttwak, *Turbo-capitalism: Winners and Losers in the Global Economy* (New York: HarperCollins, 1999).

4   Arnold Gehlen (1904–1976) was a German anthropologist and philosopher of a conservative bent. Dugin is referring to his book, *Man: His Nature and Place in the World* (New York: Columbia University Press, 1988).

Mangelwesen. Man in himself is nothing. He takes all that comprises his identity from society, history, people, and politics. So if he returns to his pure essence, he can no longer recognise anything. The abyss is hidden behind the fragmented debris of feelings, vague thoughts, and dim desires. The virtuality of sub-human emotions is a thin veil; behind it there is pure darkness. So the explicit discovery of this nihilistic basis of human nature is the last achievement of liberalism. But that is the end, and the end also for those who use liberalism for their own purposes and who are beneficiaries of liberal expansion; in other words, the masters of globalisation. Any and all order collapses in such an emergency of nihilism: the liberal order, too.

In order to rescue the rule of this liberal elite, they need to take a certain *step back*. Liberalism will reacquire its meaning only when it is confronted once more with *non-liberal society*. This step back is the only way to save what remains of order, and to save liberalism from itself. Therefore, Putin's Russia appears on its horizon. Modern Russia is not anti-liberal, not totalitarian, not nationalist, and not Communist, nor is it yet too liberal, fully liberal-democrat, sufficiently cosmopolite, or so radically anti-Communist. It is rather on the way to becoming liberal, step by step, within the process of a Gramscian adjustment to global hegemony and the subsequent transformation this entails (*trasformismo* in Gramscian language).

However, in the global agenda of liberalism as represented by the United States and NATO, there is a need for *another* actor, for another Russia that would justify the order of the liberal camp, and to help mobilise the West as it threatens to break apart from inner strife. This will delay the irruption of liberalism's inner nihilism and thus save it from its inevitable end. That is why they badly need Putin, Russia, and war. It is the only way to prevent chaos in the West and to save what remains of its global and domestic order. In this ideological play, Russia would justify liberalism's existence, because that is the enemy which would give a meaning to the struggle of the open society, and which would help it to consolidate and continue to affirm itself globally. Radical Islam, such as represented by Al Qaeda, was another candidate for this role, but it lacked sufficient stature to become a real enemy. It was used, but only on a local scale. It justified the intervention in Afghanistan, the occupation of Iraq, the overthrow of Gaddafi, and started a civil war in Syria, but it was too weak and ideologically primitive to represent the real challenge that is needed by liberals.

Russia, the traditional geopolitical enemy of Anglo-Saxons, is much more serious as an opponent. It fits the needed role extremely well — the memory of the Cold War is still fresh in many minds. Hate for Russia is an easy thing to provoke by relatively simple means. This is why I think that war with Russia is possible. It is ideologically necessary as the last means to postpone the final implosion of the liberal West. It is the needed 'one step back'.

To Save the Liberal Order

Considering the different layers of this concept of a possible war with Russia, I suggest a few points:

1. A war with Russia will help to delay the coming disorder on a global scale. The majority of the countries that are involved in the liberal economy, and which share the axioms and institutions of liberal democracy, and which are either dependent upon or directly controlled by the United States and NATO, will forge a *common front* once more behind the cause of the liberal West in its quest to oppose the anti-liberal Putin. This will serve to reaffirm liberalism as a *positive* identity when this identity is beginning to dissolve as a result of the manifestation of its nihilistic essence.
2. A war with Russia would strengthen NATO and above all its European members, who will be obliged once more to regard American hyperpower as something positive and useful, and the old Cold War stance will no longer seem obsolete. Out of a fear of the coming of the 'evil Russians', Europeans will again feel loyal to the United States as their protector and savior. As a result, the leading role of the US in NATO will be reaffirmed.
3. The EU is falling apart. The supposed 'common threat' of the Russians could prevent it from an eventual split, mobilising these societies and making their peoples once again eager to defend their liberties and values under the threat of Putin's 'imperial ambitions'.

4. The Ukraine junta in Kiev needs this war to justify and conceal all the misdeeds they carried out during the Maidan protests on both the juridical and constitutional levels, thus allowing them to *suspend democracy* that would impede their rule in the southeastern, mostly pro-Russian districts and would enable them to establish their authority and nationalistic order through extra-parliamentary means.

The only country that doesn't want war now is Russia. But Putin cannot let the radically anti-Russian government in Ukraine dominate a country that has a population that is half-Russian and which contains many pro-Russian regions. If he allows this, he will be finished on the international and domestic levels. So, reluctantly, he accepts war. And once he begins on this course, there will be no other solution for Russia but to win it.

I don't like to speculate regarding the strategic aspects of this coming war. I leave that to other, more qualified analysts. Instead I would like to formulate some ideas concerning the ideological dimension of this war.

Framing Putin

The meaning of this war on Russia is in essence the last effort of globalist liberalism to save itself from implosion. As such, liberals need to define Putin's Russia ideologically — and obviously identify it with the enemy of the open society. But in the dictionary of modern ideologies there are only three primary iterations: liberalism, Communism and fascism. It is quite clear that liberalism is represented by all the nations involved in this conflict except for Russia (the United States, the NATO member states, and Euromaidan/the Kiev junta). This leaves only Communism and fascism. Therefore Putin is made out to be a 'neo-Soviet revanchist' and a 'return of the KGB'. This is the picture that is being sold to the most stupid sort of Western public. But some aspects of the patriotic reaction emanating from the pro-Russian and anti-Banderite population of Ukraine (i.e., the defence of Lenin's monuments, portraits of Stalin and memorials to the Soviet involvement in the Second World War) could confirm this idea in the minds of this public. Nazism and fascism are too far removed from Putin and the reality of modern Russia, but Russian nationalism and Russian imperialism will be evoked within the image of the Great Evil that is being drawn. Therefore Putin is being made out to be a 'radical nationalist', a 'fascist' and an 'imperialist'. This will work on many Westerners. Under this logic, Putin can be both Communist and fascist at the same time, so he will be depicted as a National Bolshevik (although this is a little bit too complicated for the postmodern Western public). It is obvious that in reality, Putin is neither — he is not a Communist nor a fascist, nor both simultaneously. He is a *political pragmatist* in the realm of international relations — this is why he admires Kissinger, and why Kissinger likes him in return. He has no ideology whatsoever. But he will be obliged to embrace the ideological frame that he has been assigned. It is not *his* choice. But such are the rules of the game. In the course of this war on Russia, Putin will be *framed* in this way, and that is the most interesting and important aspect of this situation.

The main idea that liberals will try to advance to define Putin ideologically will be as the shadow of the past, as a vampire: 'Sometimes they come back.' That is the rationale behind this attempt to prevent the final implosion of liberalism. The primary message is that liberalism is still alive and vital because there is *something in the world that we all must be liberated from*. Russia will become the *object* from which it must be liberated. The goal is first to liberate Ukraine, and by extension Europe and the rest of humanity, who will likewise be depicted as being under threat from Russia, and in the end Russia itself will be said to be in need of rescue from its own non-liberal identity. So now we have an enemy. Such an enemy once more gives liberalism its *raison d'être*. So Russia is being made out to be *a challenger from the pre-liberal past thrown into the liberal present*. Without such a challenge there is no more life in liberalism, no more order in the world, and everything associated with them will dissolve and implode. With this challenge, the falling giant of globalism acquires new vigour. Russia is here to save the liberals.

But in order for this to happen, Russia is being framed ideologically as something pre-liberal. She must be either Communist, fascist or perhaps National Bolshevist. That is the ideological rule. Therefore, in fighting with Russia, or in considering to fight her, or in not fighting her, there is a deeper task — *to frame Russia ideologically*. It will be done from both the inside and the outside. They will try to force Russia to accept either Communism or extreme nationalism, or else they will simply treat Russia *as if* it were these things. It is a framing game.

Post-liberal Russia: The First War of the Fourth Political Theory

In conclusion, what I propose is the following:

We need to consciously counter any provocation to frame Russia as a *pre-liberal power*. We need to refuse to allow the liberals to save themselves from their fast-approaching end. Rather than helping them to *delay* it, we need to *accelerate* it. In order to do this, we need to present Russia not as a pre-liberal entity but as a *post-liberal revolutionary force* that struggles for an alternative future for all the peoples of the planet. The Russian war will not only be for Russian national interests, but will be in the cause of a just multipolar world, for real dignity and for real, positive freedom — not (*nihilistic*) freedom from but freedom for. In this war, Russia will set an example as the defender of Tradition, conservative organic values, and will represent real liberation from the open society and its beneficiaries — the global financial oligarchy. This war is not against Ukrainians or even against part of the Ukrainian populace. Nor is it against Europe. It is against the liberal world (dis)order. We are not going to save liberalism, per their designs. We are going to *kill* it once and for all. Modernity was always essentially wrong, and we are now at the terminal point of modernity. For those who rendered modernity and their own destiny synonymous, or who let that occur unconsciously, this will mean the *end*. But for those who are on the side of eternal truth and of Tradition, of faith, and of the spiritual and immortal human essence, it will be a *new beginning*, an Absolute Beginning.

The most important fight at present is the fight for the Fourth Political Theory. It is our weapon, and with it we are going to prevent the liberals from realising their wish of framing Putin and Russia in their own manner, and in so doing we will reaffirm Russia as the *first post-liberal ideological power* struggling against nihilistic liberalism for the sake of an open, multipolar and genuinely free future.

APPENDIX II

Some Suggestions Regarding the Prospects for the Fourth Political Theory in Europe

To get to the Fourth Political Theory, we must begin from three ideological points.

From Liberalism to the Fourth Political Theory: The Hardest Road

To proceed from liberalism to the Fourth Political Theory is the most difficult path, since it is the opposite of all forms of liberalism. Liberalism is the essence of modernity, but the Fourth Political Theory considers modernity to be an absolute evil. Liberalism, which takes as its primary subject the individual and all the values and agendas that proceed from it, is viewed as the enemy. To embrace the Fourth Political Theory (4PT), a liberal should deny himself ideologically and reject liberalism and its suppositions in their entirety.

The liberal is an individualist. He is dangerous only when he is an extrovert, since in doing so he destroys his community and the social bonds with which he is associated. Being an introverted liberal is less dangerous because he only destroys himself, and this is a good thing: one liberal less.

But there is one interesting fact: the 4PT diverges from the modern versions of anti-liberalism (namely, socialism and fascism) by proposing not a critique of the individual as viewed from the outside, but rather his implosion. This means not to take a step back into pre-liberal forms of society, or one step sideways into the illiberal types of modernity, but rather one step inside the nihilistic nature of the individual as constructed by liberalism. Therefore, the liberal discovers his way to the 4PT when he takes one step further and achieves self-affirmation as the unique and ultimate instance of being. This is the final consequence of the most radical solipsism, and can lead to an implosion of the ego and the appearance of the real Self (which is also the goal of the practices associated with Advaita Vedanta).[1]

Nietzsche called his *Übermensch* 'the winner of God and nothing'. By this he meant the overcoming of the old values of Tradition, but also the nothingness that comes in their place. Liberalism has accomplished the overcoming of God and the victory of pure nothingness. But this is the midnight before the breaking of dawn, so taking one step further into the midnight of European nihilism is how a liberal who wishes to leave this identity, which is more consistent with a peculiarly Western destiny of decline (because the Occident itself is nothing but decline at present — more on this later) behind, arrives at the horizon of the 4PT.

Modernity is certainly a European phenomenon. But liberalism as the essence of modernity is not so much European as Anglo-Saxon and trans-European, specifically North American. Europe was the preliminary stage of modernity, and thus Europe includes within itself the socialist (Communist) as well as fascist identities alongside the purely liberal one. Europe is the motherland of all three political theories. But America is a place where only one of them is deeply rooted and fully developed. So despite being born in Europe, liberalism has ripened in America. Europe and the

---

1   Advaita Vedanta is one the major schools of Hinduism, and teaches that the goal of life is to realise the illusory nature of one's Self and achieve liberation by losing one's personal characteristics and joining impersonal Brahman at death, which is the eternal substance that underlies the universe. In this sense it is similar to Buddhism.

US are comparable to father and child. The child inherited only one of the political possibilities from its father, albeit the most important one. As a result, liberalism in Europe is partly autochthonous and partly imposed by America (being re-exported). That is the reason why American followers of the 4PT are so important. If they manage to overcome liberalism in the Far West, they will show the path for European liberals to follow. This is something akin to Julius Evola's idea of differentiated man. This remark makes reference to my article about the 4PT in Europe and specifically to the final two propositions I make in it regarding how to overcome the individual: by method of self-transcendence by an effort of the will (a kind of polytheistic effort of pure will), or through an existential encounter with death and absolute loneliness.

Therefore, the way from liberalism to the 4PT in Europe passes through America and its inner mystics. This is the third attempt to make sense of America: the first one was that of de Tocqueville,[2] the second was that of Jean Baudrillard.[3] The third one is reserved for the European who approaches the Far West in a search for the mystery of liberalism from the 4PT perspective.

From Communism to the 4PT: From Radical Critics to the Principal Critics

The way from the Communist position to the 4PT is much easier and shorter. There are some common points: first of all, the radical rejection of liberalism, capitalism and individualism. There is a clear and definite common enemy. The problem is that the positive program of Communism is

---

2   Alexis De Tocqueville (1805–1859) was a French political thinker best known for his work, *Democracy in America*, which was based on his experiences while travelling in the US. Although De Tocqueville was a democrat who opposed the monarchy of his day, he also opposed the socialist radicals. In his study of the US, he praised America's democratic system, but disliked Americans' obsession with money and their contempt for elites, since even though the latter is what enabled them to do away with the old colonial aristocracy, it also caused them to disregard the most intelligent members of their society, coining the term 'tyranny of the majority' to describe it.

3   Jean Baudrillard (1929–2007) was a French philosopher. Dugin is referring to his book, *America* (London: Verso, 1989).

deeply rooted in modernity and shares many typically modern notions: the universality of social progress, linear time, materialistic science, atheism, Eurocentrism and so on. The battle of Communism against capitalism belongs to the past. But the 4PT is the main ideological opponent of liberalism at present, so a genuine Communist can easily become attracted to the 4PT, considering its anti-liberal aspects.

To take this step, one needs to move on from the radical critics of modernity, such as Marx, to the principal critics of modernity, such as René Guénon, according to the excellent formulation of the French author, René Alleau.[4] This brings us to the relevance of National Bolshevism. National Bolshevism is a kind of hermeneutics that identifies the qualitative features in the quantitative vision of socialism. For orthodox Marxists, society is based strictly on class principles and the socialist community is formed everywhere according to one model. But National Bolsheviks, having analyzed the Soviet, German and Chinese experiences, have remarked that, put into practice, Marxism can help to create societies with the clear features of a national culture and which possess specific and unique identities. While being theoretically internationalist, historical Communist societies were nationalist with a strong presence of traditional aspects. Therefore socialism, being the by-product of liberal modernity, can be regarded as an extreme and heretical kind of pre-modernity and an eschatological form of ecstatic religiosity — following the examples of the Gnostics, the Cathars, Bruno,[5] Müntzer[6] and so on. That was also the opinion of Eric Voegelin, who called

---

[4] René Alleau (1917–2013) was a writer on esotericism and occultism. His book on Guénon is *René Guénon et l'actualité de la pensée traditionnelle* (Braine-le-Comte: Éditions du Baucens, 1977). No English translation exists.

[5] Giordano Bruno (1548–1600) was an Italian Dominican friar and philosopher of the Renaissance who was influenced by Neoplatonism and Hermeticism, and harboured many pantheistic ideas. He also believed that all of the races were created separately, rather than possessing a common ancestor. He also claimed that the Sun was just an ordinary star and that the universe contained many inhabited worlds. He was imprisoned by the Church's Inquisition and eventually burned at the stake for his heretical views.

[6] Thomas Müntzer (1489–1525) was a German theologian who thought the ideas of the Reformation should be applied to economics, and he was one of the leaders of the German Peasants' War, for which he was executed.

this the immanentisation of the eschaton.[7] (This is a heretical notion, but it is traditional nevertheless.)

The way to the 4PT for the European Left passes through the historical and geopolitical analyses of the National Bolsheviks (Ernst Niekisch, Ernst Jünger and so on). Excellent work in this regard has been done by the European New Right and especially by Alain de Benoist.

From the Third Way to the 4PT: The Shortest Way but Problematic Nevertheless

From the European Third Way to the 4PT is only one step, because the 3PT and 4PT share the Conservative Revolution of the Weimar era and traditionalism as common starting points. But that step is not easy to take. The 4PT is strictly anti-modern, in fact counter-modern. The nation that is so dear to representatives of the Third Way is essentially a modern notion, just as are the concepts of the state and of race. The 4PT is against any and all kinds of universalism, and refuses Eurocentrism of any kind — liberal as well as nationalist.

The ethnic traditions of the European peoples are sacred in their roots and form a part of their spiritual heritage. Yet ethnic identity is something quite different from the national state as a political body. European history was always based on the plurality of its cultures and the unity of its spiritual authorities. This was destroyed, first by the Protestant Reformation and then by modernity. The liquidation of European spiritual unity was part of the origin of European nationalism. Therefore the 4PT supports the idea of a new European empire as a traditional empire with a spiritual foundation, and with the dialectical coexistence of diverse ethic groups. Instead of national states in Europe, a sacred empire — Indo-European, Roman and Greek.

---

7   In his book *The New Science of Politics*, Voegelin wrote, 'The problem of an *eidos* in history, hence, arises only when a Christian transcendental fulfillment becomes immanentized. Such an immanentist hypostasis of the eschaton, however, is a theoretical fallacy.' He was essentially writing that we should not attempt to realize on Earth what properly belongs in Heaven — utopia.

This is the dividing line between the European 4PT and the Third Way: the refusal of any kind of nationalism, chauvinism, Eurocentrism, universalism, racism, or xenophobic attitude. Historic pretensions and hostilities between the European ethnic groups existed, to be sure. It should be recognised. But it is irresponsible to construct a political program on that basis. Europe should stand for geopolitical unity, coupled with the preservation of the ethnic and cultural diversity of the various European ethnoses.

The 4PT affirms that geopolitics is the primary instrument that can be used to understand the contemporary world, so Europe should be reconstructed as an independent geopolitical power. All these points coincide with the main principles of the French New Right and with the manifesto of GRECE by Alain de Benoist.[8] Therefore we should consider the European New Right as a manifestation of the 4PT.

Here we approach the philosophy of Martin Heidegger, who is central to and the most important thinker for the 4PT. The 4PT takes as its primary subject the Heideggerian notion of *Dasein*. Heidegger is the metaphysical (fundamental-ontological) step from the Third Way toward the Fourth one. The task is to develop the implicit political philosophy of Heidegger into an explicit one, thus creating as a consequence a doctrine of existential politics.

Last point. Europe is the West, and decline is its essence. To come to the lowest point of its descent (*Niedergang*) is the fate of Europe. It is deeply tragic, and not something one should be proud of. So the 4PT is in favour of a European Idea in which Europe is understood as a sort of tragic community (as per Georges Bataille):[9] a culture that is searching for itself in the heart of Hell.

---

8 Alain de Benoist & Charles Champetier, *Manifesto for a European Renaissance* (London: Arktos, 2012).

9 Georges Bataille (1897–1962) was a French writer.

Index

0-9
9/11 21-32, 50-51, 86-97, 142-143, 189

A
Abashidze, Aslan 99-101, 128
Abkhazia 99
Abramov, Sergei 100
Abramovich, Roman 10, 116
Advaita Vedanta 306
Afghanistan 121, 189, 220, 300
Ahmadinejad, Mahmoud 82
Ajara 128
Alexei II 69
Alexeyev, Nikolai 138
Alexis 68
Alfa-Bank 158
Alkhanov, Alu 100
al-Khattab, Ibn 88
Alleau, René 308
All-Russian People's Front 41, 114, 215
Al Qaeda 88, 101, 300
Anderson, Benedict 198
Andreas-Salomé, Lou 288
Anna 25
anti-ballistic missile (ABM) 189-193
Antichrist 12, 68, 147
Arctogaia 22
Aristotle 79, 297
Armenia 169
Attali, Jacques 276
Avar 216
Aven, Pyotr 158
Avvakum 23
Azerbaijan 169, 277

B
Bagapsh, Sergei 128
Bakatin, Vadim 265
Barayev, Movsar 88
Basayev, Shamil 127
Bashkiria 94

Bataille, Georges 310
Baudrillard, Jean 307
Beckett, Samuel 43
Béhar, Pierre 124
Belarus 18, 102, 136, 165-169, 190-197, 214, 254
Belkovsky, Stanislav 205
Benoist, Alain de 280, 309-317
Berezovsky, Boris 8-14, 44-45, 116
Bilderberg Club 122, 263-269
Biron, Ernest 66
Bodin, Jean 63, 237-238
Bolotnaya 219-228, 246
Bolsheviks 69, 121, 308-309
Brazil 214, 262
Brezhnev, Leonid 62
BRICS 262, 277
Bruno, Giordano 308
Brzezinski, Zbigniew 21, 52, 88, 121-122, 211-214, 263-268
Bulgaria 194
Burckhardt, Titus 147
Burnt by the Sun (Mikhalkov) 205
Bush, George W. 73, 128, 215-221

C
Cacciari, Massimo 273-278
Cam Rahn 189
Carr, Edward 235
Carthage 25, 120
Caspian Coastal Pipeline 167
Caucasus 17, 32, 90-101, 115-129, 190-196, 211-214, 250
Central Intelligence Agency (CIA) 88, 205
Centre for Geopolitical Expertise (CGE) 123
Channel One 90
Chávez, Hugo 82
Chechen separatists 32, 86
Chechnya 10-31, 49, 87-101, 115, 135-136, 166, 196, 214, 231-234
Chernomyrdin, Viktor 110

China 50, 74, 121, 185, 214, 240, 261-262, 277-280, 298
Chubais, Anatoly 11, 36-51, 71, 92-103, 158, 203, 264-266
Churchill, Winston 84
Chuvashia 94
Cold War 76-80, 121-132, 301
Collective Security Treaty Organisation (CSTO) 101, 166, 189
Common Economic Space (CES) 18
Common Free Market Zone (CFMZ) 167-168
Commonwealth of Independent States (CIS) 18-25, 49-51, 77, 101, 126-136, 165-173, 187-190, 211
Communism 26, 44, 56-69, 113, 134, 251-308
Communist Party of the Russian Federation (CPRF) 26-53, 76, 94
Concept of the Political, The (Schmitt) 245
Conservative Revolution 6, 26, 145-157, 180, 228, 285, 309
Conspirology (Dugin) 142
Constantinople 11, 62
Contributions to Philosophy (Heidegger)
Cooper, Robert 172
Council on Foreign and Defence Policy (CFDP) 264-269
Council on Foreign Relations (CFR) 122-123, 263-266
Cox, Robert 270-271
Crime and Punishment (Dostoyevsky) 212
Crimean War 121
Cuba 189
Customs Union 136, 167-173, 190, 254-255
'Cyborg Manifesto, A' (Haraway) 59
Cyprus 252
Czech Republic 189-194

D

Dagestan 14-17, 49, 86, 115, 127-135, 214
Dasein 274-285, 310
Dashkov, Dmitri 66
'Defense Planning Guidance' (Wolfowitz) 179
de Gaulle, Charles 84, 162
de Tocqueville, Alexis 307
Deleuze, Gilles 109
Democrats (US) 101, 122-125
Deripaska, Oleg 116
Dobrodeev, Oleg 48
Domini canes 186
Dominican monks 186
Dostoevsky, Fyodor 212
Dubrovka theatre 87
Dugin, Savva 7-8, 22, 66, 317
Duma 41, 78-99, 141, 211-215, 229
Dvorkovich, Arkady 211, 266

Dyomushkin, Dmitry 205

E

East Germany 268
Ekho Moskvy 40-41, 203, 230-233
Elements 30
Empire (Hardt & Negri) 6, 63-80, 108, 120, 132-140, 156-163, 176, 212-213, 268, 299, 317
End of History and the Last Man, The (Fukuyama) 273
Energy Charter 82
England 120-124, 235
Enlightenment 5, 56, 125, 159, 295-298
Epicurus 254
Ernst, Konstantin 48, 153-154, 270, 309-317
Eurasia 7, 19-37, 49, 123-144, 156-165, 179-180, 213, 252-255, 272-287
Eurasia Movement 7, 19-37, 180, 272-279
Eurasian Economic Community (EurAsEC) 18-32, 49, 101, 166-172, 189, 254-255
Eurasian Economic Union (EEU) 252-253
Eurasianism 6, 18-38, 51, 72, 106, 124-138, 156-187, 252, 290-293
Eurasian Union 168-193, 253-254, 291-292
Eurasia Party 165, 180
Eurocentric Conception of World Politics, The (Hobson) 272
European Court of Human Rights 239
European Union (EU) 37, 50, 101, 141, 163-182, 301
Evola, Julius 147, 307-317

F

fascism 56-69, 113, 243, 272-306
Fatherland — All Russia 27, 31, 45-48, 94
Federal Security Service (FSB) 141
Federation Council 17, 31, 49-50, 87-94
Fedosevans 148
FIFA World Cup 193
Filippov, Alexander 245
Filofei 12
Foundations of Eurasianism, The (Dugin) 30
Foundations of Geopolitics, The (Dugin) 30, 81
Fourth Political Theory 6, 272-305, 317
Fourth Political Theory, The (Dugin) 6, 272-305, 317
France 65-74, 120-125, 151, 216, 269
Franco, Francisco 56
Front of National Salvation 26
Fukuyama, Francis 122-123, 149, 273, 298

G

Gaddafi, Muammar 202, 300
Gaidar, Yegor 44-46, 103-110, 197
Galkin, Maxim 102

INDEX

Gallois, Pierre 124-125
Garaudy, Roger 269
Gates, Robert 159-163
Gazprom 167, 194
Gehlen, Arnold 299
G8 130-131
Gellner, Ernest 198
Gelman, Marat 210
Géopolitique (Gallois) 124
Géopolitique pour l'Europe, Une (Béhar) 124
Georgia 51, 98-101, 126-128, 193-201
Germany 65-75, 120-124, 254, 268, 317
Gill, Stephen 263
Gilpin, Robert 236-243
Glazyev, Sergei 53
Global Revolutionary Alliance 279-287
Gontmakher, Yevgeny 203-219, 266
Gorbachev, Mikhail 77-81, 97-101, 127, 141, 201, 219-241, 268
Gozman, Leonid 264
Gräf, German 51, 102, 140, 192
Gramsci, Antonio 221, 258-270
Grand Chessboard, The (Brzezinski) 121
Great Britain 120
Greater Middle East Initiative 128
Greece 65, 252
GUAM (Organisation for Democracy and Economic Development) 166
Guattari, Félix 109
Guénon, René 147, 308
Gumilev, Lev 18, 174-183
Gumilev University 18
Gumplowicz, Ludwig 65
Gusinsky, Vladimir 9-14, 44-45, 116

H

Habermas, Jürgen 150
Haraway, Donna J 59
Hardt, Michael 108-109
Haushofer, Karl 124
Hegel 297
Heidegger, Martin 30, 153, 180, 274-287, 310
Herodotus 124
Hielscher, Friedrich 154
Higher School of Economics 266
Hitler, Adolf 124, 162, 285
Hobbes, Thomas 63, 237, 251
Hobson, John 272
Hollande, François 194
Hosking, Geoffrey 159-163
Huntington, Samuel 122-123
Hussein, Saddam 101

I

IBM 386 158
Illarionov, Andrei 47-51, 102, 203
India 50, 65, 214, 262, 277-280

Ingushetia 98, 115, 128
Institute of Contemporary Development (ICD) 200-202, 230, 266
Iran 50, 80, 194-201, 240, 266-280, 298
Iraq 32, 52, 73-80, 101, 300
Islamism 87, 164
Ivanov, Sergei 49, 218
Ivan III 49, 93
Ivan the Terrible 185-186
Izborsk Club 267, 291
Izvestija 168

J

Jakobson, Roman 181
Janissaries 186
Japan 50, 109, 165, 185
Johnson, Samuel 150
Jong-il, Kim 82
Jünger, Ernst 154, 309
Jünger, Friedrich 154, 309
justicialism 56
Just Russia, A 39

K

Kabarda 128
Kabardino-Balkaria 115
Kadyrov, Akhmad 97-100, 128, 176, 208
Kadyrov, Ramzan 97-100, 128, 176, 208
Kalmyks 216
Karachay-Cherkessia 128
Karaganov, Sergei 264
Kasparov, Garry 41, 105, 203
Kasyanov, Mikhail 46, 90-92, 105, 203, 233
katechon 12, 69
Kazakhstan 18, 165-169, 254
KGB 9, 24, 141-142, 265, 302
Khakamada, Irina 89
Khan, Genghis 183
Khanna, Parag 277
Khlyst 68
Khodorkovsky, Mikhail 20, 45-53, 71-73, 92, 116, 202
Khristenko, Viktor 102
Khrushchev, Nikita 62
Kiev 209-210, 294-302
Kievan Rus' 156
Kimry 148
Kirienko, Sergei 11
Kissinger, Henry 122, 236, 263-265, 303
Kizlyar 128
Kjellén, Rudolf 119
Klyuev, Nikolai 62
Kokoity, Eduard 128
Kosovo 194
Kovalev, Sergei 9
Krasner, Stephen 236
Krauthammer, Charles 298

Kryashens 178
Kyrgyzstan 169
Kudrin, Alexei 47, 92-102, 192, 219
Kulistikov, Vladimir 48
Kupchan, Charles 260

L

Lacoste, Yves 124-125
Laufenberg, Heinrich 152
Lavrov, Sergei 171
Lebed, Alexander 13
Lebedev, Alexander 116
Lenin, Vladimir 162, 259, 302
Leontiev, Konstantin 177
Lesin, Mikhail 48
Leviathan (Hobbes) 67, 237-239, 251
Lévi-Strauss, Claude 181-182
Liberal-Democratic Party of Russia (LDPR) 27, 40, 141, 244
Liberalism 41, 53-60, 113, 192, 208-211, 223, 256, 273-274, 295-306
Libya 52, 75, 194, 213
Limonov, Eduard 27
List, Friedrich 150, 254
Litvinenko, Alexander 194
Lomonosov Moscow State Linguistic University 82
Los Angeles Times 35
Lukashenko, Alexander 51, 167, 200, 214-215
Lutte des races, La (Gumplowicz) 65
Luttwak, Edward 299
Luzhkov, Yuri 10, 27, 45-46, 90

M

Machiavelli, Niccolò 63, 231-238
Mackinder, Halford 120, 213
Maidan protests 301
Main Intelligence Directorate (GRU) 141-142
Mallarmé, Stéphane 30
Mamleev, Yuri 24
Mamut, Alexander 10
Manifest Destiny 256
Markov, Sergei 49
Marxism 56, 69, 120, 241-243, 258, 284-285, 297-308
Marx, Karl 258, 284, 297-308
Mauss, Marcel 274
Mearsheimer, John 236
Medvedev, Dmitry 7, 35, 48-52, 106-115, 128-129, 159-168, 192-233, 247, 261
Merkel, Angela 194
Michels, Robert 65
Mikhalkov, Nikita 205
Mill, John Stuart 54-55, 274, 296
Ministry of Internal Affairs 142
Mishari 178
Mitterrand, François 124
Moeller van den Bruck, Arthur 64, 155, 317
Moldova 169
Molokan 68
Mongol Empire 213
Morgenthau, Hans 235-243
Moscow 11-28, 49-52, 68, 82-88, 101, 116-141, 174-179, 193-197, 210-214, 242, 265, 278, 294
Moscow State Institute of International Relations (MGIMO) 242
Moscow State University 174
Moya Moskva 27
multipolar world 18, 71-87, 105-119, 132-143, 168-182, 214, 252, 266-291, 304
multipolar world theory (MWT) 174-182
Munich speech (2007) 77-81, 104-116, 129-130, 168, 202, 214-220
Müntzer, Thomas 308
Muscovy 62-67, 156, 185

N

Nabiullina, Elvira 192
Narodniki 151
Narochnitskaya, Natalya 264
National Bolshevik Party (NBP) 46
National Bolshevism 27, 151-152, 308
National Socialism 56, 284, 297
National Syndicalism 56
Navalny, Alexei 203, 233
Nazarbayev, Nursultan 101, 165-178
Negri, Antonio 108-109
Nemtsov, Boris 46, 89, 110, 203, 233
neoconservatives 125, 221-230, 249
Nevzlin, Leonid 116
New START 201
Niekisch, Ernst 152-154, 270, 309
Nietzsche, Friedrich 55, 288, 306-317
Nikonov, Vyacheslav 49, 264-265
No One's World (Kupchan) 260
Nord-Ost attack 88
Norilsk 42
North Atlantic Treaty Organisation (NATO) 10, 34, 77-82, 121-144, 175, 187-195, 220-227, 296-302
North Caucasus 32, 90, 115, 127-128, 214
North Korea 50, 82, 266, 298
Nostradamus 22, 140
Novalis 162
Novaya Gazeta 40
Novodvorskaya, Valeriya 46
Nye, Joseph 275

O

Obama, Barack 197, 211
October Revolution 62
Okna 40

Old Believer 12, 25, 68
Open Society and Its Enemies, The (Popper) 297
oprichnina 184-187
Orange Revolution 114, 193
Orion 161
Orthodox Chekists 35-36
Our Home — Russia 27

P
Paisius Ligarides 68
Paraclete Union 147
Pareto, Vilfredo 184-187
Party of Russia's Rebirth 27
Parvulesco, Jean 140, 161-162
Pavlovsky, Gleb 14-21, 45-51, 71, 103, 203-210
Peresvetov, Ivan 186
Perón, Juan 56
Peter Guys 15-16, 36-43, 97-103, 202
Peter the Great 68
Petrosyan, Yevgeny 208
Philosophy of Politics, The (Dugin) 139
Pierre, Abbé 124, 269, 317
Plato 275, 297
Platonov, Andrei 62
Poklonnaya Hill 291
Pokorny, Julius 78
Poland 189-193
Popper, Karl 297
Poptsov, Oleg 44
President's thousand 115
Primakov, Yevgeny 10-13, 28, 45-46, 89, 241
Prince, The (Machiavelli) 237

P
Project for the New American Century 126
Prokhanov, Alexander 10
Prokhorov, Mikhail 217
Prozhektorperiskhilton 40
Putina, Anna 25

Q
Questions of Sociology 245

R
Rahr, Alexander 250
Raskol, see Schism
Ratzel, Friedrich 119
Republicans (US) 37, 101, 122
Retinger, Józéf 263
Rice, Condoleeza 131
Richepin, Jean 25
Right Cause, The 40, 105
Rodina 203-204
Romania 194
Romanovs 68
Rome 11-12, 120
Rose, Father Seraphim 101, 126

Rose Revolution 101
Rulers and Victims (Hosking) 159
Russia in Global Affairs 265
Russian Empire 67, 120, 132, 156-160, 176, 213
Russian Federation (RF) 18-53, 76, 94, 120-143, 176-178, 200, 216, 279-280
Russian National Unity (RNU) 46
Russian Public Opinion Research Centre 34-35, 144
Russian Union of Industrialists and Entrepreneurs (RUIE) 48, 61, 201
Russia Today 48
Russo-Japanese War 121

S
Saakashvili, Mikhail 98-101, 126-129
Saint Petersburg 11-14, 36, 66, 116
Sakha 94
Salazar, António de Oliveira 56
Sarkozy, Nicolas 194
Satarov, Georgy 110
Saudi Arabia 136
Savitsky, Pyotr 138, 174
Schism 62-68, 192
Schmitt, Carl 154, 245, 317
Schuon, Frithjof 26
Sechin, Igor 48
Second Epistle of Paul to the Thessalonians 12
Serbs 121, 133
Shanghai Cooperation Organisation (SCO) 166-167
Shevardnadze, Eduard 126
Shevtsova, Lilia 264
Shokhin, Alexander 215-217
silovik 48, 103, 116, 157, 200, 205
Skolkovo Innovation Centre 192
Skoptsy 68
Slezkine, Yuri 276
Sobchak, Anatoly 11
Sochi Olympics 193
socialism 26, 41, 54-56, 121, 151, 178, 203, 230-231, 262, 306-308
Sombart, Werner 154
Sorel, Georges 152
Soros, George 125, 297
South Africa 262
South Caucasus 98
South Ossetia 88-99, 126-129, 250
sovereign democracy 77-80, 105-107, 201
Soviet Union (USSR) 76-81, 120-141, 156-176, 196, 213-230, 256-268, 298
Spann, Othmar 154
Spengler, Oswald 154, 181, 282
Stalin, Joseph 84, 162, 195-199, 302
State Council 50
S-300 201

Sublime Porte 186
Sufis 186
Surkov, Vladislav 14-15, 45-48, 90-103, 202, 219, 267-269
Symplegades 89
Syria 80, 194, 266, 301

T
Tajikistan 169
Tatars 178
Tatarstan 86-94
Third Estate 197
Third Rome 11
third way 26, 29, 56, 284-285, 309-310
Time 5, 106-107, 121, 190, 205, 220, 293
Toynbee, Arnold 181
traditionalism 26, 146-155, 180, 291, 309
Treaty of Versailles 75
Treaty of Warsaw 76
Tretyakov, Vitaly 264
Trilateral Commission 122, 263-268
Trubetzkoy, Nikolai 138, 174-181
tsarism 156
Tsargrad, see Constantinople 62
Tskhinvali 129, 196
Turkey 136-137, 216, 266
Turkmenistan 169
Tyutchev, Fyodor 253

U
Ukraine 18, 167-169, 193, 209-216, 255, 301-303
Unified Energy Systems of Russia (RAO UES) 51
Union of Right Forces (SPS) 11, 47, 92-94, 110
Union State of Russia and Belarus 102, 136, 190-193
United Nations (UN) 171, 194
United Russia 30-53, 91-107, 202-219
United States (US) 10-37, 50-53, 74-88, 101-179, 195-200, 214-240, 257-266, 300-307
Unity 46-48
University College London 159
Ustrialov, Nikolai 152
Uvarov, Sergei 137
Uzbekistan 169

V
Vietnam 189
Voegelin, Eric 245, 308
Voloshin, Alexander 14, 43-48, 71, 92, 203
Volotsky, Saint Joseph 23

W
Wahhabism 87
Waiting for Godot (Beckett) 43
Wallerstein, Immanuel 271

Waltz, Kenneth 236-243
Warsaw treaty 76, 127
Weber, Max 237
Westphalian 172-175, 237
Witte, Sergei 150
Wittgenstein, Ludwig 162
Wolffheim, Fritz 152
Wolfowitz, Paul 52, 88, 178

Y
Yabloko 40, 92-94, 110
Yekaterinburg 197
Yakovlev, Alexander 44
Yakunin, Vladimir 218
Yalta 75
Yanukovych, Viktor 136
Yastrzhembsky, Sergei 51
Yavlinsky, Grigory 9, 40, 89, 110, 264
Yeltsin, Boris 10-24, 39-52, 71-115, 127-136, 160-171, 187-241, 265
Yudashkin, Valentin 192
Yugoslavia 166
Yukos 73
Yumashev, Valentin 45, 110
Yurgens, Igor 201-220, 266
Yushchenko, Viktor 208-210

Z
Zavtra 12, 204
Zhirinovsky, Vladimir 16-27, 60, 244
Ziegler, Leopold 147
Zubkov, Viktor 218
Zurabov, Mikhail 193
Zyuganov, Gennady 10, 26, 39, 53, 69, 113

OTHER BOOKS PUBLISHED BY ARKTOS

Virginia Abernethy	Born Abroad
Sri Dharma Pravartaka Acharya	The Dharma Manifesto
Joakim Andersen	Rising from the Ruins
Winston C. Banks	Excessive Immigration
Alain de Benoist	Beyond Human Rights
	Carl Schmitt Today
	The Ideology of Sameness
	The Indo-Europeans
	Manifesto for a European Renaissance
	On the Brink of the Abyss
	The Problem of Democracy
	Runes and the Origins of Writing
	View from the Right (vol. 1–3)
Armand Berger	Tolkien, Europe, and Tradition
Arthur Moeller van den Bruck	Germany's Third Empire
Matt Battaglioli	The Consequences of Equality
Kerry Bolton	The Perversion of Normality
	Revolution from Above
	Yockey: A Fascist Odyssey
Isac Boman	Money Power
Charles William Dailey	The Serpent Symbol in Tradition
Ricardo Duchesne	Faustian Man in a Multicultural Age
Alexander Dugin	Ethnos and Society
	Ethnosociology
	Eurasian Mission
	The Fourth Political Theory
	The Great Awakening vs the Great Reset
	Last War of the World-Island
	Political Platonism
	The Rise of the Fourth Political Theory
	Templars of the Proletariat
	The Theory of a Multipolar World
Edward Dutton	Race Differences in Ethnocentrism
Mark Dyal	Hated and Proud
Clare Ellis	The Blackening of Europe
Koenraad Elst	Return of the Swastika
Julius Evola	The Bow and the Club
	Fascism Viewed from the Right
	A Handbook for Right-Wing Youth
	Metaphysics of Power
	Metaphysics of War
	The Myth of the Blood
	Notes on the Third Reich
	Pagan Imperialism
	Recognitions
	A Traditionalist Confronts Fascism

OTHER BOOKS PUBLISHED BY ARKTOS

GUILLAUME FAYE	*Archeofuturism*
	Archeofuturism 2.0
	The Colonisation of Europe
	Convergence of Catastrophes
	Ethnic Apocalypse
	A Global Coup
	Prelude to War
	Sex and Deviance
	Understanding Islam
	Why We Fight
DANIEL S. FORREST	*Suprahumanism*
ANDREW FRASER	*Dissident Dispatches*
	Reinventing Aristocracy in the Age of Woke Capital
	The WASP Question
GÉNÉRATION IDENTITAIRE	*We are Generation Identity*
PETER GOODCHILD	*The Taxi Driver from Baghdad*
	The Western Path
PAUL GOTTFRIED	*War and Democracy*
PETR HAMPL	*Breached Enclosure*
CONSTANTIN VON HOFFMEISTER	*Esoteric Trumpism*
PORUS HOMI HAVEWALA	*The Saga of the Aryan Race*
LARS HOLGER HOLM	*Hiding in Broad Daylight*
	Homo Maximus
	Incidents of Travel in Latin America
	The Owls of Afrasiab
RICHARD HOUCK	*Liberalism Unmasked*
INSTITUT ILIADE	*For a European Awakening*
A. J. ILLINGWORTH	*Political Justice*
ALEXANDER JACOB	*De Naturae Natura*
JASON REZA JORJANI	*Artemis Unveiled*
	Closer Encounters
	Erosohpia
	Faustian Futurist
	Iranian Leviathan
	Lovers of Sophia
	Novel Folklore
	Prometheism
	Promethean Pirate
	Prometheus and Atlas
	Psychotron
	Uber Man
	World State of Emergency
HENRIK JONASSON	*Sigmund*
EDGAR JULIUS JUNG	*The Significance of the German Revolution*
RUUBEN KAALEP & AUGUST MEISTER	*Rebirth of Europe*
RODERICK KAINE	*Smart and SeXy*

OTHER BOOKS PUBLISHED BY ARKTOS

PETER KING	*Here and Now*
	Keeping Things Close
	On Modern Manners
JAMES KIRKPATRICK	*Conservatism Inc.*
LUDWIG KLAGES	*The Biocentric Worldview*
	Cosmogonic Reflections
	The Science of Character
ANDREW KORYBKO	*Hybrid Wars*
PIERRE KREBS	*Guillaume Faye: Truths & Tributes*
	Fighting for the Essence
JULIEN LANGELLA	*Catholic and Identitarian*
JOHN BRUCE LEONARD	*The New Prometheans*
STEPHEN PAX LEONARD	*The Ideology of Failure*
	Travels in Cultural Nihilism
WILLIAM S. LIND	*Reforging Excalibur*
	Retroculture
PENTTI LINKOLA	*Can Life Prevail?*
H. P. LOVECRAFT	*The Conservative*
NORMAN LOWELL	*Imperium Europa*
RICHARD LYNN	*Sex Differences in Intelligence*
JOHN MACLUGASH	*The Return of the Solar King*
CHARLES MAURRAS	*The Future of the Intelligentsia &*
	For a French Awakening
JOHN HARMON MCELROY	*Agitprop in America*
MICHAEL O'MEARA	*Guillaume Faye and the Battle of Europe*
	New Culture, New Right
MICHAEL MILLERMAN	*Beginning with Heidegger*
MAURICE MURET	*The Greatness of Elites*
BRIAN ANSE PATRICK	*The NRA and the Media*
	Rise of the Anti-Media
	The Ten Commandments of Propaganda
	Zombology
TITO PERDUE	*The Bent Pyramid*
	Journey to a Location
	Lee
	Morning Crafts
	Philip
	The Sweet-Scented Manuscript
	William's House (vol. 1–4)
JOHN K. PRESS	*The True West vs the Zombie Apocalypse*
RAIDO	*A Handbook of Traditional Living* (vol. 1–2)
CLAIRE RAE RANDALL	*The War on Gender*
P R REDDALL	*Towards Awakening*
STEVEN J. ROSEN	*The Agni and the Ecstasy*
	The Jedi in the Lotus

OTHER BOOKS PUBLISHED BY ARKTOS

Nicholas Rooney	*Talking to the Wolf*
Richard Rudgley	*Barbarians*
	Essential Substances
	Wildest Dreams
Ernst von Salomon	*It Cannot Be Stormed*
	The Outlaws
Werner Sombart	*Traders and Heroes*
Piero San Giorgio	*CBRN*
	Giuseppe
	Survive the Economic Collapse
Sri Sri Ravi Shankar	*Celebrating Silence*
	Know Your Child
	Management Mantras
	Patanjali Yoga Sutras
	Secrets of Relationships
George T. Shaw (ed.)	*A Fair Hearing*
Fenek Solère	*Kraal*
	Reconquista
Oswald Spengler	*The Decline of the West*
	Man and Technics
Richard Storey	*The Uniqueness of Western Law*
Tomislav Sunic	*Against Democracy and Equality*
	Homo Americanus
	Postmortem Report
	Titans are in Town
Askr Svarte	*Gods in the Abyss*
Hans-Jürgen Syberberg	*On the Fortunes and Misfortunes of Art in Post-War Germany*
Abir Taha	*Defining Terrorism*
	The Epic of Arya (2nd ed.)
	Nietzsche's Coming God, or the Redemption of the Divine
	Verses of Light
Jean Thiriart	*Europe: An Empire of 400 Million*
Bal Gangadhar Tilak	*The Arctic Home in the Vedas*
Dominique Venner	*For a Positive Critique*
	The Shock of History
Hans Vogel	*How Europe Became American*
Markus Willinger	*A Europe of Nations*
	Generation Identity
Alexander Wolfheze	*Alba Rosa*
	Rupes Nigra

www.ingramcontent.com/pod-product-compliance
Lightning Source LLC
Chambersburg PA
CBHW030239170426
43202CB00007B/49